# At the End
## *of the*
# American Century

# At the End
## *of the*
# American Century

## America's Role
## in the Post–Cold War World

*edited by*
ROBERT L. HUTCHINGS

THE WOODROW WILSON CENTER PRESS
Washington, D.C.

THE JOHNS HOPKINS UNIVERSITY PRESS
Baltimore and London

Editorial offices:
The Woodrow Wilson Center Press
370 L'Enfant Promenade, S.W., Suite 704
Washington, D.C. 20024-2518
Telephone 202-287-3000, ext. 218

Order from:
The Johns Hopkins University Press
Hampden Station
Baltimore, Maryland 21211
Telephone 1-800-537-5487
www.press.jhu.edu

2 4 6 8 9 7 5 3 1

Library of Congress Catologing-in-Publication Data

At the end of the American century : America's role in the post–cold war
    world / edited by Robert L. Hutchings.
        p.   cm.
    Includes bibliographical references and index.
    ISBN 0-8018-5915-8 (alk. paper). — ISBN 0-8018-5916-6 (pbk. :
alk. paper)
    1. United States—Foreign relations—1989-  I. Hutchings, Robert L.,
    1946-   .
E840.A86     1998
327.73—dc21                                                    98-4022
                                                                  CIP

# Contents

## PART II  The Changing Shape of International Politics

## PART III  The United States in the Global Economy

## PART IV  American Foreign Policy in the Post–Cold War Era

# A Second
# American Century

## THOMAS S. FOLEY

*Thomas S. Foley was the 49th Speaker of the U.S. House of Representatives, in which capacity he earned a reputation for statesmanship and foreign policy bipartisanship. He was elected to represent the State of Washington's Fifth Congressional District fifteen times, serving from 1965 to 1994 and rising to the positions of majority whip, majority leader, and Speaker. He is now U.S. Ambassador to Japan. He is a member of several public and private boards, including the East-West Center, the Center for National Policy, and the Center for Strategic and International Studies. He is an honorary Knight Commander of the British Empire, a holder of the Cross of the Order of Merit of the Federal Republic of Germany, and a member of the French Legion of Honor.*

The end of the Cold War has had a serious impact, not only on international affairs, but also on the domestic consciousness of the American people. For two generations, we had the concept in the United States that we were the leader of the so-called Western alliance and the free world—that we had the responsibility of con-

Keynote address by Thomas S. Foley, former Speaker of the U.S. House of Representatives, to the conference on *End of the American Century? Searching for America's Role in the Post–Cold War World*, Woodrow Wilson International Center for Scholars, 3 June 1996.

fronting Soviet communism, both its intellectual challenge and its military threat. This idea provided a real identity for the country. It even softened, to some extent, the political dialogue. The columnist George Will once suggested that conservatives, in their attack on the domestic role of the government, should be careful not to paint with too broad a brush because the public needed to have confidence in the security capacity of the United States and its pivotal role in leading the Western alliance. If there was a loss of confidence or morale on the part of the American people in that key challenge and role, then there would be enormous consequences for the alliance and the cause of freedom.

The end of the Cold War resulted, in large measure, from a consensus of the American people and of the two political parties to stand together over a period of two generations. This is to take nothing away from President Bush, who deserves great credit for his skillful handling of foreign policy issues at the time of the collapse of the Soviet empire. But even more remarkable was the bipartisan consensus that held together since the late 1940s. Democrats and Republicans in the Congress and administration supported the cause of the West and the key principles of U.S. foreign policy, including support for NATO and support for the American security relationship with Japan. Rarely was there serious disagreement and political controversy over foreign policy issues. There were, of course, important exceptions with attitudes toward South Africa and the controversies over Nicaragua, but for the most part one could argue that American foreign policy had strong bipartisan support.

It is an interesting question whether this happened as a result of the public's conscious understanding and allegiance to those ideas, or its lack thereof. To some extent one might argue that the basic tenets of American foreign policy in the Cold War endured because they were never debated much. In no presidential campaign was it suggested that we withdraw from Europe. There was the Mansfield Amendment, which threatened a pullback of U.S. forces, but most Americans had no knowledge of it. For most Americans the idea of our relationships with Europe and Japan and our other alliances were taken for granted. Because they have not been debated, one might argue that to some extent they will be more vulnerable in the future if they are called into question.

For the most part, the alliances have held firm. They have enabled the United States and its allies to play a role in bringing about the end of the Cold War, the unification of Germany, the revitalization of middle

Europe, the collapse of the Soviet Union, the beginning of a sustainable peace process in the Middle East, the peaceful transformation of South Africa, the democratization of Latin America, and the beginnings of economic transformation in Asia.

All of these events took place in less than a decade—one of the most remarkable times in modern history. The role of the United States during this period cannot be overestimated. Indeed we have seen recently in Bosnia that without the United States continuing to assert its leadership, Europe is not able to function effectively in meeting the problems in the former Yugoslavia. It took the United States and the determination of the Clinton administration to move strongly to bring Europe together in a cohesive and coordinated way. Similarly, the rise of China and the need to incorporate China into the modern state system are supported by the continuation of our security relationships in Japan and Korea. For the foreseeable future, the broad outline of both an expanded NATO and our security relationships in Asia will continue to give the United States a key role.

One could argue convincingly that the "American century" was a result of military power, economic power, and what Joseph Nye calls "soft power"—the power of institutions, the power of culture, and the power of motivating ideas. All of those forces will remain strong for the foreseeable future and will, in fact, become even stronger guarantees of American preeminence.

Today, we are the lone military superpower in the world, and that power will be enhanced, not reduced, even as budget reductions take effect in the coming years. The development of precision bombing and the ability to take control of the so-called digital battlefield give military commanders unprecedented knowledge of the battlefield and an enormous capacity to launch specific, precision attacks on the enemy. American military power will probably become even more exceptional in the coming years, even though our force levels may decline.

The American economy is still a great engine of the world economy. We have increased productivity, continued strong economic growth, and have every prospect of continued prosperity into the next century. American cultural influence around the world is unprecedented. Popular culture in particular is dominated by the United States—in films, music, and art. The English language, enhanced by our cultural dominance around the world, is now the second language in almost every country. English has become the international language and is likely to continue dominating world cultural and literary patterns.

The United States has been and will continue to be an influential power in every sense—militarily, economically, culturally, and institutionally. What are we going to do with that power? What is the role for the United States if it is not defeating communism or leading the Western alliance in resisting the Soviet threat? What is our new purpose? Is it the promotion of democracy around the world? There are some who have suggested that the democratic model is not necessarily the best for all countries. African leaders often comment that multiparty democracy as practiced in the West leads almost inevitably to tribalism in their countries. Asian leaders have remarked that certain kinds of guided democracy are a better pattern for Asia. Maybe the role of the United States is to emphasize the constitutional limits on government—a recognition of constitutional human rights as well as the benefits of economic and political freedom—rather than a particular political model.

## AN OVERDUE PUBLIC DEBATE

The American people need to undertake a debate over what our power and influence should accomplish in the post–Cold War world. We have not had that debate. Most Americans have a very foggy and distant notion about what the United States' role should be in the world. We want to do good. We have a tinge of that Wilsonian ideal of being the good people who would advance the values, ideas, and concepts that will help our fellow human beings. But as soon as we run into trouble or difficulty, there is a tendency to harken back to the old Washington notion of not getting involved in entangling alliances.

In order to maintain our power and influence into the next century, we need to inform the American public about the fundamental tenets of our foreign policy. And in turn, it is important that the public informs the leadership as to what it is willing to support in the way of a new role in the post–Cold War period. If we are to be strong and influential abroad, there needs to be a consensus on our foreign policy objectives and on our role in the world.

The Council on Foreign Relations of Chicago has for many years conducted a poll about whether the country supports an active foreign policy. Now perhaps the question is put too starkly—do you favor a strong, active foreign policy or a withdrawal from foreign affairs? Still the results are very dramatic. According to the most recent polls, 65 percent of the country supports a strong foreign policy—the highest level of support since the Chicago Council began these surveys in 1974.

If the American people are interested in a strong foreign policy, are they then willing to put the needed resources behind it? Certainly in a military sense I think they are. The military component of our foreign policy has always been well funded; in fact, some feel that there is still an opportunity for reductions in the cost of the defense budget. Others, myself included, believe that we can reestablish the balance in our military budget in a way that allows arming the country with the most technically advanced weapons with some minor reduction in force levels.

On the civilian side of foreign policy—the State Department, the Agency for International Development, and the United States Information Agency—the reductions have been more precipitous. The closing of some of our consulates is perhaps not critical and may even be appropriate. But I worry that there is a tendency within Congress to weaken and restrict the budgets of these organizations to such a degree that the consequences may become harmful.

Now, the public has an exaggerated notion of how much this civilian side costs. If you ask the public how much we are spending on international affairs apart from defense and including foreign assistance, the figures are somewhere between 10 and 25 percent of the budget—which, of course, are wildly inflated. Because these figures clearly overestimate the actual percentage, and the public still favors a strong foreign policy, we can hope that with a serious public debate the American people can be led to support an active foreign policy and provide the resources needed to carry it out.

## THE DECLINE OF BIPARTISANSHIP

I am disappointed, however, in the failure of our political system to focus on serious questions, both in international and domestic issues. Our politics have become trivialized. There seems to be a growing tendency in the press to sensationalize the coverage of the news. And there is now a disturbing precedent to try to bring about domestic political change through the instruments of our legal system—as seen publicly through the prosecutions of Watergate and Iran-Contra. With the combination of these latest tendencies, we are now in a situation where each party seems to have grievances about the criminalization of the political system and is anxious in its turn for revenge or retaliation. It is amazing to think that a country this strong and this powerful should be focused on events that took place more than a decade ago when the current head of state and government was, in a sense, a parochial governor. This sensationalism sets up the danger that our politics will become, as it has been called, a blood sport of prosecution and destruction.

Members of the House run every two years. As a result, they are always in a political environment and almost always in a campaign environment. The press is anxious and energetic in demanding that members respond to every issue and problem, and there is a tendency to fall into a pattern of easy criticism. With a divided government, which we have experienced more often than not in the period since the end of World War II—usually with Republican presidents and Democratic congresses, but now with a Democratic president and a Republican Congress—there is a special need to pull back from a permanent campaign environment.

I used to face a certain amount of criticism from my own party because I did not think that we should continue the campaign after the election. Once the public had decided they were going to give responsibility to President Bush or President Reagan and to the Democrats in Congress, I thought we ought to try to work together. There ought to be a respite from the easy partisan attacks until the political debate returns sometime in the latter part of the presidential or congressional term. This tendency to carry on forever in an unending partisan debate explains in part the public's current disgust with politics and the negative advertising associated with it.

The media deserves some criticism for its own tendency to portray the institutions of government and public officials so harshly. If you listen to leading network programs, every night you will hear something fundamentally critical of the policies of government. Now, a certain amount of that is both healthy and a part of democracy. But when the pattern is almost entirely negative and without any positive or constructive balance, then it can have the dangerous effect of reducing public support for these institutions.

When I was growing up in the 1930s, it was a family ritual to gather around the radio and listen to Franklin Roosevelt, the president of the United States, make an address to the nation. Even in my best friend's house next door, where his father forbade the mention of Roosevelt's name, they were listening, too. The bully pulpit in the 1930s, particularly with Roosevelt's use of radio, had a great capacity to command the attention of the country.

In today's political arena, because there is such a profusion of voices, media, and speeches, it is difficult for any president to command the same attention and have the same influence on public opinion that Roosevelt had. Thus there is a tendency among today's leaders, even when convinced of the rightness of their positions, to doubt that the public can be persuaded. Yet, the public expects leadership that will command its attention and influence its opinion. Those who engage in that kind of leadership effort will win the respect of a responsive public.

## A SECOND AMERICAN CENTURY?

As a country we face other dangers and risks. Obviously we could slip back into the isolationism of the past. The current House of Representatives shows the least amount of interest and engagement in international issues of any Congress in the last two generations. There is the danger that the public attitudes of dissatisfaction and even disgust with government will continue and deny legitimacy to those who would want to lead the country.

Consider a series of polls that asked the public, "How much of the time can you trust the government to do the right thing?" In the late 1950s and early 1960s when the options were "all of the time," "most of the time," "some of the time," "little of the time," or "none of the time," an amazing 75 percent of the public chose all or most of the time. Last year, those who chose all or most of the time numbered only 19 percent of the responding public. This illustrates all too well an enormous shift away from public confidence in government institutions and perhaps public institutions in general. Business institutions, institutions of organized labor, and religious institutions all have suffered a loss of public confidence.

The military is the only institution of serious importance to this society that is in better shape today and that earns more public confidence and appreciation than twenty years ago. I think the public sees the military in general as being well motivated and as performing well. The success of Desert Storm is a recent vindication of that view.

The Henry Luce "American Century" essay was a clarion call for the involvement of the United States in world affairs. He began the essay with a contemporary statement on our society: "We Americans are unhappy. We are not happy about America. We are not happy about ourselves in relation to America. . . . We look to the future—our own future and the future of other nations—and we are filled with foreboding." But he concluded the essay with hope: "America as the dynamic center of ever-widening spheres of enterprise, America as the training center of the skillful servants of mankind, America as the Good Samaritan, really believing again that it is more blessed to give than to receive, and America as the powerhouse of ideals of Freedom and Justice—out of these elements surely can be fashioned a vision of the 20th Century to which we can and will devote ourselves in joy and gladness and vigor and enthusiasm." A very enthusiastic homily! "Other nations," he went on to say, "can survive simply because they endured so long—sometimes with more and sometimes with less significance. But this nation, conceived in adventure and dedicated to the progress of man–this nation cannot truly endure unless there courses strongly through its veins from Maine to California the blood of purpose and enterprise and high resolve. . . . It is in this spirit that all of us are called, each to his own measure of capacity, and each to the widest horizon of his vision, to create the first great American Century."[1]

That century was created. There is no question that at least in the last half of the twentieth century the United States filled the role and vision that Henry Luce announced. It remains to be seen whether we have the ability to come together as a country to find a new purpose and spirit of enterprise and whether we have a commitment to values that can carry us forward as the leader in the next century—making it a second great American century.

NOTE

1. Henry Luce, "The American Century," *Life* 10, no. 7 (1941): 61–65.

# At the End
## *of the*
# American Century

# INTRODUCTION

## ROBERT L. HUTCHINGS

*Robert L. Hutchings has spent a career bridging the worlds of learning and public affairs. He is currently assistant dean for academic affairs of the Woodrow Wilson School of Public and International Affairs at Princeton University, where he also teaches international politics. His diplomatic career included service as director of European affairs with the National Security Council, 1989–92, and special adviser to the secretary of state in 1992–93, with the rank of ambassador. He formerly served as deputy director of Radio Free Europe and on the faculty of the University of Virginia. His latest book is* American Diplomacy and the End of the Cold War.

After a century of world dominance, the country seemed to have become a "weary Titan, [staggering] under the too vast orb of its fate." The reference was to Great Britain at the close of the nineteenth century; the speaker of the time was British colonial secretary Joseph Chamberlain.[1] Writing around the same time, a prominent British journalist asked, "Will the Empire which is celebrating one centenary of Trafalgar survive for the next?"[2] Others decried the country's lack of "competitiveness" and called for educational reform and "national efficiency."[3]

These commentators might have been describing the American mood at the end of the twentieth century. For two generations, the United States had borne the burdens of world leadership with impressively few complaints. The dust had not settled from World War II before the United States had willingly undertaken another grand struggle, this one a protracted Cold War against Soviet communism. Both contests ended in decisive victory that vindicated the heavy prices we paid for waging them. Yet, the very thoroughness of victory seemed to vitiate the purposes of continued global leadership.

Have we reached the end of what Henry Luce famously called "The American Century"?[4] Is the leadership role the United States played for most of the twentieth century—certainly for the last half of it—a semipermanent feature of international politics, or is it the product of the unique circumstances of Cold War confrontation, which could not and should not be extended into a new and very different era? Are we "bound to lead"[5] because there is no power or combination of powers capable of replacing us, or will we gradually extricate ourselves from the burdens of global leadership? Or, as seems likely, will America's global role be neither the dominant one of the Cold War nor a turning away from global problems, because neo-isolationism is probably precluded by the demands and opportunities of an interdependent world?

Such questions seemed to be at the heart of numerous informal discussions in the fall of 1995 at the Woodrow Wilson International Center for Scholars, where I was finishing up a book on American diplomacy and the end of the Cold War. Like many others who concern themselves with international affairs, I was becoming preoccupied with the strategic confusion besetting American foreign policy in the aftermath of the confrontation that had defined world politics for two generations.

Public discussion was needed. It was all too predictable that the 1996 American presidential election, then just a year away, would come and go without any serious examination of the country's global role five years after the collapse of the Soviet empire. The foreign affairs journals were filled with learned treatises on "enlarging the zone of peace," "the clash of civilizations," and a "new concert of powers"—all weighty and important matters, to be sure, but oddly detached from the concerns and priorities of the wider public.

In thinking through these issues, I sought out fellows and guest scholars at the Woodrow Wilson Center whose areas of interest were not in international affairs—thoughtful people who were by no means ignorant of the wider world but who did not necessarily follow the latest new paradigm trotted out in the foreign policy journals. An expert on constitutional law, a specialist on American federalism, a novelist, a historian doing a book on railroads: what did they think about American foreign policy at the crossroads of a new century?

Jonathan Clarke, a former British diplomat who was then a guest scholar at the Wilson Center, had been nagged by similar concerns that were reinforced by his many speaking tours around the United States. On the basis of our discussions with colleagues, we sketched out questions that we would like to see addressed as part of a more coherent discussion about America's role in the post–Cold War world.

A yearlong series of lectures and symposia, provocatively entitled "End of the American Century?" ensued. It brought together prominent thinkers from the academic, policy-making, business, foundation, and journalistic communities. Their presentations are gathered and edited in this book. The idea was to broaden the foreign policy debate by expanding the range of perspectives and bringing together people who would not normally sit around the same table. The participants found the theme so provocative that it inspired them to think through these issues in ways that they probably would not have done but for the series and the question it proposed to address.

The issues raised in these discussions are less about the *loss* of American power than about the appropriate *uses* of that power absent the threat that lent focus and purpose to American policy for two generations. Former Soviet president Mikhail Gorbachev once said—in a prediction that became more literally true than he intended—that he was going to deprive us of any enemy. Absent a generally shared sense of external threat, what was the United States to do with its power and legacy of world leadership? If America's mission was no longer that of leading the free world, how, then, should the country think about its proper role in the post–Cold War world? The question is a very different one from those raised by British commentators a century ago. They wanted their country to regain competitiveness for the sake of preserving its international position; when Americans of today embrace the same term, they are thinking of the country's domestic well-being, not its global role. For Britons, the empire was more than a "mere geographical unit" but an "elaborate abstraction of ideas, loyalties, fancies, bluffs, [and] aspirations" that were bound up in their self-image as a global power.[6] The British governing class in particular was attached to the empire—on which "the sun never set"—and feared its loss.

Americans are not so sure. It was one thing to lead an alliance of Western democracies in a grand struggle against Soviet communism; quite another for the accumulated obligations of forty years of Cold War confrontation to ensnare us in a continued international role against no certain foe toward no clear end.

In this sense, the American condition at the end of the twentieth century was more like the Athenian empire during the Peloponnesian war. It was the "course of events"—for Thucydides, the struggle against Sparta; for us, the demands of the Cold War—"which first compelled us to increase our power to its present extent."[7] Yet the exigencies of war entailed the acquisition of a far-flung alliance system that seemed to many to have become a "tyranny" from which it was impossible to escape. Here is how Pericles put it in trying to stiffen the resolve of the Athenians: "You cannot continue to enjoy the privileges unless you also shoulder the burdens of empire. . . . Nor is it any longer possible for you to give up this empire, though there may be some people who in a mood of sudden panic and in a spirit of political apathy think that this would be a fine and noble thing to do. Your empire is now like a tyranny: it may have been wrong to take it; it is certainly dangerous to let it go."[8] "Bound to lead," in other words?

Thus this book is not part of the declinist debate over whether the United States, like great powers before it, was entering a period of inevitably diminishing power and influence.[9] For the immediate future, the problem seems to be, quite literally, that we have more power than we know what do with.

Americans have always been ambivalent about the exercise of power in international relations; this ambivalence has become particularly acute with respect to the country's status as the sole remaining superpower in a world without a compelling rationale and logic for the continued exercise of its unrivaled power. Even those reveling in what they saw as the "unipolar moment" of American predominance were by no means disposed to exercise American power with the sense of purpose and mission that Luce so enthusiastically evoked in 1941.[10]

The foreign policy elite (if it can be so called) searches for an elusive new paradigm to explain and justify America's continued global leadership, yet it does so with manifestly less assurance than was the case in the euphoric aftermath of the Cold War. The public at large is less interested in grand theory than in looking for a compelling rationale for American involvement in global issues as they arise—in the Persian Gulf, Haiti, Bosnia, or central Africa.

Americans know that their country's well-being is connected to international events; they understand that drugs, crime, terrorism, and environmental threats transcend national borders. Chicagoans and San Franciscans can see that their mayors must now travel to Tokyo and Frankfurt to do their city's business and know that their local prosperity is bound up in an interdependent global economy in ways that were not true fifty or even twenty-five years ago. Yet, they know as well that not every problem around the world is America's responsibility and are wary of being dragged into intractable local conflicts far from our shores and remote to our interests. Skepticism, rather than isolationism, is the prevailing frame of mind.

It has now been several years since the collapse of the Soviet Union. Yet, two presidential elections have come and gone without a serious public debate about American foreign policy approaching the twenty-first century, absent the threat that lent focus and purpose to American policy for two generations. Of course, a lively after the Cold War debate has been taking place in think tanks, foreign policy institutes, and foreign affairs journals, but it has conspicuously failed to resonate among the wider citizenry. Indeed, much of the debate has been framed in a way that is inaccessible to the informed general public and oddly disconnected from the other public issues that do prompt informed and spirited discussion.

This volume of essays aims at framing and catalyzing such a debate. Written by prominent legislators, foreign policy makers, scholars, and business leaders, the essays reflect a wide range of perspectives and judgments. Indeed, the group of contributors makes this volume unique among those dealing with American foreign policy issues. At least four different career paths are represented: there are leading academics, prominent thinkers identified with a particular issue area, officials with high-level experience in the executive branch, and well-known elected officials with experience in Congress. Several have had careers that bridged two or more of these paths.

The essays are organized around broad themes that go to the heart of America's international engagement, rather than highly specialized foreign policy topics accessible only to the foreign policy *illuminati*. They are arranged to make the connections across regions and issues, including domestic ones, that are too often missed in the fragmented national foreign policy debate. Finally, the book aims at framing a debate, not driving it toward a predetermined set of conclusions. Among the contributors one will find ardent internationalists alongside proponents of

American disengagement, realists together with idealists, hawks along-side doves and birds of a different feather. Most defy easy categorization; they reflect elements of several perspectives and indeed wrestle, as thoughtful people usually do, with the contradictory impulses that are manifest in international politics. This spirit of inquiry was very deliberately presaged by the question mark in the title of the series from which the book came: "End of the American Century?"

In his foreword to this volume, former House Speaker Thomas Foley contrasts the unrivaled power and influence the United States enjoys in the post–Cold War world with the great domestic uncertainties about how to wield this power. The remarkable level of foreign policy consensus during the Cold War caused public officials to get out of the habit of communicating with their constituents, he observes. "Because they have not been debated," key elements of the country's international engagement may be "more vulnerable in the future if they are called into question." Similarly, the breakdown of foreign policy bipartisanship and the shrillness of our public discourse risks undermining support for a continued American leadership role. Foley concludes by posing a question and a challenge: "Whether we have the ability to come together as a country to find a new purpose . . . that can carry us forward as the leader in the next century—making it a second great American century—remains to be seen."

## THE AMERICAN FOREIGN POLICY TRADITION

In his chapter, "Searching for the Soul of American Foreign Policy," Jonathan Clarke goes back to basics, examining the core principles, interests, and approaches that undergird American foreign policy. A former British diplomat, Clarke sometimes seems to know us better than we know ourselves. He describes what he calls the "soul" of American foreign policy and its three key elements: avoidance of "foreign entanglements," a "don't tread on me" readiness to fight when vital interests are at stake, and a moralistic impulse that is neither mere pose nor a reliable indicator of a willingness to act. Clarke disputes the notion that public ignorance of world affairs renders Americans incapable of discriminating judgment; to the contrary, he finds among ordinary Americans "a rather consistent, well-developed, and finely calibrated feeling for what does and what does not make sense for their nation's foreign engagements." Their attitudes toward the conflict in

Bosnia, Clarke contends, were consistent, predictable, and unpersuaded by the "passionate urging of the foreign policy *illuminati* that [this was] the paradigm of the post–Cold War world." Those who seek to guide or merely to understand American foreign policy, he concludes, would do well to consider the "soul" and its "sanctioned field of operation."

In "Exemplary America versus Interventionist America," historian H. W. Brands expands on the same theme. Given the contemporary disputes over America's post–Cold War leadership role, it is reassuring to follow Brands as he traces elements of the current debate back to recurrent themes from the very beginning of the republic. He identifies two broad conceptions: America as an example for the rest of the world, and America as the vindicator of liberty everywhere. The "exemplarists" called for the perfection of the institutions of freedom at home and warned that "foreign entanglements" risked sullying our own democracy. The "vindicators" saw the risk as arising from too little involvement, for "an America alone in a world of aggressors would be an America intolerably endangered." Every generation of Americans has had advocates of both schools, and U.S. policy in the post–Cold War world will have to balance these two historical visions. As Brands puts it, "Ambivalence comes with the territory of American foreign relations. Americans can't save the world, but neither can they leave it alone."

"Rethinking Cold War History," an essay based on a roundtable discussion with historian John Lewis Gaddis, examines new evidence and perspectives on our recent past in order to help us think about our country's role going forward. "Up until the collapse of the Soviet Union, the great majority of Americans experienced no other history than Cold War history." How should we think about this period now that it is over? "In retrospect, the Cold War does not seem quite the epic struggle that we may have taken it for as we were waging it." The bipolar world that seemed a semipermanent feature of international politics "in the long-term scheme of things was just a blip." Yet the Cold War was no mere historical accident. Perhaps the most important lesson we can draw is that "the broad course on which [the United States] embarked four decades ago was vindicated. At the beginning of the new era, we could do worse than to look back to those core values and principles to draw our bearings."

"The American Century and Its Discontents" draws different lessons. Joseph Duffey, director of the United States Information Agency and former president of the American University and the University of Massachusetts, goes back to Luce's "American Century" article and its

ringing call for internationalism against the backdrop of domestic isolationist sentiment. Turning to NSC 68 (National Security Council
Document 68) of April 1950, he argues that the us-against-them character and unprecedented secrecy of America's Cold War strategies left a
corrosive legacy of public cynicism and mistrust. The American century,
Duffey suggests, may be giving way to a new "century of modernity"
that is shaped by American technology and popular culture but is not
coequal with American values. "When we peel back all the layers of what
it means to be an American," our historical experiences "in the crucible
of modern democracy are what best define what is unique, and worth
preserving, of the American Century."

## THE CHANGING SHAPE OF
## INTERNATIONAL POLITICS

The relative clarity and simplicity of Cold War confrontation have given
way to a world situation of much greater complexity; instead of bipolar
confrontation between two rival alliance systems, we now face a multiplicity of foreign policy actors operating outside established structures
of international relations. My essay on "World Politics in the Twenty-
first Century" foresees an international system that remains militarily
unipolar, with no state or group of states matching the global reach of
American power, but with a tripolar distribution of economic power
among North America, Europe, and a dynamic East Asia. Yet, beneath
these familiar yardsticks of global power and influence, there will be an
increasing diffusion of power. In the parts of the world Robert Kaplan
describes, the very existence of states is at risk. Even the advanced
Western democracies will confront a combination of factors—including
the globalization of the economy and the rise of non-state actors
like multinational corporations, international financiers, and crime
syndicates—that will make it increasingly hard for governments to effect
outcomes for which they are nonetheless held accountable by their
publics. The chief dangers will come not from aggression by one state
against another, the predominant threat to international security in the
modern era, but from a complex of factors arising within states.

In "An Anarchic World," Robert Kaplan examines worrying global
trends springing from environmental degradation, population pressures,
and related factors that may no longer be possible to contain or compartmentalize. He offers a sobering survey of these patterns—not only

in sub-Saharan Africa and South Asia, where collapsing states are descending into chaos, but also in relatively more stable countries like Mexico, where entire regions have become "brown zones" in which the state has no authority or legitimacy. In the Middle East, he argues, the next thirty years are likely to be much more volatile than the last, as rapid population growth and mass urbanization will produce socioeconomic pressures and fundamental political change. This new array of issues, for which there are no adequate historical antecedents, risk overwhelming the established international order; they call for a fundamental restructuring of the international system that reflects and harnesses the growing influence of multinational corporations.

In "The United States in a Turbulent World," James Rosenau coins the term "fragmegration" to connote the interplay between the forces of fragmentation and of integration at every level. The world, he argues, "is undergoing a profound transformation that is far deeper and far more pervasive than any of us appreciate, so much so that it amounts to a new epoch." And it is a world of contrary trends. "States are changing, but they are not disappearing. State sovereignty has eroded, but it is still vigorously asserted." It is an open question, Rosenau concludes, whether the United States, beset with sharpening societal divisions and growing political disaffection, can adapt successfully to the coming age of turbulence.

Thus the modern state system, as it emerged after the peace of Westphalia in 1648, is alive but not entirely well. In his essay on "Strategy and Ethics in World Politics," Father Bryan Hehir observes that the three pillars of that system—the sovereignty of states, the principle of noninterference in internal affairs, and the separation of religion and politics—are all eroding. There has been an empirical shift toward intervention in the internal affairs of states: Bosnia, Haiti, and Somalia are among the recent cases in point. And there is a normative shift as well, as the doctrine of a "just war" transmutes into the doctrine of "just intervention." In cases of massive humanitarian or human rights abuses, the question is posed, "Is there a duty to intervene?" But the modern state system, however eroded, is not to be abandoned lightly. The answer, Hehir argues, may be to strike "a new Westphalian bargain" that mediates between "the wisdom of Westphalia with its understanding of the centrality of sovereignty and the necessity of peace and the limits of Westphalia, both morally and politically, when faced with the kind of intrastate violence and injustice that Haiti, Somalia, Rwanda, the Sudan, and other failed or divided states can produce."

THE UNITED STATES IN
THE GLOBAL ECONOMY

The three essays on the global economy reinforce the sense of an eroding international order. In "A New International Economic Order?"
Bowman Cutter, a former senior economic adviser to President Clinton,
depicts the changing shape of the modern developed economy, driven by
radical shifts in information technology and world financial markets, and
the arrival of major new economic powers like China and India on the
world stage. Taken singly, these two trends are of profound importance;
taken together, they are fundamentally altering the character of the
global economy as we have known it for half a century. "Economic eras
do not begin or end with sharp edges," he observes. Yet, if the United
States fails to see how different the economic context is becoming, "we
will never be able to summon the capacity to create the institutions and
the community that the next era's economy will demand." It is an open
question whether the future will see "vicious circles" of protectionism
and North-South conflict or "virtuous circles" of integration and cooperation, especially between the developed and developing economies.
Cutter concludes with a cogent set of prescriptions for U.S. policy,
including "an agenda for American leadership."

In "The New Mercantilism" Michael Oppenheimer expands on this
theme, exploring the likely consequences of America's headlong rush
into big emerging markets like China, India, Indonesia, Brazil, and,
potentially, Russia. The subtitle of his essay—"Where Is Business
Leading Our Foreign Policy?"—previews his provocative conclusion
that "the commercialization of our foreign policy [may be] tantamount
to its marginalization." For forty years, the United States' main commercial partners have also been its principal allies. That situation is
changing fundamentally, as American business moves into new markets
in countries where our interests traditionally have been remote, or with
which our relations are complicated or even antagonistic. The implications of this underexplored trend are profound, as Oppenheimer shows.
"A mercantilist foreign policy," he concludes, "can take us only so far."
It offers significant commercial advantages, but "it cannot deliver the
strategic goal of a sound global economy . . . or redress burgeoning
global problems that ultimately could overwhelm our own prosperity
and well-being."

In "A New Protectionism? Tariffs versus Free Trade," Alfred Eckes, a
historian and former chairman of the U.S. International Trade

Commission, makes it clear that the choices for American commercial policy are more stark than the rhetoric of "free trade" and "global integration" suggest. He provocatively and persuasively challenges the "euphoric predictions of today's free trade enthusiasts." Economic internationalism helped promote world prosperity and served several strategic interests, but it left a legacy of unequal access to markets whereby we open ours but tolerate restrictions in others'. The ambitious trade liberalization commitments of the past decade have exposed American workers to burdens whose full magnitude will not be known for years to come. One possible remedy is temporary import restraints, which "can work without perpetuating the inefficiencies of permanent protectionism"; another is to encourage regional economic groupings among countries with similar income levels. "Economic nationalism is very much alive in the world," Eckes warns, "and ideologues and polemicists who ignore this point do so at their own peril."

## AMERICAN FOREIGN POLICY IN THE POST–COLD WAR ERA

The growing complexity of the global economy and world politics generally poses new challenges for the conduct and execution of American foreign policy. National Security Adviser Samuel Berger, in "Challenges Approaching the Twenty-first Century," outlines four dimensions of America's global role approaching the end of the century: the nation's military and economic strength, its unique capacity as peacekeeper, its continuing role in reducing the nuclear threat, and its promotion of democracy around the world. He identifies the chief threat to America's ability to play a strong global role as coming "not so much from traditional isolationism" as from "those who 'talk the talk' of internationalism but 'walk the walk' of isolationism," who "argue that we must lead, but say we must not spend." When it comes to American engagement, "they say yes in the abstract, but then say no to Bosnia, no to Haiti, no to Russia." But "America cannot lead in the abstract. . . . We cannot do so on the cheap, or simply through rhetoric." Although "we cannot and should not go it alone," Berger concludes, "American leadership in the world today is more important than ever."

Ronald Steel disagrees. In "The Internationalist Temptation," he argues that greater complexity does not necessarily mean greater danger, nor do proliferating problems around the world necessarily demand

American involvement. His is a warning to instinctive internationalists looking abroad for new dragons to slay. The habits of Cold War leadership have become so ingrained, he argues, that even a modest call to fulfill the country's "international responsibilities" can lead to a frame of mind that sees "any breakdown of order in the world as a crisis, and transforms every such event into a vital interest." Rather than strengthening American security, Steel contends, "the globalist strategy has the perverse effect of undermining it." "The American economy cannot indefinitely sustain it; rising rival powers will not accept it; and the American public will not support its enormous costs." He argues for a "new concept of national interest" that no longer assumes that "every problem anywhere must have an American solution, but working with others to establish a consensus for joint action."

Can such a consensus be forged to replace the broad public support that American foreign policy enjoyed for most of the Cold War period? In "Searching for a New Domestic Consensus," Milton Morris reviews recent public opinion polling and inquires into the prospects for rallying public support behind a post–Cold War U.S. leadership role. The polling data contradict the conventional wisdom. The first surprise is the remarkable, and encouraging, similarity of public attitudes across racial and ethnic lines. On the U.S. role in world affairs, including specific aspects like foreign aid and peacekeeping operations, there is hardly a difference worth noting among African American, Hispanic, and white respondents. The second surprise concerns the differences between political elites and the public; while leaders are significantly more internationalist, the gap is not so great when it comes to specific objectives. Leaders, according to the polling data, assign relatively low priority to democratization, human rights, and protecting weaker nations. So does the public. Yet, reading between the lines, it is clear that what leaders say about these issues is at odds with public attitudes, suggesting that political leaders would be better advised to speak honestly with the American people than to wrap their initiatives in ambitious rhetoric that they themselves do not believe.

One way of rebuilding domestic support is for the government to cultivate new public constituencies. In "Building Domestic Constituencies for Global Action," Undersecretary of State Timothy Wirth argues that the end of the Cold War severed the connection between the foreign policy agencies and the American public. The post–Cold War foreign policy environment demands that these agencies cultivate new domestic constituencies to support their missions. In a series of vivid examples,

Wirth shows that such constituencies exist, at least potentially, and are sometimes to be found in unexpected places . . . like the Garden Clubs of America. For foreign service officers, the task of building domestic constituencies is not the job they were trained to do and is foreign to their professional culture. Yet attitudinal changes are coming, as "every American ambassador abroad now sees the promotion of U.S. commercial interests as absolutely integral to his or her portfolio." The next step is for the foreign policy community to acquire sensitivity to another range of issues and constituencies. "This historic transformation," Wirth concludes, demands that we liberate ourselves "from outworn policies, from old assumptions, from fixed views that only yesterday seemed to be the dividing and defining lines of our policies."

In the afterword to this volume, Senator Carol Moseley-Braun returns to the issue of political leadership. She argues that U.S. foreign policy must have "full reference to one consent" (as Shakespeare wrote) that reflects American values, interests, and sense of community" if the country is to resist the "siren song of the isolationists." American workers fearing competition from cheap foreign labor need assurance that through education, retraining, and other measures, America's participation in the global economy will yield new opportunities for them; they need to know that "by assisting development abroad, we can create business at home" and provide new jobs in the process. She calls for a "new paradigm of shared prosperity through partnership" that "proceeds from an understanding that we are all in this together, that as Americans our well-being is directly linked to the well-being of people throughout the world." In our domestic debate, Moseley-Braun concludes, a "people-centered approach to public policy" must extend also to foreign policy, if we are to forge the "one consent" to which Shakespeare referred.

### NOTES

1. Cited in Paul Kennedy, *The Rise and Fall of the Great Powers* (New York: Random House, 1987), 229.

2. Ibid.

3. Ibid., 529–30.

4. Henry Luce, "The American Century," *Life*, 17 February 1941, 61–65.

5. Joseph S. Nye, Jr., *Bound to Lead: The Changing Nature of American Power* (New York: Basic Books, 1990).

6. Jan Morris, *Fisher's Face: or, Getting to Know the Admiral* (New York: Random House, 1995), 5.

7. Thucydides, *The Peloponnesian War*, trans. Rex Warner (Baltimore: Penguin Books, 1954), 80. Cf. President Bush's address to a NATO summit meeting in Rome in November 1991: "The alliance is not an American enterprise nor a vehicle of American power. We never sought preponderance, and we certainly do not seek to keep it." ("A Time of Decision for the NATO Alliance," U.S. State Department *Dispatch*, 11 November 1991.)

8. Ibid., 161.

9. In addition to Kennedy and Nye, above, see, among others, Henry R. Nau, *The Myth of America's Decline* (New York: Oxford University Press, 1990); and Samuel P. Huntington, "The U.S.—Decline or Renewal?" *Foreign Affairs* 67, no. 2 (Winter 1988–89): 76–97.

10. Charles Krauthammer, "The Unipolar Moment," *Foreign Affairs* 70, no. 1 (Winter 1989–90): 23–33.

# PART I

# The American
# Foreign Policy Tradition

# CHAPTER ONE

## Searching for the Soul
## of American Foreign Policy

JONATHAN CLARKE

*Jonathan Clarke, a former British diplomat, is now working as a foreign policy analyst, author, and journalist, and is a foreign policy scholar at the Cato Institute. He has served in Germany, Zimbabwe, and the United States, working on security policy as well as political, economic, and development issues. In 1995, he was a Guest Scholar at the Woodrow Wilson Center. He has a column syndicated by the* Los Angeles Times, *and has contributed to* Atlantic Monthly, Foreign Affairs, Foreign Policy, National Interest, Orbis, *and* Journal of Strategic Studies. *His most recent book, coauthored with James Clad, is* After the Crusade: American Foreign Policy for the Post–Superpower Age.

Several years have passed since the fall of the Berlin Wall signaled the end of the Cold War. American foreign policy, however, continues to struggle to adapt to the momentous implications of this event.

Why have practical results been so disappointing? Why do so many uncertainties still bedevil America's position in the world? Why, despite the intellectual exertions of the foreign policy establishment, does the public at large remain so unenthusiastic about and disengaged from foreign policy?

This essay examines some of these questions from what, it is hoped, is a fresh perspective. Its aim is to look beyond the feverish pressures of day-to-day business and instead to focus on "the basics." The assumption behind this approach is that if foreign policy reform is to be successful, the first need is to achieve a measure of clarity about the core character of the American role in the world.

The Bosnian tragedy illustrates why such an approach may be of value. Landing as it did on policy makers' desks in mid-1990 when other issues such as the impending implosion of the Soviet Union and the gathering storm in the Persian Gulf were preempting top-level attention, the Yugoslav crisis caught the West unprepared. Less obviously but more seriously, Bosnia exposed a deep confusion in the United States about the fundamental identity of American foreign policy. Brave words and fine promises abounded but, in the absence of agreement on what these stirring statements meant in terms of practical policy, action limped behind. An alarming gap opened between elite opinion, which tended to treat Bosnia as the post–Cold War "paradigm," and wider public sentiment, which accorded a more modest priority to events there.

This confusion will only get worse unless we reestablish contact with what might be called the long-term center of gravity of American foreign policy. That such an entity as center of gravity exists in the foreign policy context—let alone that it can be discovered by intellectual exploration—may be a controversial proposition. Certainly, to anyone schooled in the national interest-based tradition of Lord Palmerston, Hsun Tzu, or Hans Morgenthau, this may appear to be an alien idea.

Seen from the longer perspective of the totality of American diplomatic history, however, American foreign policy seems to possess certain long-term continuities. This accumulated experience appears to have bequeathed something akin to a transcendent foreign policy character that, in its form of a uniquely American blend of moral and practical impulses, plays an important—albeit little acknowledged—role in the outcomes of foreign policy discussions.

## THE HIDDEN LOGIC

A possible word for this character is "soul." This is not the only possibility. A more down-to-earth expression might be gut instinct. For those who prefer a more scientific feel to their foreign policy analysis, other words with a greater resonance of rationality about them may suggest themselves. Global positioning satellite or inertial navigation system come to mind. The precise terminology is less important than the essential idea that there is an underlying guidance mechanism or operating system that has enabled (and enables) Americans to plot their foreign policy journey according to two or three fixed points.

In essence, the soul (or whatever appropriate concept the reader may wish to substitute) functions as a sort of "referee" in shaping America's foreign policy choices. Inconspicuously tucked away in the background, it adjudicates the endless debate between isolationists and internationalists, realists and idealists, know-nothings and know-it-alls. If this sounds impossibly ethereal, the soul also has a very practical side to it. At the end of the day, when all the experts have had their say, the soul determines when American armies march and when they stay at home.

To lose touch with the soul—as we have done over the past few years—is therefore a serious affair. Without a close relationship with the soul, the professional diplomatic skills such as area specialization, political-military knowledge, or national security expertise count for little. We will be navigating blind. The result will be a disjointed and ineffective foreign policy.

Searching for souls is a chancy enterprise, so it may be best to start with a down-to-earth story from the diplomatic archives. In 1906 William Jennings Bryan was on a visit to the American embassy in Constantinople. At this stage in his career, Bryan had been twice the Democratic nominee for the presidency, but his secretary of stateship in the first Wilson administration still lay ahead. When, the story goes, Bryan was taking his leave from the embassy before continuing his journey through southern Europe, his hosts wished him a pleasant visit to the Balkans. "What," Bryan is reputed to have asked—and remember, this is the question of a future secretary of state—"are the Balkans?"

When foreigners, particularly former British diplomats like the present author, mention stories such as these, American readers are likely to bridle. It may be acceptable for distinguished Americans such as Ralph Waldo Emerson, Walter Lippmann, or George Kennan to make observations of a similar nature, but foreigners should not trespass onto this delicate ground of American self-esteem.

In fact, the purpose of the story is not to poke fun, but to crystallize—and then emphatically reject—a common caricature of the American approach to foreign affairs: namely that Americans' ignorance of world affairs puts them in emotional thrall to the latest outrage purveyed on

CNN and renders them incapable of discriminating judgment or sustained engagement. From de Tocqueville onward, this has been a widely held conception. However flattering it may be to European sensibilities, it is nonetheless a bad error.

Viewed over the historical record, Americans have in fact developed a rather consistent, well-developed, and finely calibrated feeling for what does and what does not make sense for their nation's foreign engagements. If a proposition looks reasonable, they are capable of immense, sustained effort. In 1951 John Foster Dulles said that "nothing could be more dangerous than for the United States to operate on the theory that, if hostile and evil forces do not quickly change, then it is we who must change to meet them." Americans understood what that meant. Over the fifty years of the Cold War, they proved that they could rise to such sentiments—in striking contrast to many Europeans who, smiling at what they regarded as unsophisticated American anticommunism, showed troublesome signs of succumbing to the fellow-traveling blandishments of Mikhail Gorbachev's Common European Home.

The corollary, however, is that they will not buy damaged goods, however plausible the salesman. An example might be the Nicaraguan opposition movement, the Contras, for whom President Ronald Reagan sought to win support by commending them to the American people as the moral equivalents of the Founding Fathers. His efforts foundered because American foreign policy is not made in a vacuum. Instead, guided by the soul's prompting, Americans are able to discriminate between courses of action with a far greater degree of subtlety and judgment than their relative unfamiliarity with the detailed facts of a particular case would suggest.

To illustrate how the soul operates, a brief review of some aspects of American diplomatic history may be useful. Although this review will necessarily be both broad-brush and highly selective, it is hoped that, by looking at some of the choices that Americans have made in reacting to the various calls on their attention by events around the world, it may be possible to bring some of the continuities into focus. Once made, these choices function like precedents in common law. They condition the present and the future.

A salient example might be the American experience in the Philippines early in this century following its annexation by the United States after the Spanish-American War. After a brief period of euphoria and enthusiasm for "civilizing" the Philippines, American ardor quickly cooled when the inhabitants of the Philippines showed themselves highly resistant to these supposed benefits.

A few years later in Mexico, Wilson encountered a similarly lukewarm reception for his efforts to restore the legitimate rights of President Venustiano Carranza. The upshot was not gratitude for American intervention but the issuance in 1919 of a sharply anti-Yanqui proclamation, the sentiments of which have bedeviled relations with Mexico to this day.

In contemporary parlance, these efforts to bring good government to foreign countries by means of direct intervention would be called nation building or enlarging democracy. The fact that America's first experiments in this area were less than happy means that it is perhaps no accident that Americans brought little commitment to similar exercises in Lebanon, Afghanistan, and Somalia. Nor is it surprising that recent efforts in Haiti attracted only shallow support.

In exploring what history says about the soul, neither advocacy nor criticism is the appropriate frame of mind. Like teenagers, souls come as they are, not as we might always like them to be. The Mexican war happened; the United States did not react militarily to the occupation of the Rhineland in 1936; China received an extension of MFN in 1994. For present purposes, the fact that these events took place is more important than whether they meet a particular moral standard. Rather than taking sides, let us treat these and other events as raw data and examine what they may say about the American foreign policy soul.

That the soul is not merely an intellectual abstraction becomes apparent in Bosnia. Events there bring to life the soul's most practical implications for policy makers. Seen from the soul's perspective, it becomes clear that, despite all the rhetorical sound and fury, American actions in Bosnia were of a piece with long-established American foreign policy traditions, and were thus not unpredictable. This makes the soul's importance crystal clear. Had we had a better understanding of its true makeup, that is, had we understood ourselves better, some of the tragic miscalculations, both here and in the Balkans, might have been avoided.

## THE THREE CHAMBERS OF THE SOUL

Souls are elusive entities, but in terms of foreign policy, it makes sense to regard the American soul as subject to three main themes or vectors. First is the "frankly, I don't give a damn" spirit emanating from Washington's

Farewell Address of 1799 in which he warned of the dangers of entangling alliances with Europe; second is the "don't tread on me" syndrome from the 1823 Monroe Doctrine that warned the European powers not to interfere with American prerogatives; and third is the "we are spiritually superior" conviction taken from Wilson's declaration that the United States was going to war against Germany in 1917 not to guard its national interests but to make the world "safe for democracy."

Starting with Washington's warnings against entanglements, this is clearly an enormously powerful theme. Arising partly from America's geostrategic strength and partly from a conscious rejection of the rest of the world's petty quarrels, this has been reaffirmed time and time again throughout American history and has survived several significant challenges.

Consider, for example, the foreign policy of the Progressive era beginning with the presidency of William McKinley and coming to full bloom under Theodore Roosevelt. Those who controlled the levers of foreign policy at that time (and most later historians) regarded this as starting a new period in American history in which, following the victory over Spain, American power came of age and irrevocably committed the nation to a posture of enthusiastic global engagement.

From today's perspective, a very different interpretation is possible. Like the "curious incident" of the dog in the Sherlock Holmes mystery that did not bark, the activist engagement of the Progressives was short-lived. Far from overturning the cautious instincts expressed in the Farewell Address and launching an enduring culture of instinctive internationalism, the progressive era was—in foreign policy terms—a false start.

In sharp contrast to Britain where, following the extravagant celebrations of Queen Victoria's Diamond Jubilee in 1897, imperialist fervor ran deep, the allure of foreign power projection proved notably short-lived in the United States. Organized groups with significant legislative backing such as the Anti-Imperialist League sprang into being to oppose the expansionists every inch of the way. No sooner had Rudyard Kipling penned his famous invocation to the United States to take up the "white man's burden" in the Philippines, than parodies began circulating asking how to put it down. World War I found America once again preferring caution over adventure until submarine warfare brought home the threat. The United States took part in that war as an "associate" power rather than as an ally.

That cautious culture seems to have returned today. It is all too easy to dismiss it as ignorant isolationism, readily curable by a sharp dose of internationalist shock therapy. Another reading is possible, however. Even if it is true that the events of this century have accustomed Americans to see their interests on a much more global scale than was the case at the dawn of the Republic, nonetheless the Cold War's globalism may not—any more than was the Progressive era's activism—have been the irreversible phenomenon that it is commonly taken to be.

Rather than representing a permanent shift in American attitudes, the Cold War consensus may have been simply a response to the unique circumstances represented by the challenge of the Soviet Union. With the demise of this challenge, the soul may be reminding Americans of their alternative foreign policy traditions. This is not to suggest that America can ever return to an unencumbered pre-GATT, pre-NAFTA, pre-NATO state of what Reinhold Niebuhr called "innocency in our foreign relations," but simply that a less activist, less forward style of foreign policy may also suit the national purpose. Today's skepticism about the worth of America's role as world policeman echoes similar doubts expressed in 1905 when Roosevelt issued his "corollary" to the Monroe Doctrine to legitimize American police action in the less civilized parts of the globe.

If it is correct that deep historical patterns are reasserting themselves (and clearly this is not yet an established fact), a practical consequence may be to place a question mark over the reliability of the American commitment to the collective defense agreements inherited from the activist Cold War period—or at least to warn that they cannot be easily continued as effective organizations of deterrence, let alone expanded as is proposed for NATO, unless a new basis for public support is generated.

In effect, the soul erects an extraordinarily high barrier for American involvement in the world. In general, Americans look for reasons to stay out of the rest of the world's conflicts, not how to get into them. Foreigners ignore such attitudes at their peril. It is, for example, ill-advised to argue for NATO expansion—as did a group of senior Czech parliamentarians making the rounds in Washington in 1996—by reference to the presumptive American interest in mediating ethnic conflict in Central Europe. For Americans, this is not an argument to stay in Europe; it is an argument to get out.

This is not to suggest, however, that the American foreign policy soul is dogmatically isolationist. On the contrary, it is open to internationalist argument, but of a rather specific kind. This is the soul's second main vector: namely, the existence of a manifest and imminent threat by a credible adversary. The two world wars and the Cold War (including the latter's regional manifestations) fit this categorization, and the threshold becomes slightly lower as the action moves closer to home. Witness the massive assistance for Mexico that was arranged with quiet dispatch over the New Year weekend 1994–95, far outstripping the volume of aid for Russia and yet attracting only token congressional opposition. The precipitate departure from Somalia makes the point from the opposite direction.

An interesting aspect here is the degree of sobriety of Americans in their approach to external threat. Whereas during the Cold War people placed relations with Russia near the top of their list of concerns—witness the rapturous reception of Kennedy's call in his inaugural address to "pay any price, bear any burden"—they did not go overboard. They expect sensible moderation from their leaders. In 1964 Barry Goldwater strayed beyond what was acceptable and crashed to defeat. In other words, Americans have brought a sophisticated sensibility to the threat issue. Those who today see new Hitlers in every strutting provincial dictator have discovered how hard it is to make their case persuasively.

To turn now to morality, the third chamber of the soul. Over the years this has been the noisiest. Consider this, for example: "The reports from the most reliable sources indicate that the worst stories are less than the truth. Meanwhile, what is Europe doing? Practically nothing. If the civilized world delays too long, there will be few witnesses left to tell the tale."

A quotation from a *Washington Post* story about the killing of Bosnian Muslims outside Srebrenica? In fact, this comes from an editorial in the *New York Times* of January 1895, a hundred years ago, about the massacres of Armenians in the Ottoman empire. Yet, despite an incandescent debate in the Senate (reminiscent of contemporary debates about Bosnia, and other instances of egregious human rights outrages), the two American naval ships stationed nearby took no action other than to evacuate American missionaries.

Time and time again this pattern repeats itself. In 1852, for example, the Hungarian patriot Louis Kossuth visited Washington, where he was given a hero's reception for his attempts to secure Hungarian independence from Austria. "Hungarian independence, Hungarian selfgovernance, Hungarian control of Hungarian destinies" thundered Secretary of State Daniel Webster at a legislative banquet. But privately he was more circumspect. In response to Kossuth's entreaties for direct

American intervention, Webster declared he had "ears more deaf than adders'."

Over a century later Kossuth's spiritual heirs suffered a like fate. Visiting Washington in 1990, Hungary's first democratically elected post–Cold War leaders heard similarly uplifting rhetoric—and encountered a similarly modest amount of substantive aid. At that time speechwriters in the White House considered explaining Washington's attitude by dusting off the standback sentiments uttered by John Quincy Adams in his well-known address of July 4, 1821: "[America] is the well-wisher to the freedom and independence of all, but"—and the speechwriters intended this to be the punch line—"she is the champion and vindicator only of her own." The quotation was rejected by the foreign policy experts as sending the wrong message. In retrospect, perhaps the non-specialist speechwriters were more in touch with the national mood than the experts!

The point here is not that American morality is merely a pose. This is far from the case. Hitler and Stalin both sought to overturn American values and both came up short. The world would be a very different place today had not the United States stood up for human freedom. What needs to be noted for contemporary policy formation, however, is that this tension between morality and action has been a perennial feature of the American foreign policy debate. If, as this essay asserts, previous decisions act like the precedents of common law, then those who wish to understand the practical implications of today's moral oratory would be well advised to study how these debates have turned out. There has rarely been a straight-line progression from moral outrage to action.

## UNDERSTANDING BOSNIA

To turn now to Bosnia: in addition to the technical mistakes that were undoubtedly made, there may be value in analyzing how the interplay of these themes of caution, threat, and moral sensibility helps explain what went and could still go wrong. The continuities of American foreign policy are important. To ignore them is to court disaster.

In this context, the statement of Assistant Secretary of State Richard Holbrooke opening the 1995 peace talks in Dayton, Ohio, is worth considering. "The eyes of the world are on us," he pronounced. This was understandable rhetoric, but appeared to miss an important point of substance. If there has been one consistent thread to Bosnia in the United States, it is that, when all is said and done, Americans generally are neither very interested in nor troubled by events there. Sarajevo 1995, they say, does not presage the dangers of world war as did the Sarajevo of 1914.

Those who put faith in opinion polls can quote Gallup surveys showing how consistently flat has been the popular interest in Bosnia. While they have supported humanitarian relief and endorsed the administration's human rights positions, Americans do not buy the passionate urging of foreign policy *illuminati* that Bosnia is the paradigm of the post–Cold War world—no matter that this viewpoint has dominated the print and electronic media. Those who have expected or advocated a major American involvement in Bosnia have learned the hard way and may still have unpleasant truths to discover about the strength of the American commitment to Bosnia.

There are those who argue that the reason for this assessment is that Americans are ignorant and willfully provincial. Once again, however, reference to the soul's guidance system suggests the precise opposite. Americans have been here before. Talking about possible deployment of American troops to Bosnia, Representative Tony Hall of Ohio said that this was "a new idea" for Americans. From a historical perspective, this seems to get things exactly backwards.

The discussion on whether to dispatch troops overseas is as old as the Republic—with a multitude of recent updates. On October 24, 1983, the day after more than two hundred Marines were killed in their barracks by a suicide bomber, the *Atlanta Constitution* editorialized: "It is time to abandon the fiction of peacekeeping—there is no peace to be kept—and to go over to peacemaking." Despite this expression of firm purpose that was echoed around the country, a few days later the Marines had quit Beirut. This confirms the point. With the exception of the Caribbean and Central America where the burden of proof is slightly lighter—although by no means straightforward, as the Clinton administration discovered in seeking to justify its intervention in Haiti—Americans require an exceptionally persuasive case before they agree to send troops into harm's way.

For the decision to be different, Jefferson's expeditions to the Mediterranean or the world wars, for example, the threat contour has to be scaled. As suggested earlier, this requires some significant ropework. Over Bosnia, valiant efforts have been made. Words like Munich, Hitler, vital national interest, and NATO credibility have been thrown around with abandon.

It is perhaps not surprising that these arguments failed to convince. Apart from the odd occasion like the shelling of the Sarajevo market-place in 1995 that did appear directly provocative, most Americans do not think the violence in Bosnia is aimed at them. Given that over their history this is the reason they have been moved to action, it would have been wholly uncharacteristic had they reacted differently in this case. The book is not yet closed on this story, of course, but the weight of precedent points to extreme caution.

What confused and confuses participants in the Bosnia conflict is that the soul's third theme of offended morality has sounded with full orches-tral support from the beginning. President Bush started out neutral, but by fall 1992 sounded as morally critical of the Serbs as candidate Clinton. Most Americans were and are genuinely sickened by events in Bosnia. But they have also been there before. Greece 1823, Hungary 1848, Cuba throughout the late nineteenth century, Belgium 1914, Ethiopia and China in the 1930s, Hungary again in 1956: the list goes on and on.

Sympathy or moral outrage have frequently led to humanitarian activ-ities like Clara Barton's mission to the Armenians in the 1890s or to individual volunteerism like the American fliers in the Esquadrille Lafayette prior to 1917. Action in terms of military intervention has been much less frequent. Nor, as the recent apparent acceptance by the United States of cold-hearted European ideas of partition shows, is moral sympathy necessarily a good predictor of where policy will end. Once again, the uncharacteristic reaction would have been a strong American engagement based on sentiment alone.

All in all, therefore, Bosnia shows the American soul working on long-established, understandable lines. Few Americans are familiar with the details of the situation there or of the particular rights and wrongs. Yet their basic instincts have been consistent. They are appalled by the human tragedy and have been very supportive of humanitarian assis-tance. But, absent an intimate connection with threat and obvious potential for American intervention to do some good, they are loath to make an open-ended commitment to engage on the ground.

## THE SOUL, PRACTICAL POLICY, AND LEADERSHIP

To turn now to the implications for practical policy. If it is accepted that such a thing as a foreign policy soul exists (and there will probably be many who find this a difficult concept), what does this mean for policy makers? Do the soul's dictates reduce them to automatons?

As previously noted, souls come as they are, not as we might wish them to be. This does not mean, however, that leaders have no role other than, in the words of a critic of President McKinley, "leading wherever the people seem willing to push." On the contrary, great scope exists for political leadership and vision. The soul does not proscribe or prescribe any specific set of action. What it does is to set the parameters of the possible. For example, given the instinctive American caution about foreign engagements, an extraordinary commitment of elite leadership is required to overcome this factor. The demands on presidential time to marshal support for the Gulf War illustrate the degree of effort required.

Bosnia shows what can happen when policy strays from the soul's sanctioned field of operation. Political leaders and members of the foreign policy elite made statements about the potential for American involvement that went beyond the natural bounds of what was acceptable to public opinion. But they then failed to follow up these statements with concerted leadership or public education.

This is why it is important to return to the basics and to get them right. The errors over Bosnia have had tragic but, in the greater scheme of things, containable consequences. Yet there are other issues waiting in the wings, particularly in Asia, that will test leaders' skills to the utmost.

Among these skills should be an effort to stay in touch with the soul. Intangible and elusive though this idea may be, the American soul equips the nation more than adequately for its world role, so long as we understand it. Dwight Eisenhower summed things up well: "We are not saints, we know we make mistakes, but our heart is in the right place." Many peoples' hearts are not in the right place, so the fact that America's is should be a source of considerable comfort.

CHAPTER TWO

# Exemplary America versus
# Interventionist America

H. W. BRANDS

*H. W. Brands is a historian whose twelve books span the past century of American history. They include* TR: The Last Romantic; The Restless Decade: America in the 1890s; Lyndon Johnson and the Limits of American Power; *and* The Devils We Knew: Americans and the Cold War. *The recipient of numerous scholarly awards, he is a professor of history at Texas A&M University and serves on the editorial board of* Diplomatic History.

Two sets of influences, broadly speaking, determine the kinds of foreign policies the United States can profitably pursue. The first involves the condition of the countries on the receiving end of prospective American policies. Will Bosnia dissolve after the withdrawal of American peacekeepers? Can Chinese palace politics allow enforcement of a copyright deal? Whither Russia? These are complicated questions—and will be left to others to address.

The second set of determinants, which *will* be dealt with here, has to do with the condition of the American political mind. In foreign policy the president proposes, but the American public disposes. How many casualties in Bosnia will Americans tolerate before demanding a pullout? The government might support a trade war over software, but will

Peoria? Having spent trillions to defeat Russian communism, will voters back a few billion more to keep it from making a comeback?

I do not propose to examine such specific questions—which in any event will fade into others within a few weeks or months—but rather to trace the broader outlines of American thinking about the world. Americans have been in the business of foreign policy for over two hundred years, and during that time they have displayed certain characteristic attitudes toward the world.

Of these, one stands out—namely, an abiding belief that the United States has an obligation to improve the world. Americans are hardly alone in conceiving a mission to better humanity; most powerful nations and empires have demonstrated the tendency in one form or another. But in America the tendency has been particularly noticeable. John Winthrop and the Puritans established their "city on a hill" for the edification of all the world; Thomas Jefferson propounded the unalienable rights of "all men," not just Americans; the Manifest Destinarians of the mid–nineteenth century insisted on enlarging the area of democracy; William McKinley announced his intention to "uplift and civilize and Christianize" the Filipinos; Woodrow Wilson wanted to make the world "safe for democracy"; Franklin Roosevelt pledged to extend the "four freedoms" to humanity at large.

Yet Americans have hardly been of a single mind regarding how humanity ought to be regenerated. Two predominant schools of thought emerged early in America's national history, and they have informed the debate on the subject ever since.

The first school comprises those who might be called "exemplarists." Following (and expanding upon) Winthrop, this group has held that America's highest obligation to the world is the perfection of the institutions of freedom at home. The United States should shine as a beacon of virtue to the other nations and peoples of the planet, providing an example for emulation. At times the exemplarists have been misleadingly labeled isolationists; the label misleads because it fails to encompass the element of moral engagement that has underpinned, and in most cases informed, the political distancing the exemplarists have prescribed. In exemplarist thought, foreign adventures are not merely unnecessary but counterproductive and downright dangerous. In the end, each nation must save itself, and for Americans to attempt to do for others what those others must do for themselves risks all kinds of evil consequences for both parties, including, most perniciously, the corruption of American democracy.

The second school contends that America's benign example is necessary but insufficient. In this benighted world here below, evil goes armed, and so must good. Americans must actively seek to vindicate the right; the sword of wrath must accompany the beacon of virtue. The "vindicators," to give the advocates of this philosophy a name, concur with the exemplarists in seeing the welfare of the world and the welfare of the United States as being of a piece, but where the exemplarists argue that too much involvement overseas will endanger democracy at home, the vindicators see the danger as arising from too little involvement. A forward defense of democracy is the only reliable one; an America alone in a world of aggressors would be an America intolerably endangered.

I I

The debate between the exemplarists and the vindicators emerged with the birth of American foreign policy during the 1790s. The French revolution broke out just months after George Washington took office as the first American president, and as it proceeded to rend French society, it also drove a wedge through his administration and through the American public. On one side were those sympathetic to the goals of the revolutionaries, even if sometimes put off by their methods. Thomas Jefferson, Washington's secretary of state, an admirer of things French, and a boat-rocker by nature, was the leader of this group. On the other side, Alexander Hamilton, Washington's treasury secretary, a notorious Anglophile and an unabashed elitist, decried the revolution as destructive of order, peace, and most other attributes of settled society.

For the first few years after the fall of the Bastille, the difference of opinion in America on the merits of the revolution in France was mostly academic; but France's 1793 declaration of war against Britain and Austria made it a matter of policy. The Franco-American alliance of 1778 remained in effect, and the French government called on the Americans to aid their ally. Jefferson and James Madison, Jefferson's collaborator in Congress, were strongly inclined to do so. Jefferson saw republican France's struggle against the monarchies of Europe as nothing less than a contest between freedom and tyranny. The "liberty of the whole earth," he said, turned on the outcome of the contest. Madison contended that the "cause of liberty" required the United States to honor its commitments under the 1778 treaty and to aid France in that country's hour of need, as France had aided America earlier.[1]

Alexander Hamilton adamantly opposed American assistance to France. The treasury secretary had no desire to abet revolution, which he—quite unlike Jefferson—considered dangerous to the values and aspirations America ought to stand for. Besides, he held, the France that had signed the 1778 treaty no longer existed, having been drowned beneath the blood of the Terror. By their own actions the French had nullified the treaty, freeing America of any obligations under it. Finally, for Americans to enmesh themselves in Europe's troubles would jeopardize the example the United States was setting for other countries. If the United States entered the European war, the rest of the world would see Americans as no different from the other belligerents. By contrast, if the United States remained aloof from the fighting, the other nations would see something unique:

> They will see in us a people who have a due respect for property and personal security, who in the midst of our revolution abstained with exemplary moderation from every thing violent or sanguinary, instituting governments adequate to the protection of persons and property; who since the completion of our revolution have in a very short period, from mere reasoning and reflection, without tumult or bloodshed adopted a form of general Government calculated as well as the nature of things would permit, to remedy antecedent defects, to give strength and security to the nation, to rest the foundations of Liberty on the basis of Justice, Order and law; who at all times have been content to govern ourselves, unmeddling in the Governments or Affairs of other nations.[2]

This early exposition of the exemplarist position was followed shortly by a similar analysis in George Washington's farewell address. The similarity was hardly coincidental: Hamilton strongly influenced Washington's thinking on foreign affairs and guided the hand that drafted Washington's message. "Observe good faith and justice toward all nations," the retiring founder counseled. "Cultivate peace and harmony with all." By such means would the United States serve itself and humanity at large. "It will be worthy of a free, enlightened, and at no distant period a great nation to give to mankind the magnanimous and too novel example of a people always guided by an exalted justice and benevolence."[3]

## III

It wasn't easy to argue with the Father of His Country, as Jefferson discovered on assuming the presidency himself. Indeed, Jefferson may have been the original neoconservative (in an appropriately nineteenth-century sense): abandoning vindicationism, he swung around to an arch-exemplarist stance. To some extent the transformation reflected changing circumstances across the Atlantic: Napoleon was hard for even a Francophile like Jefferson to stomach. To some extent it reflected changing circumstances on the Atlantic: the resumption of war between Britain and France had both belligerents seizing American vessels by the score. Honor dictated defiance; prudence counseled caution. Jefferson embraced prudence by persuading Congress to declare an embargo of American trade. While his opponents—including the Federalist merchant types on whom the embargo fell most heavily—hurled vitriolic abuse upon him, he calmly urged Americans to tend to their own affairs in a world gone mad. "A single good government," he reasoned, "thus becomes a blessing to the whole earth."

James Madison, too, found that exemplarism comported better with responsibility than vindicationism. Unlike Jefferson, he was unable to avoid war; America's embarrassing experience in the War of 1812 made Madison only more desirous of seeing his country left alone to perfect its republican institutions. With the mature Jefferson he held that setting a good example for other countries would satisfactorily discharge America's obligations to the world. "The free system of government we have established is so congenial with reason, with common sense, and with a universal feeling, that it must produce approbation and a desire of imitation . . .," he wrote. "Our Country, if it does justice to itself, will be the workshop of liberty to the Civilized World, and do more than any other for the uncivilized."[4]

The most compelling statement of the exemplarist position, though, came from John Quincy Adams. As James Monroe's secretary of state, Adams was besieged by advocates of American intervention in the anti-imperialist struggles of the day. In the continent-and-a-half to the south of the United States, aspiring republicans had raised the banner of revolt against imperial Spain. American partisans of their cause, led by the dashingly ambitious Speaker of the House of Representatives, Henry Clay, demanded that Monroe and Adams lend assistance. The extreme vindicators insisted on military intervention on the side of the revolutionists; Clay suggested he would settle for "all means short of actual war."[5]

A second revolt during this same period inflamed the vindicators even more. Then, as seventeen decades later, the Balkans were in turmoil: Greek nationalists were rebelling against the Ottoman sultan. The cause of the Greeks was made to order for American freedom fighters. The Greeks were Christians, as opposed to the Muslim Turks. Greece had been the cradle of democracy and was now fighting for its national independence; the nicest thing anyone could say about Turkish politics was that it was Byzantine, with all the intrigue and corruption that word implied. Greek culture was the glory of Western civilization; what had Turkey given the world? Edward Everett, editor of the influential *North American Review*, published an appeal by the Greek nationalists to the conscience of America, and went on to urge Americans to furnish material and political sustenance to the noble cause of Greek freedom. The Greek appeal, Everett declared, "must bring home to the mind of the least reflecting American the great and glorious part which this country is to act in the political regeneration of the world." The curtain had risen; the moment of truth was at hand.[6]

Daniel Webster lent sonorous support to the Greek cause. The Massachusetts orator stopped short of calling for the enlistment of armed soldiers on behalf of Greek independence, but he judged prompt political recognition to be an absolute necessity. The heroes of Hellas deserved no less. "I cannot say, sir, that they will succeed," the great Daniel granted his fellow congressmen. "That rests with Heaven. But for myself, sir, if I should tomorrow hear that they have failed, that their last phalanx had sunk beneath the Turkish scimitar, that the flames of their last city had sunk into ashes, and that naught remained but the wide melancholy waste where Greece once was, I should still reflect, with the most heartfelt satisfaction, that I have asked you in the name of seven millions of freemen, that you would give them at least the cheering of one friendly voice."[7]

Against this swelling tide of vindicationist enthusiasm, John Quincy Adams stood as an exemplarist rock. Speaking on the forty-fifth anniversary of American independence, Adams answered any who would have the United States intervene in the affairs of foreign countries, even for the noblest purposes. Once America took it upon herself to place others' feet on the right path, he said, she would begin to lose her own way.

> Wherever the standard of freedom and independence has been or shall be unfurled, there will her heart, her benedictions, and her prayers be. But she goes not abroad in search of monsters to

destroy. She is the well-wisher to the freedom and independence of all. She is the champion and vindicator only of her own. . . . She well knows that by once enlisting under other banners than her own, were they even the banners of foreign independence, she would involve herself beyond the power of extrication, in all the wars of interest and intrigue, of individual avarice, envy, and ambition, which assume the colors and usurp the standard of freedom. The fundamental maxims of her policy would insensibly change from liberty to force. . . . She might become the dictatress of the world. She would no longer be the ruler of her own spirit.[8]

IV

For the next two generations, Adams's formulation remained the clearest statement of American exemplarism, and exemplarism remained the primary mode of American interaction with foreign countries. The vindicators tested the primacy of exemplarism during the hothouse years of Manifest Destiny in the 1840s, with some contending that the only way to redeem Mexico, for instance, was to annex it. But the annexationists lost out, not least because the Mexicans made plain that they would not be annexed easily, and most Americans were not inclined to force the issue.

The vindicators tried again a few years later when Louis Kossuth, the Hungarian patriot, toured America to drum up support for his country's rebellion against Russian hegemony. Gamaliel Bailey, editor of the reformist *National Era*, succumbed to Kossuth's considerable appeal. "Intervention in behalf of Freedom, Justice and Humanity is the maxim of Democracy," Bailey proclaimed. Pierre Soulé, senator from Louisiana and himself a refugee from an earlier round of European uprisings, argued that the genius of American democracy lay in action, not mere exhibition. "Do we mean to hide it under a bushel, from fear that its light might set the world in flames?" Let the burning begin, for the fire of liberty would cleanse the earth of corruption. "Onward! onward! is the injunction of God's will as much as Ahead! ahead! is the aspiration of every American heart."

Yet again the vindicators failed to rally the country. Even Henry Clay—like Jefferson and Madison, a convert in maturity to exemplarism—now cautioned against entanglement in the coils of European politics. Clasping Kossuth's hand, the aging Kentuckian said, "God bless your country! May she yet be free!" But he asserted that America must not make Hungary's cause her own, for if Hungary went down, America might go down too. "Where then would be the last hope of the friends of freedom throughout the world?" Far better that Americans "keep our lamp burning brightly on this Western shore as a light to all nations" than to hazard "its utter extinction amid the ruins of fallen or falling republics in Europe."[9]

V

At the time Clay spoke, pessimists could easily class the United States as one of the falling republics, for sectional crisis threatened to tear the nation in two. The exemplarists have generally been bears in the market of foreign affairs, with troubles at home seeming to claim first call on American energies. America's troubles were never greater than during the 1850s and 1860s, and these contributed significantly to the persuasiveness of the exemplarists' arguments.

Conversely, the Union victory in the Civil War, followed by the burst of industrialization in the North and Midwest, fostered a feeling of national self-confidence and a resurgence of vindicationism. No one exhibited more national self-confidence than John Fiske, whose 1885 essay "Manifest Destiny" stole the label and consciously echoed the themes of the bullish 1840s. Fiske did not have the slightest doubt that the expansion that had marked three hundred years of American history was bound to continue. "The work which the English race began when it colonized North America," he declared, "is destined to go on until every land on the earth's surface that is not already the seat of an old civilization shall become English in its language, in its political habits and traditions, and to a predominant extent in the blood of its people. The day is at hand when four fifths of the human race will trace its pedigree to English forefathers, as four fifths of the white people in the United States trace their pedigree today."[10]

Josiah Strong joined Fiske in forecasting a gloriously expansive future for the United States. The general secretary of the American Evangelical Alliance, Strong put a predictably more religious spin on his message, but it came out about the same: "I believe it is fully in the hands of the Christians of the United States, during the next ten or fifteen years, to hasten or retard the coming of Christ's kingdom in the world by hundreds, and perhaps thousands, of years. We of this generation and nation occupy the Gibraltar of the ages which commands the world's future."[11]

Fortified by the message of Fiske and Strong, Americans of vindication-ist mind were prepared to move into action as soon as the opportunity arose. It did in the second half of the 1890s, when Spanish savageries against Cuban nationalists provoked outrage in most civilized quarters, as well as in the New York editorial offices of Joseph Pulitzer's *World* and William Randolph Hearst's *Journal.* The dueling press barons did their utmost to incite interventionist sentiment in the United States, on the rea-soning that a war would certainly boost circulation and might even miti-gate the suffering of the Cubans. From their pages poured a potent brew of investigative (and often imaginative) reporting and impassioned editori-alizing, not to mention tales of the daring exploits of guerrilla correspon-dents who made hairbreadth rescues of damsels in distress and generally vindicated America's hemispheric honor while Washington dithered.

The press lords got their way and the vindicators their war. Cuba won its freedom from Spain, although not entirely from the United States. In addition, the war yielded America an unanticipated (by those who did-n't keep up with the designs of naval enthusiasts like A. T. Mahan and Theodore Roosevelt) bonus: control of the Philippines. Actually, the Spanish war didn't quite deliver control of the Philippines; this remained to be contested with the Filipinos. But the treaty that terminated the war delivered nominal sovereignty over that distant archipelago, and it prompted the most searching examination in decades of the role of the United States in world affairs. The debate cast into sharp relief the dif-ferences between the exemplarists and the vindicators.

The exemplarists opposed annexation of the Philippines. Some held that annexation was immoral; others said it was simply stupid. The most politically compelling aspect of the anti-annexationists' argument was that it would poison the well of American democracy. Lapsed-businessman-turned-Harvard-professor Charles Eliot Norton warned that the acquisition of an overseas empire would bring upon America "the misery and burdens that war and standing armies have brought upon the nations of the Old World." The misery had already set in: seeking to fathom the lust for empire that had bewitched certain circles in America, Norton lamented, "All the evil spirits of the Old World which we trusted were exorcised in the New, have taken possession of her, and under their influence she has gone mad." Lapsed-lawyer-turned-dyspeptic-journalist E. L. Godkin, a longtime opponent of territorial expansion (earlier he had declared, "We do not want any more States until we can civilize Kansas"), joined Norton in bemoaning the outcome of the war and of the peace-making. "I can not help thinking this triumph over Spain seals the fate of the American republic." Irregular Republican and regular reformer Carl Schurz predicted that the Filipinos would rise up against their new American rulers, just as they had risen up against their erstwhile Spanish rulers. The likely result would be the militarization of American society. "The character and future of the Republic," wrote Schurz, "and the welfare of its people now living and yet to be born are in unprecedented jeopardy." Steel king Andrew Carnegie dismissed claims that American soldiers would bring civilization or anything else beneficial to the Filipinos. "Soldiers in foreign camps," Carnegie said, "far from being missionaries for good, require missionaries themselves more than the natives." Americans and Filipinos both would suffer from their forced encounter. "Has the influence of the superior race upon the inferior ever proved beneficial to either? I know of no case in which it has been or is."

The annexationists showered scorn upon the negativism of the anti-imperialists. Theodore Roosevelt declared that to abandon the Philippines would dishonor those (including himself, although this went without saying) who had fought in the late war. "We have hoisted our flag," the Rough Rider stated, "and it is not fashioned of the stuff which can be quickly hauled down." Republican senator Henry Cabot Lodge characterized the war with Spain as "not only righteous but inevitable." Inevitable also was an expansion of American territory: "We are going to hold possessions over the seas, be they more or less." Senator Albert Beveridge likewise discerned destiny in an imperial role for the United States, although he saw destiny's roots running rather deeper than Lodge did. "It is elemental," the Indiana expansionist declared. "It is racial. God has not been preparing the English-speaking and Teutonic peoples for a thousand years for nothing but vain and idle self-contemplation and self-admiration." Quite the contrary: God had far larger plans for Americans. "He has made us the master organizers of the world to establish system where chaos reigns. He has given us the spirit of progress to overwhelm the forces of reaction throughout the earth."[12]

VI

The annexationists won the battle but lost the war. Or, rather, they won two wars but lost the third. They had already won the war against Spain; then, after the Senate approved the Paris treaty and annexation of the

Philippines, they won the war there that Schurz and other anti-imperialists had predicted. But the experience soured the American public on vigorous vindicationism, especially the imperialist subclass of that category. The Philippines had been and would remain a Republican project in American politics; as long as the Republicans controlled the executive branch (which was to say, during the administrations of McKinley, Roosevelt, Taft, Harding, Coolidge, and Hoover), the uplifting mission proceeded—to the frequently problematic degree the Filipinos allowed. But when the Democrats occupied the White House (Wilson, Franklin Roosevelt), American ties to the Philippines loosened. Wilson introduced virtual home rule (which Harding attempted to reverse); the second Roosevelt oversaw passage of the legislation that cut the Philippines loose from the United States.

Wilson's anti-imperialism suggested an exemplarist streak. So did his studied neutrality between the belligerents during the first two-and-half years of World War I. But beneath this outward appearance lurked a vindicationism of the progressive variety. Progressives had few compunctions about telling Americans who didn't meet their bourgeois standards how to live; why should they hesitate to tell foreigners who fell similarly short? In fact they usually didn't. Wilson started by telling Mexico what kind of president it ought to choose. "They say the Mexicans are not fitted for self-government," he declared, suggesting for the briefest moment that he was about to distance himself from such misguided reactionaries. "To this I reply"—correcting the misimpression—"that, when properly directed, there is no people not fitted for self-government." Wilson determined that, in Mexico's case, proper direction included seizing the port of Vera Cruz and dispatching an expeditionary force of more than 15,000 under General John Pershing.[13]

But it was the European war that gave Wilson the opportunity to show his true vindicationist colors. Though Wilson hesitated to enter the European conflict, when he did so he insisted that America fight for nothing so narrow as neutral rights or the security of American nationals abroad, but for the purpose of making the world "safe for democracy." Not only would Germany be chastised, but the entire international order would be reconstructed under an appropriately progressive League of Nations.

Most American progressives fell over themselves applauding Wilson's audacity and vision. The *New Republic*, established in 1914 as the self-conscious mouthpiece of American liberalism, and edited by Herbert Croly,

Walter Weyl, and Walter Lippmann, the best and brightest of that generation, positively exulted in what Wilson was leading the country into.
"Only a statesman who will be called great could have made America's
intervention mean so much to the generous forces of the world," the *TNR*
troika declared. "No other statesman has ever so clearly identified the
glory of his country with the peace and liberty of the world." After further
such effusions, the three predicted confidently, "It is now as certain as
anything human can be that the war which started as a clash of empires in
the Balkans will dissolve into democratic revolution the world over."[14]

Not everyone was quite so sure. Unreconstructed radical Randolph
Bourne blistered his former allies on the progressive front for selling out
to the party of war. Bourne warned—as exemplarists before him had and
exemplarists after him would—that a foreign war, far from safeguarding
democracy, would be democracy's death. Bourne could understand the
frenzy for war among those bankers, munitions makers, and shippers who
stood to gain directly from belligerence, but he couldn't understand, and
certainly couldn't forgive, the war fever that was inflaming intellectuals
like Lippmann, Weyl, and Croly. "The intellectuals . . ." Bourne asserted,
"have identified themselves with the least democratic forces in American
life. They have assumed the leadership for war of those very classes whom
the American democracy has been immemorially fighting." They might
win the war, but they would surely lose the peace.[15]

VII

When events came closer to proving Bourne right than Lippmann and
the others, American opinion took a sharp turn toward exemplarism.
Vindicators were thin on the ground in America during the 1920s, and
they grew thinner after the stock market crash and the Great Depression
fostered the Great Introspection of the 1930s. With democracy disappearing in Italy and Germany and wobbling elsewhere, most Americans
thought they would have their hands full merely preserving democracy
at home.

Much of the American exemplarism of the 1930s was emotional
rather than philosophical, a visceral reaction to the failed vindicationism
of the world war and the collapse of the world economy rather than a
careful assessment of competing arguments. Yet rising above the
emotion to develop a historically informed and intellectually coherent
theory of contemporary exemplarism was Charles Beard. The most

popular historian of his day (or many other days: his books sold more than ten million copies), Beard had made his reputation tweaking the noses of the American establishment. His *Economic Interpretation of the Constitution* suggested that America's founding charter was something less (and something more interesting) than the product of the disinterested deliberations of the demigods of democracy. The framers had a financial stake in the outcome of the constitutional convention. Similarly during the 1930s, when assorted establishment types argued that the national interest required attention to the affairs of Europe and East Asia, Beard replied by asking: Whose national interest? Exporters, bankers, one-crop farmers, and their intellectual associates, he answered—but not the American people as a whole.

Beard believed in a fundamental connection between American domestic security and American international security. So did the internationalists of his day, but they had it just backward, he said. Rather than foreign adventures being necessary to protect democracy at home, domestic reform would render foreign adventures unnecessary. By cultivating the American garden—by enhancing the purchasing power of the poor, by loosening the hold of the monopolists, by refusing to underwrite an unnecessary military establishment—Americans could cure their depression without having to dump their excess production overseas. And in doing so, they would remove most of the incentive to meddle overseas. Of course, this would not do much immediately for those Chinese and Koreans being savaged by Japan, for the Ethiopians being massacred by Italy, or for the numerous peoples being menaced by Germany. But evil was always with us, and just because other countries were going insane did not mean America had to. When everyone else was hell-bent on destruction, the United States could best serve humanity by being an oasis of composure and stability. Besides, those do-gooders who absolutely had to save other people hardly needed to venture abroad. "Anybody who feels hot with morals and is affected with delicate sensibilities can find enough to do at home, considering the misery of the 10,000,000 unemployed, the tramps, the beggars, the sharecroppers, tenants and field hands right at our door."[16]

## VIII

Americans found Beard's exemplarist arguments very persuasive until March 1939, when Hitler revealed that he had been lying at Munich;

somewhat less persuasive until September 1939, when Hitler and Stalin swallowed Poland; still less persuasive but not completely without merit until December 1941, when Japan reminded Americans that a global power couldn't simply sit out a world war. The sneak attack on Pearl Harbor and the conflagration that followed knocked American exemplarism back a generation. It wouldn't recover until the 1960s.

Meanwhile it was replaced by the most thoroughgoing vindicationist consensus in American history. The consensus rested on two legs, the first being the comparatively incontrovertible assertion that appeasing Hitler had failed, the second being the more problematic postulate that Stalin was essentially Hitler in red. Problematic though this was, after their experience with Hitler most Americans were unwilling to gamble on any meaningful distinctions between the two dictators.

Yet within the vindicationist consensus of the Cold War there emerged tactical differences. George Kennan prescribed "a policy of firm containment, designed to confront the Russians with unalterable counter-force at every point where they show signs of encroaching upon the interests of a peaceful and stable world." Americans must prepare to act energetically all along the border between the Soviet sphere and the rest of the planet. This would require a greater commitment to the welfare of others than Americans had been accustomed to, and greater perseverance than Americans had ever demonstrated. But though the struggle would be long, it need not be endless. Writing in 1947, Kennan suggested that the Soviet threat might already have peaked—that Soviet power bore within itself the seeds of its own decay, and that the sprouting of these seeds was well advanced. Kennan projected a period of ten to fifteen years of maximum danger; after that, the threat would diminish and perhaps disappear. Moreover, the challenge to American society was equally an opportunity. In words that might have been spoken by John Fiske, Josiah Strong, or Albert Beveridge, Kennan declared that Americans should be thankful to "a Providence which, by providing the American people with this implacable challenge, has made their entire security as a nation dependent on their pulling themselves together and accepting the responsibilities of moral and political leadership that history plainly intended for them to bear."[17]

Walter Lippmann accused Kennan of wishful thinking. By now an institution of American journalism, Lippmann saw no reason to believe that the Soviet system was rotting from within. Nor did he think Americans were temperamentally suited to the kind of defensive everreadiness containment demanded. "The genius of American military power does not lie in holding positions indefinitely. That requires a massive patience by great hordes of docile people." Lacking hordes and patience, Americans would be reduced to reliance on others. "The policy can be implemented only by recruiting, subsidizing and supporting a heterogeneous array of satellites, clients, dependents and puppets. The instrument of the policy of containment is therefore a coalition of disorganized, disunited, feeble or disorderly nations, tribes and factions around the perimeter of the Soviet Union." This reliance on proxies, Lippmann said, was the fatal weakness of Kennan's policy. "They will act for their own reasons, and on their own judgment, presenting us with accomplished facts that we did not intend, and with crises for which we are unready." Identifying what would become the crux of America's Cold War dilemma, Lippmann concluded, "We shall either have to disown our puppets, which would be tantamount to appeasement and defeat and the loss of face, or must support them at an incalculable cost on an unintended, unforeseen and perhaps undesirable issue." In place of Kennan's open-ended vindicationism, Lippmann proposed a more modest version: an immediate American push for peace treaties that would require the evacuation of Soviet occupation forces from Eastern Europe, and would thereby return control of those countries to their inhabitants.[18]

Lippmann lost this argument, and unlimited vindicationism became the watchword of American policy. The policy was enshrined in NSC 68, a 1950 position paper that described the Soviet threat to world peace in apocalyptic language. "The issues that we face are momentous," the paper intoned, "involving the fulfillment or destruction not only of this Republic but of civilization itself." The new barbarians of the Soviet Union confronted the world with "a basic conflict between the idea of freedom under a government of laws, and the idea of slavery under the grim oligarchy of the Kremlin." The United States no longer enjoyed the luxury of choice as to whether to fight for the right. "In the context of the present polarization of power a defeat of free institutions anywhere is a defeat everywhere." If the United States did not defend democracy and order, no one would. "Unwillingly our free society finds itself mortally challenged by the Soviet system. . . . The absence of order among nations is becoming less and less tolerable. This fact imposes on us, in our interests, the responsibility of world leadership. It demands that we make the attempt, and accept the risks, inherent in it, to bring about order and justice by means consistent with the principles of freedom and democracy."[19]

IX

Americans made the attempt and took the risks. And in doing so they collided with the conundrum Lippmann had foretold. The conundrum—whether to defend unsavory allies or disown them—assumed its most spectacular and tragic form in Vietnam. The fighting and defeat there produced yet another shift in American thinking, this time back toward exemplarism. The shift involved far more than Vietnam, however, and mushroomed into a wholesale revision of recent American history.

Principal among the revisionists was William Appleman Williams, a neo-Beardian who taught history at the University of Wisconsin. Williams had caused a minor splash with the 1959 publication of *The Tragedy of American Diplomacy*, a skeptical view of American foreign policy in the twentieth century. The splash grew into a tsunami as events of the next several years made Williams look like a prophet, and a 1962 revision of *The Tragedy* became a campus classic. In Williams's view, American policy in the Cold War was the ill-conceived extension of an ill-begotten tradition in American dealing with the world. Rather than meeting the world on its own terms, Williams said, Americans insisted on treating the world on American terms. Those terms, in themselves, weren't all bad, but they didn't fit everyone else. Williams summarized the American approach as an extrapolation of the Open Door principles first espoused with regard to China at the turn of the century. American leaders ceaselessly demanded access to foreign markets and investment opportunities; they justified their pushiness on the reasoning that the expansion of American capitalism would be accompanied by the expansion of democracy. The tragedy of American diplomacy, Williams averred, lay in the conflation of these two institutions: capitalism and democracy. Intertwined in American history, they were not so intertwined in other people's history. Yet Americans acted as though they were, and when some country cast aspersions on capitalism, Americans interpreted this as an attack on democracy. Lately, the confusion in American thinking had led the United States into sordid alliances with dictators who ignored democracy but pledged to uphold property rights against the encroachments of communism. Most distressing, it had led to the morass Southeast Asia was becoming.

Williams advocated a shift from the misguided vindicationism of the Open Door to the exemplarism of genuine American democracy. "Isn't it time to stop defining trade as the control of markets for our surplus products and control of raw materials for our factories?" he asked. "Isn't it time to stop depending so narrowly—in our thinking as well as in our practice—upon an informal empire for our welfare? Isn't it time to ask ourselves if we are really so unimaginative that we have to have a frontier in the form of an informal empire in order to have democracy and prosperity at home? Isn't it time to say that we can make American society function even better on the basis of equitable relationships with other people?" Williams thought so. Instead of an Open Door for American exports, he called for "an open door for revolutions"—a willingness to let other people solve their problems as they saw fit. Besides benefiting those others, it would allow Americans to concentrate on solving their own problems. As they did so, the American example once again could shine as a beacon to humanity.[20]

The approach Williams espoused gained followers as the situation in Vietnam got worse, and it increasingly informed American policy during the late 1960s and 1970s. Although Richard Nixon and Henry Kissinger were hardly disciples of Williams, they were revisionists after their own fashion, and an essential aspect of détente and the Nixon doctrine was a recognition that the United States no longer possessed the capacity to police the world—if it ever had. They accepted the need to accommodate the Soviet Union, and they understood that while America might offer advice and assistance, other countries would have to find security and salvation on their own.

Jimmy Carter carried the retreat from vindicationism even further. Carter denounced what he labeled the "inordinate fear of communism" that had led the United States to cozy up to dictators and to deny its better impulses. He called on Americans to live up to their hopes rather than down to their fears. He emphasized human rights and the need to mitigate world poverty. America could employ political and economic devices, such as the withholding of American aid, to encourage other governments to embrace the same values Americans did, but by far the most effective tool would be the example of an America that practiced what it preached.[21]

X

Though Vietnam forced a vindicationist retreat, it didn't drive the vindicators from the field. A variety of vindicationist types reviled détente and plotted a countercoup. The most articulate, determined, and organized of these were the neoconservatives—those refugees from the Old Left who had managed to trade their former views in for new ones without denting the self-confidence that had made them sure they were right the first time and even surer when they changed their minds. The most combative of the neoconservatives was Norman Podhoretz, the agitprop editor of *Commentary*, polemicist par excellence and all-purpose political pyromaniac.

In 1980, just in time for the presidential election of that year, Podhoretz published *The Present Danger*, a scorching assault on détente and everyone associated with it. Like other neoconservatives, Podhoretz longed for the good old days of the early Cold War, when everything had been so clear. Things still were clear to him, if not to the Carter administration and America's policy elites. Détente had been a fool's game from the start, he asserted, a form of neo-appeasement. While the United States had cut back on weapons construction, the Soviet Union had raced forward. While the United States had backed away from Third World struggles, the Soviets had forged ahead. Unless Americans awakened to the danger into which the delusions of the détentists had delivered them, they would find themselves beyond rescue. The recent Soviet invasion of Afghanistan demonstrated how little détente had altered Moscow's designs. The continuing hostage crisis in Iran revealed to what depths American prestige had sunk. Podhoretz asked why the Iranian mob hadn't stormed the Soviet embassy in Teheran. "Might it have something to do," he answered archly, "with a fear of Soviet retaliation as against the expectation that the United States would go to any length to avoid the use of force?" Podhoretz applauded Carter's recent conversion to a stauncher line against the Kremlin, but wondered darkly, "Is it too late?" The "culture of appeasement," he feared, might already have taken too firm a hold on the nation. The "Finlandization of America" was well (or ill, rather) begun. Podhoretz called for the most strenuous efforts to reverse the trend of the last ten years, to recapture the spirit that had motivated America in the days when George Kennan's words had inspired the country to heroic measures. "In 1947 these words pointed the way to the containment of Soviet expansionism," Podhoretz said. "Today, if we but consent, they can energize our resistance to Finlandization and our determination to marshal the power we will need 'to assure the survival and success of liberty' in the new and infinitely more dangerous age ahead."[22]

Podhoretz and the other neoconservatives paved the path for Ronald Reagan's victory over Jimmy Carter and for a revival of the Cold War. For five years they thrilled to see America "standing tall" again, arraying its resources against the "evil empire," supporting subversion against leftist regimes around the world, planning to launch the arms race into outer space, and generally acting to vindicate American values against the communist challenge. For many neoconservatives, the revival of the Cold War also paid off vocationally: with jobs in the Republican administration.

But all good things end, and starting in 1985 the revised (for the third time in quick succession) leadership of the Soviet Union deprived the New Cold Warriors of their *casus belli* and raison d'être by unilaterally—albeit tacitly—conceding defeat. The gloating that followed the collapse of the Soviet empire and then of the Soviet Union itself soon gave way to conceptual confusion and the gnashing of think-tank teeth. "Nations need enemies," wrote Charles Krauthammer, an adjunct neoconservative. "Take away one, and they find another."[23]

This was easy to say, hard to do. Americans spent the first half of the 1990s groping for an enemy to replace the one they had grown codependent on since 1945. Saddam Hussein served briefly. But despite efforts by the Bush administration to make a Hitler out of him, the Iraqi leader was a one-year wonder. Somalia and Haiti likewise were nonstarters when it came to generating recurrent and reliable mass-market indignation.

As a result, the 1990s produced a crisis in American thinking about the world. Not since 1945 had Americans had to determine from first principles what their country's mission ought to be. A school of American decline (headed by transplanted Briton Paul Kennedy, who presumably had prior knowledge of these things) asserted that America's best days were past, that ambitious efforts to save the world—on the order of the Truman Doctrine and the Marshall Plan—were now beyond America's capacity. A competing school of American triumphalism (headed by Joseph Nye, who, significantly, landed a top job in the Clinton administration) held that while America's comparative lead over its nearest rivals might have diminished, the United States remained the world's only full-service superpower. If America did not provide the leadership the world required, no one would.

Amid the confusion, the Cold War began to look better and better. Though resuscitating it again seemed out of the question, many of those who had derived careers from it and now faced premature retirement managed to transfer to the postmortem department. The debates over what caused the Soviet collapse were almost as heated as the earlier fights over how to provoke that collapse. Neo-, meso-, and paleoconservatives contended that containment had been vindicated, with the different vintages of conservatives variously crediting Ronald Reagan, Harry Truman, and Adam Smith. Liberals, among others, held that it wasn't the use or threat of American force that had done the Soviets in, but the force of America's example.

Perhaps the most intriguing of the morning-after musings came from George Kennan, the christener of containment and the father of Cold War vindicationism. Speaking at a ninetieth birthday party thrown for him by the Council on Foreign Relations, whose journal had run his seminal containment article, Kennan refused to accept congratulations for what he had wrought. He complained (as, in fact, he had for quite some time) that containment had been overmilitarized. He pointed out that the costs of victory in the Cold War included a horribly expensive and otherwise unnecessary arms race, as well as the consignment of Eastern Europe to forty years of domination by Moscow. Had American leaders been willing to negotiate peace terms with the Russians, instead of insisting on what amounted to the Kremlin's unconditional surrender—in other words, if the United States had followed Walter Lippmann's advice instead of his own—this unfortunate outcome might have been averted.

Looking to the future, Kennan recommended something more akin to exemplarism in American dealings with the world. He cited John Quincy Adams's warning about involvement in other people's affairs to the detriment of America's own. He urged Americans to examine their society and country, building on their strengths and remedying their weaknesses:

> And then ask yourselves how such a country ought to shape its
> foreign relations in such a way as to help it be what it could be to
> itself and to its world environment, bearing in mind, of course,
> that it is primarily by example, never by precept, that a country
> such as ours exerts the most useful influence beyond its borders,
> but remembering, too, that there are limits to what one sovereign
> country can do to help another, and that unless we preserve the
> quality, the vigor and the morale of our own society, we will be of
> little use to anyone at all.[24]

XI

So what did it add up to? Or, as McGeorge Bundy used to say, when aides to the Kennedy-Johnson national security adviser launched into involved explanations of how the United States had gotten into a particular fix: "The fact of the matter is: We're here, and what do we do tomorrow?"[25]

Bundy was searching for a simple answer, or at least a straightforward one. Unfortunately, the world is rarely so obliging—which may explain how Bundy and his colleagues got the United States into its deepest fix of the last half-century. Neither does any simple, straightforward answer to America's foreign policy problems emerge from the two centuries of debate over the nation's proper role in the world.

Yet all the arguing has not been wasted, for if it does not yield simple answers, it does afford certain insights into the way America interacts with the world. Of these, the most important is that Americans are profoundly and, on historical evidence, incurably ambivalent regarding their international obligations. In two hundred years of trying, neither the exemplarists nor the vindicators have won the debate. This inconclusive outcome has been partly the fault of the world, which has refused to respond consistently to either the beacon of American virtue or the sword of American wrath, and partly the fault of Americans, who have refused to relinquish their sense of obligation to save, or at least substantially improve, the world.

Human nature changes, but slowly; consequently, there is no reason to think that the world is suddenly going to become appreciably more amenable to American influence, or that Americans are suddenly going to lose all feeling for that majority of humanity living beyond their country's borders. American leaders, charged with acting on behalf of the American people, need to keep this ambivalence in mind.

Doing so won't be easy, for ambivalence is the enemy of action, as everyone from Hamlet to Dean Acheson has understood. The Democratic secretary of state, who was as responsible as anyone else for persuading Harry Truman to sign off on NSC 68, conceded the hyperbolic character of that charter of Cold War mobilization. But Acheson nonetheless defended the document as necessary "to so bludgeon the mass mind of 'top government' that not only could the President make a decision but that the decision could be carried out."[26]

Although bludgeons may suppress ambivalence momentarily, they cannot eradicate it, not when its roots run two centuries deep. Acheson won his vindicationist point in 1950, but at the cost of an exemplarist backlash when the world proved less monolithically malleable than Acheson and his brass-knuckle gang made it out to be.

For better or worse, ambivalence comes with the territory of American foreign relations. Americans can't save the world, but neither can they leave it alone. Any policy that aims for consistency—and, beyond consistency, efficacy and wisdom—must balance the two historical aspects of American thinking about international affairs. The latter-day Kennan comes close to such a balance, substituting some of the exemplarism of John Quincy Adams for a part of the vindicationism of Cold War containment. Other formulations are possible, but all will share this same duality (duality being merely another, more positive, label for ambivalence). In particular, an enduringly successful American policy will manifest sufficient self-confidence to assert and demonstrate that America can act as an effective agent for good in the world, but sufficient humility to recognize that whatever good America accomplishes will be limited by the degree to which Americans hold true to their own democratic ideals.

## NOTES

1. Lawrence S. Kaplan, *Jefferson and France*, (Vol. 3 New Haven, Conn.: Yale University Press, 1967), 51; Irving Brant, *James Madison* (Indianapolis: Bobbs-Merrill, 1950), 375.

2. Harold C. Syrett, ed., *The Papers of Alexander Hamilton*, vol. 16 (New York: Columbia University Press, 1972), 18–19.

3. James D. Richardson, ed.,. *A Compilation of the Messages and Papers of the Presidents*, vol. 1 (Washington, D.C.: "Published by Authority of Congress," 1896), 221.

4. Norman A. Graebner, ed., *Ideas and Diplomacy: Readings in the Intellectual Tradition of American Foreign Policy* (New York: Oxford University Press, 1964), 86.

5Arthur Preston Whitaker, *The United States and the Independence of Latin America*, 1800–1830 (Baltimore: Johns Hopkins University Press, 1941), 344–45.

6. Edward Everett, "Affairs of Greece," *North American Review* (October 1823).

7. Paul Constantine Pappas, *The United States and the Greek War for Independence*, 1821–1828 (New York: Columbia University Press, 1985), 68.

8. Walter LaFeber, ed., *John Quincy Adams and American Continental Empire* (Chicago: Quadrangle Books 1965), 45.

9. Donald S. Spencer, *Louis Kossuth and Young America: A Study of Sectionalism and Foreign Policy* (Columbia, Mo.: University of Missouri Press, 1977), 53, 93–94, 108–9, 138–39.

10. John Fiske, "Manifest Destiny," *Harper's* (March 1885).

11. Josiah Strong, *Our Country: Its Possible Future and Its Present Crisis* (New York: Baker and Taylor, 1885, 1891), 227.

12. H. W. Brands, *Bound to Empire: The United States and the Philippines* (New York: Oxford University Press, 1993), 26–33.

13. Walter LaFeber, *The American Age* (New York: Norton, 1989), 264–65.

14. "The Great Decision," *New Republic*, 1917.

15. Randolph Bourne, "War and the Intellectuals," *Seven Arts* (June 1917).

16. "A Reply to Mr. Browder," *New Republic*, 2 February 1938.

17. "The Sources of Soviet Conduct," *Foreign Affairs* (July 1947).

18. Walter Lippmann, *The Cold War* (New York: Harper, 1947), 20–23.

19. NSC 68, April 14, 1950, *Foreign Relations of the United States*, 1950, vol. 1 (Washington, D.C.: Department of State, 1977), 237–41.

20. Williams, *The Tragedy of American Diplomacy* (New York: Dell, 1959, 1962), 296–97, 305.

21. *Public Papers of the Presidents: Jimmy Carter*, 1977 (Washington, D.C.: Government Printing Office, 1977), 956.

22. Norman Podhoretz, *The Present Danger* (New York: Simon and Schuster, 1980), 49, 54, 58, 79, 101.

23. Charles Krauthammer, "Beyond the Cold War," *New Republic*, 19 December 1988.

24. *New York Times*, 14 March 1994.

25. H. W. Brands, *The Wages of Globalism: Lyndon Johnson and the Limits of American Power* (New York: Oxford University Press, 1995), 10.

26. Dean Acheson, *Present at the Creation* (New York: Norton, 1969), 374.

# CHAPTER THREE

# Rethinking Cold War History:
# A Roundtable Discussion

JOHN LEWIS GADDIS[1]

*John Lewis Gaddis is widely regarded as the preeminent scholar of the Cold War. His many books include* The United States and the End of the Cold War, The Long Peace, Strategies of Containment, The United States and the Origins of the Cold War, *and* We Now Know: Rethinking Cold War History. *He was distinguished professor of history at Ohio University and has taught at the U.S. Naval War College, the University of Helsinki, Princeton University, and Oxford University. He is now Robert A. Lovett Professor of History at Yale University.*

U p until the collapse of the Soviet Union, the great majority of Americans experienced no other history than Cold War history. Even now, we refer to the "post–Cold War" era. Our brave new world has no name of its own nor any generally accepted characteristics, so we name and define it by the era just ended.

Not that most Americans gave much thought to the history of the Cold War as they were living through it: to the contrary, our engagement came to be taken so much for granted that it evoked little debate and indeed little interest, except episodically. But ordinary Americans absorbed and internalized more Cold War history than they may have realized.

Certainly, they understood enough to accept and support, with impressively few complaints, the burdens of leadership that attended the Cold War.

How then should they—or rather we—think about the Cold War now that it is over? Were the underlying premises of the containment strategy valid? Was the Soviet threat what we took it to be? Was it, after all, a clash of titans? In the final analysis, was the game worth the candle?

We can now think about these questions in new ways, both because of the new evidence that sheds new light on the thinking of the "other side" during this period, and because we can now view it with a certain perspective that we could not have as we lived through it. Paraphrasing Mark Twain—or was it Will Rogers?—it isn't what we didn't know that concerns us here; it is what we knew for sure but just wasn't so.

A growing public interest in Cold War history is evident: research originating in the scholarly journals is finding its way into the mass circulation press, and television networks are preparing retrospectives that draw on new evidence and fresh perspectives. It is not just curiosity that drives this interest, but an instinctive awareness that these questions about our recent past bear importantly on how we think about our country's role going forward. If, as we sort through the new Cold War history, serious public doubts arise about how well and for what purposes we were led, it will compound the difficulty of forging a new domestic consensus behind America's current international role. If, on the other hand, we emerge generally satisfied with the role we played during this period, it augurs well for our ability to work through our present uncertainties and begin fashioning new strategies appropriate to the challenges ahead.

### COMPETING INTERPRETATIONS
### OF THE COLD WAR

Any discussion about the "new" Cold War history obviously should begin with some explanation of what the "old" Cold War history was all about. For many years, three approaches dominated the field of Cold War history:

#### *Orthodoxy*

The first accounts of Cold War origins largely reflected the official American view, which was that the Soviet Union, acting out of an ideologically motivated drive for world revolution, had started it. Stalin's totalitarian threat was little different from that of Hitler, and had to be contained. The heroic Americans, who would rather have been doing other things, stepped in just in time to plug the hole in the dike that the Europeans themselves were too weak to fill; they then proceeded to rebuild the whole structure and thereby save Western civilization.

### Revisionism

These accounts, which began to appear in the mid–1960s, were almost a mirror image of orthodoxy. They saw the United States as the aggressive destabilizing power on the world scene, and they viewed it as acting out of an ideologically motivated drive to spread capitalism as widely as possible throughout the world—purely for selfish ends. The heroic Russians, Chinese, Vietnamese, and Cubans (Sandinistas had not yet come on the scene) resisted this process, as did a few enlightened American patriots who happened to be mostly countercultural university students. In time, the argument ran, they would prevail, thereby saving world civilization.

### Postrevisionism

This tendency began to develop during the early 1970s out of a sense of dissatisfaction with both orthodoxy and revisionism. Both, it argued, were too simplistic, too much given to single-cause explanations, too inclined to assume blame. The postrevisionists—without realizing that they were Hegelians—sought a kind of Hegelian synthesis of orthodoxy and revisionism, taking the strongest elements of each argument and rejecting the weakest. The result was largely mush, leaving it quite unclear as to whether Western or world civilization or anything else was worth saving.

### Corporatism

A more sophisticated version of revisionism, this sees American capitalism, not as a competitive process setting domestic economic interests against one another, but rather as a cooperative one based on enlarging the pie for everyone. The Americans sought to become the world hegemon, in effect, by buying it out, or co-opting it, or by smothering everyone in a kind of warm, fuzzy blanket of corporate consumerism.

## *International history*

These historians made the entirely correct point that too much of Cold War history had been written from the perspective of the United States. They sought to expand diplomatic history to become international history, focusing to a considerable extent on Europe and the Third World.

## *Cultural history*

In a reflection of the social history movement that has been sweeping the profession, particularly in the United States, these historians insisted that diplomatic history reflected the cultures that lay behind it. It was, therefore, subject to largely unconscious influences that only historians in retrospect could ferret out.

## *Postmodernism*

The idea here is that anything we can say about the past is socially or culturally constructed, therefore we can't say anything at all that is not subject to challenge. To insist on firm interpretations of anything is itself an act of imperialism, which progressive forces of course will want to resist.

This "old" Cold War history, despite its diverse manifestations, does have certain common characteristics. The first is not knowing how things came out. All of these interpretations originated and evolved while the Cold War was still going on, so that none of them was in a position to view that conflict as a whole, from beginning to end.

A second common characteristic of the "old" Cold War history is that it said almost nothing about the "other side." Almost all of this writing was done from the standpoint of the United States, its allies, and its clients—very little of it took cognizance of the fact that there were two super-powers, not just one. There was, in short, a bipolar international system, and as time went on it spawned a complex set of subsystems on each side; the "old" Cold War history gave us very little sense of the dynamics of all of this.

A third characteristic of the "old" Cold War history was that it gave surprisingly little attention to the role of ideas. All of these interpretations emphasized the role of interests, which were mostly defined in material terms—what people possessed or wanted to possess. They neglected the role of ideas—what people believed or wanted to believe.

It is not so difficult, in retrospect, to see how these deficiencies arose. Not only was there no certain way, while the Cold War was going on, to know how it was going to come out, there was also no assurance that it would ever end at all. The conflict had gone on for so long that it was the only condition of international affairs several generations of experts on international relations had ever known. Even historians, who should have known better, fell into the habit of characterizing the Cold War as a "long peace."

It was difficult to know very much about the other side of Cold War history because the other side made a point of keeping its history hidden. There was no Freedom of Information Act, or mandatory review declassification process, in the Soviet Union, China, and the other Marxist-Leninist states; indeed, the tradition in these countries had long been that of insisting that all historians serve as official historians, in that they were expected to write about the past only in the way that the state wanted it remembered.

As far as the role of ideas was concerned, our most distinguished theorists of international relations had long since assured us that only interests, and the power relationships they reflected, were important. The world of theory provided surprisingly few mechanisms for understanding how ideas—even ideas that might appear, at least at first glance, to be at odds with material interests—can take hold and shape the course of history; although the historians were perfectly prepared to acknowledge this when studying more distant topics like the rise of Christianity or the subordination of women or the emergence of national consciousness, they gave rather little attention to the possibility that ideas might be important in shaping Cold War history.

### A NEW COLD WAR HISTORY

What will the "new Cold War history" be like? First, it will treat the Cold War as a discrete historical episode with a known beginning and a known end, not as a continuing or even permanent system. It will place the Cold War within the stream of time, but it will not confuse the Cold War with the stream of time itself. It will acknowledge fully that there have been, and certainly will be, other ways of organizing international affairs. It will place the Cold War in much more of a comparative perspective across time than the "old" Cold War history managed to do.

Second, it will be a genuinely multiarchival history, in that it will draw symmetrically rather than asymmetrically on the archival sources of all major participants in that conflict. It will move away from the old pattern where we knew both the public and behind-the-scenes face of Western diplomacy, but could only speculate about the latter when it came to the Marxist-Leninist world. Third, it will take more seriously the ideas people had in their heads. The reason the Cold War ended when it did, and in the peaceful manner that it did, can only be explained in these terms: there was no military defeat or economic collapse as such, but there was a collapse of legitimacy. People of one Cold War empire suddenly realized that its emperor had no clothes on—but as in the classic fairy tale, that realization resulted from a shift in the way people thought, not from the circumstances that actually existed before their eyes.

Will the "new Cold War history" alter the way Americans view their recent past? Perhaps, perhaps not. But, this "new" history will certainly test some of the basic assumptions that we had during the Cold War—such as bipolarity, the utility of nuclear weapons, and the role of ideology.

### BIPOLARITY: A STRATEGIC ACCIDENT?

Was bipolarity—and the Cold War that grew out of it—a historical accident, or was it a permanent shift in the nature of the international system? One of the assumptions underlying the writing of much Cold War history was that bipolarity was firmly rooted; that whereas the history of international relations prior to 1945 had been multipolar in character, that was all behind us now, and bipolarity stretched out indefinitely into the future.

Some of this came from the rediscovery and popularization of Alexis de Tocqueville's great prediction, from 1835, that the Russians and the Americans would one day each dominate half the earth. Some of it came from the way World War II ended: the great powers of Europe seemed to have committed a kind of collective suicide, leaving the United States on one side and the Soviet Union on the other as—or so it appeared—the only great powers. Some of it came from international relations theory.

There were serious deficiencies, it is now clear, in the way we were measuring power in international affairs. We tended to look at it almost entirely in monodimensional terms, when a multidimensional framework would have been preferable. The end of the Cold War revealed that there were in reality several different kinds of power—military, but also economic, ideological, cultural, moral—all of which contributed toward a determination of great power status.

The Soviet Union, which had started out the Cold War possessing several different kinds of power, found itself over the years confronting a contraction in the varieties it could draw upon. It once had power in economic, ideological, moral realms, but this gradually dropped away, leaving only the shell of military power. Had we adopted that multidimensional framework, we would probably have seen sooner than we did that bipolarity was more an artifact of the way World War II had ended—and of the improbable series of events that had brought about World War II—than of any fundamental change in the nature of the international system.

That system, we can now see, has remained multipolar—bipolarity in the long-term scheme of things was just a blip—and that implies a less stable framework for international relations than the Cold War in fact provided. The Cold War ended, by this logic, when the international system finally got back to normal in all the dimensions of power, including the military.

## THE NUCLEAR PARADOX

The proposition that nuclear weapons kept the Cold War from getting hot is a familiar one, although still not universally accepted. The argument is that nuclear weapons created new constraints against escalation and other forms of risk-taking that had not been present at other points in the history of international relations. As a result, crises that in other periods would have caused wars in the Cold War did not.

Have we, however, fully considered the price we paid for this? Some historians are coming around to the view that nuclear weapons created rigidities that made a political settlement impossible, even when conditions otherwise might have been propitious. Consider the period 1962–63. The pattern, already mentioned, of diminishing power diversity on the Soviet side, as against continuing diversity on the American side, was already by then fairly clear.

Capitalism had not collapsed, as Marxist-Leninist theorists had fully expected it to do. Instead the United States had presided over a remarkable recovery of the world economic system that had, by about 1960, pretty effectively wiped out whatever bad reputation capitalism retained from the memory of the Great Depression. Communism, in the meantime, had come close to failing. Neither the Russians nor the Chinese had worked out how to manage an economy that would elevate standards of living. Khrushchev's agricultural policies had failed, and Mao's Great Leap had produced even more devastating results.

An asymmetry in alliance structures had by this time emerged. Events in Eastern Europe in 1956 had made it clear that the Warsaw Pact would never be NATO. Meanwhile the breakup of the Sino-Soviet alliance was making it clear that Mao's disruptive influence was much greater than that of de Gaulle in the Western alliance. Also evident, by this time, was an asymmetry in military capabilities. Khrushchev's effort to gain strategic superiority by rattling rockets he did not have had ended in near disaster with the Kennedy administration calling his bluff in 1961, thereby setting off the desperate and ultimately unsuccessful quick fix of putting intermediate range ballistic missiles in Cuba. American nuclear superiority, in turn, negated whatever conventional force superiority the Russians may have had, a fact Khrushchev had tacitly acknowledged by cutting back on Soviet conventional forces.

Finally, the virtues of cooperation had begun to surface with formal agreements such as the Limited Test Ban Treaty of 1963 and the hot line arrangement. Perhaps even more important were informal agreements on the mutual toleration of satellite reconnaissance. By all material indices at this time, it should have been clear that the Soviet Union's power base was contracting, that it would not be able to keep up with the West, that capitalism's grandchildren were not going to live under communism. Why didn't the Cold War end at that point?

It was probably because power was still chiefly calculated in the particular currency in which the Soviet Union had the most impressive capabilities, which was nuclear weapons. The Soviet decision, in the wake of the missile crisis, to push for strategic parity provided the basis for a long-term and, in retrospect, quite misleading assessment of Soviet capabilities in the West; it was also the basis for the underlying (but false) assumption of détente, which was that the West, not the Marxist-Leninist world, was declining. This almost caused us to give up on our goals just as they were being realized. There also developed from this the preoccupation with arms control as the major focus of Soviet-

American relations, something that is going to be hard for future generations to understand. This should raise questions in our minds about how accurately we were assessing the strength of our chief adversary, the extent to which nuclear weapons got in the way of such assessments, and whether the Cold War might have ended earlier.

## THE ROLE OF ROMANTICISM

Being ideological during the Cold War led to romantic illusions. In his latest book, *Diplomacy*, Henry Kissinger faults Hitler for having fallen prey to romantic visions based much more on emotion than on rational calculation. But Stalin, he claims, was brutally realistic, perfectly prepared to take as long as necessary to achieve his objectives, perfectly willing to adapt ideology as needed to justify them. For Hitler, Kissinger seems to be saying, ideology determined objectives, and practical difficulties were not allowed to stand in the way. For Stalin, it was the other way around; the objectives determined the ideology, which was revised and updated as needed.

That certainly has been the standard view of the relationship between ideology and Soviet foreign policy over the years; and perhaps even more so with Mao Zedong, who achieved the remarkable feat of rearranging Marx and Lenin to make them fit China. As a consequence, Cold War historians did not take ideology very seriously.

This was partly because we assumed too easily that regimes that depend on propaganda know that it is propaganda, and hence don't believe in it themselves. It was partly also because our own realist and neorealist theories of international relations gave us few tools for understanding the role of ideology. The new sources for Cold War history seem to call rather strongly the neglect of ideology into question, for what they are suggesting is that ideology went much further as a determinant of action in Marxist-Leninist societies, that it was not just a justification for actions already decided upon.

In one sense, this should hardly surprise us. The Soviet Union, the People's Republic of China, and the other Marxist-Leninist governments based their very legitimacy upon ideological arguments; and ideology—with its premium on orthodoxy and its deep distrust of heresy—permeated all aspects of daily life. What the new sources often reveal, though, are actions taken by Soviet and Chinese leaders that make no sense apart from ideological explanations.

One is Stalin's persistent belief that, sooner or later, conflict was going to break out within the capitalist world. When the September 1946 Novikov dispatch—the Soviet equivalent of Kennan's "long telegram"—was first released, what was striking about it was its emphasis on Anglo-American conflict.[2] Stalin actually believed that Great Britain and the United States were destined to clash, and soon. This came, of course, from Lenin's teachings on the contradictions of capitalism, but it severely impaired Stalin's ability to see the extent to which coalitions were building against him in the West. This helps to explain his surprise over the Marshall Plan.

Another one is Stalin's curious belief that the Europeans, and particularly the Germans, would welcome the Red Army as liberators—that there could be an empire by invitation. This is clearest in what we now know of his plans for Germany: he intended to build a socialist state in the east that would serve as a magnet for the rest of Germany by the sheer force of ideological example. This was at a time when the examples sticking in the minds of Germans were those of forced expropriation of property and mass rape.

A third example has to do with Mao Zedong, who it now seems had always been more worshipful of Stalin than suspicious of him. Far from letting China's geopolitical interests suggest wariness of Russian intentions, it now looks as though Mao consistently put ideological interests above national interests in his relations with Moscow—at least as long as Stalin was alive.

A fourth example has to do with both Stalin and Mao: it now appears that far from opposing the Chinese Communist revolution, Stalin welcomed it as a great but beneficial surprise, as evidence that the forces of revolution were swinging to the east. As a consequence, in his old age he fell into a kind of revolutionary romanticism, encouraging the Chinese to take the lead in sparking revolutionary movements throughout Asia.

A fifth example has to do with Khrushchev, who seems—along with his advisers—to have responded to Fidel Castro in much the same way. It was not strategic advantages that made Khrushchev, but latent revolutionary romanticism.

The conclusion that seems to come from all of this is not that Marxism-Leninism promoted realistic thinking, as Kissinger seems to suggest; rather, that it encouraged a kind of unrealistic emotional romanticism that was often profoundly at odds with the stark evidence that lay before the eyes of those who practiced it.

## THE COLD WAR WAS AN
## IDEOLOGICAL STRUGGLE

*Webster's Ninth New Collegiate Dictionary* defines power as the ability to get the outcome one wants or the ability to achieve one's purposes. The next level of understanding within this definition is that power among nations has two dimensions.

The first is the aspect that power is the ability to make others do what you want them to do. The sources of this national ability are what some analysts have called hard power resources—military, technological, and economic. This is the traditional definition of power among nations. The second face of power is what some scholars have dubbed soft power resources. This is the idea that power is the ability to get others to want what you want. The source of this comes from a nation's culture, ideology, and its ability to control international institutions.

Being idealistic during the Cold War produced realistic results. Idealism, at the time the Cold War began, had a bad name in the West, and has had since in most historical treatments of the Cold War. The founding fathers of realism, inside and outside the government, saw Wilsonian idealism as having led to the League of Nations, the Washington Naval Treaties, the Kellogg-Briand Pact banning aggression, and the whole series of developments that had so conspicuously failed to prevent World War II.

Their basic argument was that none of these initiatives had taken into account the actual power relationships that determined the course of international relations. If the Western democracies were to survive in the postwar world—which was likely to be as cold and cruel as the prewar world had been—they would have to abandon the illusion that they could conduct foreign policy in the same genteel way they conducted their domestic affairs. It would be necessary to learn about balances of power, about covert operations, about the permanent peacetime uses of military force—in short, it would be necessary to learn the cynical art of realpolitik. And surely, we did find ourselves skewed toward a global military presence that many felt was inconsistent with our history and values.

But with Kennan at least, there was an interesting ambivalence here, as in so much else about him. On the one hand, he had little use for the influence of democratic procedures on the conduct of foreign policy. On the other, though, he expected containment to work by having the United States remain true to its fundamental principles, which presumably included those of democratic politics. What is significant about the Cold War in retrospect is the extent to which the United States and the other democracies did in fact do this—not only did they remain democracies at home, but they allowed their democratic instincts to shape their policies abroad.

This happened not so much as a matter of deliberate policy as by instinct. When confronting situations in which they did not otherwise know what to do, Americans behaved democratically and encouraged others to do so as well. Far from being the impractical idealism that the realists thought such practices would be, they turned out to be eminently realistic because they provided a key lubricant in keeping the Western coalition together and attracting those farther east.

To see this, it is useful to go back to Marxist-Leninist thinking on the internal contradictions of capitalism, and ask the question: why did the contradictions of Marxism-Leninism turn out to be so much more severe? One reason, frequently written about, is that the United States managed, through the Bretton Woods system and later the Marshall Plan, to stave off a postwar depression and revive capitalism. Surely there is something to this.

But another less well-known lubricant was surely democratic politics, and here there are three key episodes, all relating to the conduct of U.S. foreign policy: the democratization (by way of occupation) of Germany and Japan, the management of the NATO alliance, and the encouragement of European integration. What all of these had in common was the ability of the Americans to give the others involved a stake in the success of the enterprise. This was more than just the tangible benefits of market economics; it also involved a good deal of flexibility in letting the others design the enterprise altogether.

Flexibility was the least, obviously, in the German and Japanese occupations, and yet even there one cannot help but be impressed by the extent to which the Americans were able to adapt their reforms to local conditions and, for the most part, make them stick. NATO was very much a joint enterprise—it would not have existed had it not been for the Europeans, and the Americans allowed them a great deal of influence over its organization, its membership, its operations. European integration was even more a European initiative, although one much encouraged by the United States. The Americans created the environment, and then the integrative process became a self-organizing system, taking on a life and character very much its own. Some Europeans came to resent American preponderance, to be sure, but the remarkable achievement was the enduring democratic character of the Western alliance system.

It is difficult to conceive of the Russians managing any of these things in this way. Their own occupation policies in Germany for the most part backfired on them, and they were never able to establish a regime there that had the support the West German regime could command. The Warsaw Pact never operated in the same way as NATO. There was little sense of mutual interest, and especially after the events of 1956 the Russians could hardly count on its loyalty if an emergency had come. The Sino-Soviet alliance operated no better. Nor was there any kind of self-organizing economic or political integration within the Soviet sphere—instead, everything had to be routed through Moscow, in the classic imperial manner.

The reason the Americans succeeded at this, it would seem, is simply the fact that they were, by habit, history, and instinct, democratic in their politics. They were used to the bargaining, deal-making, coercion, and conciliation that takes place within a democratic political system; they did not automatically regard resistance as treason. Their system, as a result, spread easily; it also coexisted easily with other democratic systems where they already existed.

The Soviets, coming out of their authoritarian tradition, had no means of dealing with independent thinking. The slightest signs of independence, for Stalin, were heresy, to be rooted out with all of the thoroughness of the Spanish Inquisition. The result was surely subservience, but it was not self-organization, it was not spontaneity, it was not the way of operating that could give those involved a stake in the success of the enterprise. In this sense, then, the preservation of democratic ideas—free markets, free speech, free association, and the processes of compromise and conciliation that come with these—turned out to be a very realistic thing for the Western democracies to have done.

Perhaps Samuel Huntington is behind the times: the Cold War, rather than the post–Cold War era, may best fit his description of a clash of civilizations.[3] That is to say, the domestic institutions that existed on each side proved decisive in determining the outcome of the competition. De Tocqueville had caught the difference in these civilizations as early as 1835 when he commented on the difference between the authoritarian system of the Russian tsar, where the opinion of one man determined everything that happened, and the remarkable cacophony of opinions that somehow coalesced to shape what happened within the American political system. Perhaps the real significance of the Cold War was that it was a clash between democratic and authoritarian forms of culture, or civilization, and that democracy won not so much because of the wisdom of the West and its leaders—although surely some of that was there—as because it happened to take place just at the moment in world history in which the environmental conditions that had for so long favored authoritarian forms of government had ceased to do so.

## CONCLUSIONS

Do any of these considerations fundamentally alter the way we should think about the Cold War? Do they confirm the rightness of our policies or call them into serious question? Of course, the new evidence is ambiguous, and new perspectives are contested. The end of the Cold War was not the end of history, and it was not the end of historical debate. Yet, a few tentative conclusions suggest themselves.

In retrospect, the Cold War does not seem quite the epic struggle that we may have taken it for as we were waging it. Certainly, it was not a foreordained clash between two rival power systems that had its genesis in World War I or even earlier.

Epic or not, the struggle was not merely a historical accident. Certainly, there is little in the "new Cold War history" that suggests the whole thing could have been averted had only the two sides shown greater flexibility. That said, it is also evident that nuclear weapons imposed unusual rigidities on the Cold War system—rigidities that helped prevent conventional war (because of the danger of escalation) but also made political settlement elusive so long as the nuclear threat remained.

It is worth recalling that no Soviet or American leader since Stalin seriously called for the overthrow of the adversary. American policy during the Cold War was meant to tame, not defeat, the Soviet Union. Thus the Cold War ended unexpectedly for both sides. The American side was left with an adversary not only defeated but physically dismembered; the other side, with an empire lost but without the finality of defeat that attended Germany and Japan at the end of World War II.

Americans and Russians knew when V-E Day and V-J Day were. But when, exactly, did the Cold War end? Both sides mobilized as if for war, and both sides incurred huge costs and burdens. Yet the victor felt little sense of exhilaration and the loser, little remorse. Small wonder that both are experiencing a prolonged period of disorientation.

Yet for Americans, perhaps the most important lesson we can draw from the "new Cold War history" is that the values, principles, and assumptions that guided our policies during the Cold War proved generally sound. Neither the new evidence nor our new, post–Cold War perspective should cause us to be more critical in retrospect than we were at the time. At various points we may have lost sight of our principles or, as in Vietnam, lost confidence in our political leadership. But in the end, the broad course on which we embarked four decades ago was vindicated. At the beginning of the new era, we could do worse than to look back to those core values and principles to draw our bearings.

## NOTES

1. This essay is based on a roundtable discussion with John Lewis Gaddis on March 6, 1996, at the Woodrow Wilson International Center for Scholars. It was edited by Robert Hutchings and rapporteur Michael K. Vaden on the basis of Gaddis's prepared remarks and reflects the views and perspectives of other scholars and specialists who participated in the discussion.

2. The nineteen-page cable from the Soviet ambassador to the United States, Nikolai Novikov, to Foreign Minister Molotov describing the likely direction of U.S. foreign policy in the postwar period as well as the February 1946 "Long Telegram" from George Kennan, the U.S. charge d'affaires in Moscow, to the U.S. Secretary of State may be found in Kenneth M. Jensen, ed., *Origins of the Cold War: The Novikov, Kennan, and Roberts 'Long Telegrams' of* 1946 (Washington, D.C.: United States Institute of Peace, 1991).

3. Samuel P. Huntington, "The Clash of Civilizations," *Foreign Affairs* 72 (Summer 1993): 22–49.

# CHAPTER FOUR

## The American Century
## and Its Discontents

JOSEPH DUFFEY

*Joseph Duffey has served at the most senior levels of both government and academia. Currently director of the United States Information Agency, he previously served as president of the American University in Washington, D.C., and from 1982–91 as chancellor of the University of Massachusetts at Amherst. He was assistant secretary of state for educational and cultural affairs and chair of the National Endowment for the Humanities under presidents Carter and Reagan. He has taught at Yale University and holds fifteen honorary degrees from colleges and universities in the United States and abroad.*

In the month of February an American journalist wrote the following about the national mood: "We Americans are unhappy. We are not happy about America. We are not happy about ourselves in relation to America. We are nervous . . . gloomy . . . apathetic."[1]

These words did not come from a recent Sunday morning television show or a contemporary speech about the so-called funk in America. Rather, they were written more than a half-century ago. They were written in February of 1941, the first sentences of Henry Luce's essay "The American Century."

Those who view America's current uneasiness as something extraordinary need occasionally to be reminded that "there is nothing new under the sun"—even nervousness, gloominess, and apathy in America.

Yet we should also be cautious about too quickly dismissing the current national mood as merely a periodic recurrence of normal populist dissatisfaction. In 1941, when Henry Luce penned those words, America had good reason to be unhappy. The nation still struggled with the great economic challenges brought on by the Depression; a terrible war was engulfing Europe and threatening the Far East; and it seemed that America would soon have to choose once again whether to send its young men to fight and die on the fields of Europe and perhaps in the Pacific, or remove itself entirely from the world with the foolish hope that the world would in turn ignore America.

It is useful and necessary to put current American unhappiness in perspective: as Robert Samuelson has reminded us in his recent book, *The Good Life and Its Discontents*, things aren't as bad as we make them out to be. The world is, relatively speaking, at peace. While many Americans have undergone economic dislocation, the economy today is significantly more healthy than it was over fifty years ago.

It is all the more perplexing then that there should seem to be such a pervasive sense of anxiety. Despite all of our apparent successes—the greatest of which is certainly the utterly unexpected collapse of the Soviet Empire now more than a half-decade ago—Americans express levels of discontent that have not been seen since the Vietnam War. While analysts can point to the purported irrationality of American's disenchantment, it persists nevertheless, and its source remains elusive.

The difficulty in specifically locating America's discontent arises precisely from the vague, indefinable uneasiness that arises from these broad sea changes in American and international life. There is no specific event such as economic depression or war that would, on the one hand, elicit a sense of national nervousness, and that might in turn inspire a united and definite response. Rather, our uneasiness arises from a general uncertainty about the future: economic insecurity; a loss of old certainties—those represented by the fading realities of neighborhood, community, and civic associations; and an uncertainty about the role that America can and should play in world affairs.

Henry Luce's essay on the American Century in 1941 sounded some themes that are familiar to those who are following the current debate about America's role in the world. I must say that, reading the article again after some years, I was impressed by the force of rhetoric and international idealism that animates Luce's arguments. He champions what might today be called assertive unilateralism. Like some who try to define a world role for America today, Luce puts the issue in stark, mutually exclusive terms. He wrote: "And so we . . . come squarely and closely face to face with the issue which Americans hate most to face. It is that old, old issue with those old, old battered labels—the issue of isolationism versus internationalism. . . . We detest both words. We spit them at each other with the fury of hissing geese. We duck and dodge them."

After Luce published his essay there ensued a long and respectful correspondence with Henry Wallace, who wrote a rejoinder, "The Century of the Common Man." The nuances and differences of the two positions expressed by Luce and Wallace must have made for a stimulating exchange on the role America might aspire to play on the world stage four decades into the twentieth century. I frankly doubt that Luce would have prevailed on argument alone in his effort to define a new, more assertive role for the United States. But ominous events intervened. Ten months after the essay appeared, the Japanese attack on Pearl Harbor and the outbreak of war ended the debate. America became by fate, if not by choice, the Arsenal of Democracy, the Leader of the Free World.

The task of fighting the war focused the attention of the nation for the next four years. But, as is always the case, euphoria after the victory in World War II was followed by a time of confusion and depression of spirit. Soon, however, world events gave rise to a new debate about the role that America should assume and aspire to in world affairs. This time the terms of the debate took a different twist. In 1949 the Soviets tested a nuclear bomb, and at approximately the same time, a secret document began to circulate in the high levels of our government that argued for a major new strategic commitment to international leadership. I refer to National Security Council Document 68.

These were the opening moments of the Cold War. In those crucial months a number of influential Americans came to the realization that a new ideological and perhaps military showdown with the Soviet Union loomed—a showdown whose consequences threatened the virtual annihilation of mankind.

## COLD WAR STRATEGY
### AND ITS CONSEQUENCES

NSC 68 was written primarily by Paul Nitze in April 1950. It was a classified memo from the National Security Council for the eyes of

President Truman only about how best to confront the looming threat from the Soviet Union. It is a remarkable document in many ways. For one thing it was written in a style of breadth and purpose that is rare in government documents today. NSC 68 was a sequel to Luce's earlier essay, but it defined America's role in the world even more out of the case of necessity than out of aspiration. NSC 68 called for major sacrifices from the American people in order to begin the largest and most expensive peacetime buildup of military forces in world history. Stating the issue frankly, Nitze wrote that "there are risks in making ourselves strong. A large measure of sacrifice and discipline will be demanded of the American people. They will be asked to give up some of the benefits which they have come to associate with those freedoms." In other words, in defense of America's freedom, some of those freedoms would have to be sacrificed for the sake of national strength. In this effort, Nitze concluded that "Nothing can be more important than that they [the American people] fully understand the reasons for this."[2]

Yet, despite NSC 68's appeal to the understanding of the American public, paradoxically the document remained classified until 1975. The fundamental blueprint of America's Cold War strategy was kept secret from the same American people whose support it so explicitly appeared to require.

The authors of NSC 68 did not conclude that the persuasiveness of their own document should be used to encourage the public's support for the Cold War; rather, the document suggests that the American people should be told only "sufficient" information that would elicit the necessary support for the Cold War buildup. The authors wrote, "Having achieved a comprehension of the issues now confronting this Republic, it will then be possible for the American people and the American Government to arrive at a consensus. Out of this common view will develop a determination of the national will and a solid resolute expression of that will. The initiative in this process lies with the Government."[3]

What is noteworthy about these words from our perspective is the presumption that the American government could, entirely of its own initiative, mold the national will in support of an unprecedented military buildup whose justification was in part withheld from the nation. This pronouncement is all the more remarkable because the authors of this document were fundamentally correct about the extent to which the government could lead the formation of the national will—after all, trust in national institutions in previous decades ran so deep that the authors of NSC 68 could write without self-consciousness about a unanimous "consensus"—a near indivisibility of opinion—between the "American people" and "the American Government."

I cite NSC 68 not only as an example of a bygone era in which trust in institutions and fellow citizens was more pervasive in America than at present, but further to suggest that NSC 68's very presumption of trust without a simultaneous willingness to engage the American public in a more fundamental debate about the effects that the Cold War might have on democracy was, in the end, a corrosive combination. The authors recognized that the military buildup would require some sacrifice of the freedoms that Americans otherwise enjoyed. However, not only was this statement never aired for democratic debate, but its fulfillment—the curtailing of democratic freedoms—was essentially guaranteed by NSC 68's division of the world into "us"—America—versus "them"—the Kremlin. The architects of the Cold War realized that American opinion could most easily and fiercely be motivated, and a willingness to sacrifice be encouraged, by stressing American-Soviet differences in the starkest terms. But the very creation of a well-defined enemy had the simultaneous effect of narrowing the definition of what it meant to be an American. And the vast mobilization of American society guaranteed a garrison mentality that only fed the demands for social and political conformity. As the sociologist Robert Bellah and his colleagues suggested in their book, *The Good Society*, "A vast military mobilization carried out for the sake of preserving dignity and freedom might actually destroy freedom, since a massive military establishment can smother the rest of society and sow the seeds of paranoia among the citizens."[4]

Of course, I am not suggesting that NSC 68 or any single document alone could have this sweeping effect on American society. But, at the same time, I agree with Bellah that inasmuch as NSC 68 can be pointed to as a definitive blueprint for the Cold War, it did sow some rather potent seeds of mistrust in our polity. The sense of paranoia that was exhibited at its worst during the McCarthy hearings can also be identified in the way which the Vietnam War was conducted, creating in turn a sense of us-against-them that led to the Watergate break-in and cover-up, and motivated ignoble efforts of the government to protect our so-called security, such as testing the effects of nuclear weapons on its own servicemen. Increasingly, our mistrust of the other has been turned inward: a government that did not trust democracy enough to disclose its original intentions has found that mistrust returned tenfold from its citizens.

This roundabout examination of some of the corrosive effects of the Cold War on trust in America has profound implications for America's role in the post–Cold War era. With the conclusion of the Cold War, the old debate, as Luce describes it, isolationism versus internationalism, has once more come to the fore, albeit in new terms and categories. Some argue now that American foreign policy should be conceived and undertaken as a more direct outgrowth of domestic policy. In particular, they argue that the nation's role in international affairs is finally either limited or enhanced by its domestic strength, both economic and political.

It can be argued, with some credibility I believe, that it was the very strategy adopted by the United States during the Cold War—one that proved successful in strictly foreign policy terms—that has undercut America's domestic ability to creatively respond to challenges posed in the international arena today.

Without downplaying the continued necessity of maintaining an adequate defense structure, it must be recognized that today struggling nations around the globe do not urgently require arms and military training to resist tyranny, but rather new and transformed civil, economic, and political structures. Our government, in concert with nongovernmental organizations (NGOs) and American business, should be able to play some role in that transition. But the very mistrust of government—partly a legacy of the Cold War—now stands ironically as a roadblock in the creation of a post–Cold War foreign policy of assisting democracy overseas.

The United States Information Agency recently celebrated the fiftieth anniversary of the enactment of the legislation that created the Fulbright Program. I enjoyed reacquainting myself with this program's history, the senator for whom it was named, and the era from which it arose—an era that spanned the New Deal, the Marshall Plan, the Fair Deal, and the Great Society. That era which demonstrated that the American government at its best could make positive contributions, both domestically and internationally, to the betterment of society. But I have been startled by the contrast with today's widespread belief that government is incapable of improving society, and the concomitant faith that only the free market holds the key to human progress.

We in the international affairs community have been too complacent about this pervasive American cynicism toward government and public life, mistakenly thinking that foreign policy is immune from its effects, and worse yet, that we are wholly innocent of the cause of this cynicism. Much of the recent analysis of the decline of trust in government, the dwindling participation in our nation's civic life and institutions, and the sense of frustration and anxiety that arises from this civic isolation has emphasized the negative effects on our domestic political life. But it is also the case that widespread citizen apathy and mistrust must ultimately affect negatively the conduct of foreign policy as well.

## THE CENTURY OF MODERNITY?

In the absence of a conscious and concerted effort toward improving international political and civic structures, it is likely that a different American role in international affairs will predominate: a de facto Americanization in the cultural sphere. Even as confidence in our public institutions has waned, the American public's affection for the icons of movies, television, and popular culture has proven internationally contagious. It was primarily this facet of American life that prompted Henry Luce to announce the beginning of "The American Century." Even as early as 1941 he was able to write that "there is already an immense American internationalism. American jazz, Hollywood movies, American slang, American machines and patented products are in fact the only things that every community in the world, from Zanzibar to Hamburg, recognizes in common."[5]

Luce's comments contain the seeds of irony that are blooming around the world today. It may very well be that the "American Century" is giving way to the "Century of Modernity." Modeled on American cultural iconography and norms, modernity has enveloped the world, creating a standardless standard that makes everyone and everywhere identical and interchangeable. In a commencement address at Harvard University in 1995, Czech President Vaclav Havel reminisced about a recent evening he had spent drinking traditional Czech cocktails in an entirely familiar setting, sitting on familiar furniture and listening to universal Western rock music—except that he was sitting at a bar in Singapore. Havel simultaneously marveled and lamented over the rigid standardization of life after the prevailing American-Western model, and wondered whether native cultures and folkways would soon succumb to the enchanting contagion that is modernity.

Havel's observations have further implications on the question we consider today: is this the end of the American century? In the vacuum created by the mistrust of the public sector's ability to contribute to civic improvements, what we are likely to see—what we are already seeing— is the American Century, solely defined by American entertainment, culture, and sports, folding effortlessly and unnoticed into the Century of Modernity. I think many wish for this consummation, equating America almost purely with the popular culture it has created. But just as the world will lose its distinctiveness, so too will America. And what was truly distinctive about the great American project—its great experiment with democracy—will fade quietly into the background of a Technicolor future.

As we contemplate what America's role should be in the next millennium, we should reflect on what is uniquely worth preserving from the American Century. Among the American accomplishments that Luce thought America could offer the world—technological advancement, its culture, its ideals of freedom—there is no mention of its historic experience with democracy, both its triumphs and the lessons to be learned from its shortcomings. When we peel back all of the layers of what it means to be an American, perhaps these lessons in the crucible of modern democracy are what best define what is unique, and worth preserving, of the American Century.

But as long as mistrust marks the relationship between citizens and their government, and toward one another, America is unlikely to be successful as an example to the world of the virtues of democratic life. Before we can even contemplate taking on a greater role in the post–Cold War world, we must attend to the problems in our own democracy that may prevent us from successfully assuming that larger role. While many of the challenges facing our American democracy involve budget and spending decisions, I believe that our greatest challenge lies in rebuilding the trust between citizen and citizen, between citizen and government, and ultimately among citizens of the world. The belief that one's own self-interest is directly linked to the interests of others, both in one's own nation and throughout the world, is the vital imaginative bridge of sympathy that allows democracy to function. And to whatever extent the foreign affairs community might have contributed to the decline of trust, it is necessary for us to assist in its reinvigoration. For without attending to the re-creation of trust in America, and dispelling the deep anxieties of America's citizens about their future in an uncertain world, we may then indeed see an ending to the American Century.

## NOTES

1. Henry Luce, "The American Century," John K. Jessup, ed., *The Ideas of Henry Luce* (New York: Athenaeum, 1969), 106.

2. "NSC 68: United States Objectives and Programs for National Security," Ernest R. May, ed., *American Cold War Strategy: Interpreting NSC 68* (New York: St. Martin's Press, 1993), 54.

3. Ibid., 43.

4. Robert Bellah, et al., *The Good Society* (New York: Vintage Books, 1991), 228–29.

5. Luce, "The American Century," 117.

# PART TWO

# The Changing Shape of International Politics

# CHAPTER FIVE

# World Politics in the
# Twenty-first Century[1]

## ROBERT L. HUTCHINGS

*Robert L. Hutchings is assistant dean for academic affairs of the Woodrow Wilson School of Public and International Affairs at Princeton University, where he also teaches international politics.*

We refer, awkwardly, to the "post–Cold War era," as if our brave new world could be defined by the era that preceded it. Our new world has no name, for it is still in a state of becoming, not yet of being. History will record the 1990s not as a postrevolutionary period but as the midpoint of an era of revolutionary upheaval in the wake of the Cold War.

This essay attempts to look beyond the present transitional period to project the kind of world we are likely to confront in the year 2020. It is a year sufficiently distant to be interesting: one could not plausibly argue that nothing much will have changed by that time. Yet it is near enough to impose a certain discipline, for most of the key features of that world should be already visible, if only dimly.

Prior examples of planning for a postwar order should instill caution about bold forecasting. President Wilson launched "The Inquiry" in the midst of World War I to engage the brightest minds in and out of government on the nature of a postwar order and America's place and purposes in it. In 1939, President Roosevelt approved the "Committee on

Postwar Planning" with a similar mandate and mission. Neither body did much to inform a postwar order. Both suffered from the inherent difficulties, vastly greater than the participants realized, of divining the real power relationships that would emerge after the dust of war had settled.

Still, it should be possible to suggest some of the main features of world politics in the early twenty-first century. Indeed, it may be liberating to leapfrog over the immediate foreign policy debate, most of whose issues will have been resolved one way or another by the year 2020, and look instead to deeper and more durable patterns. However uncertain we may be about Russia's future or China's prospects, we can speak with somewhat greater confidence about the basic structure of power in world politics and the principal global trends, some only beginning to be apparent, that will shape the world of 2020 and the environment in which American foreign policy will operate.

## THE STRUCTURE OF WORLD POWER

Militarily, the world of 2020 is likely to remain unipolar, with several regional centers but with no other power or group of powers capable of matching the global reach of the United States. Russia will not be able to regenerate the military capacity of the former Soviet Union within twenty-five years, no matter the character of its political leadership. Neither can China develop a global capacity so quickly, though a continuation of its current military spending spree and rapid economic growth could transform it into a dominant regional power.

Economically, there will be a multipolar distribution of power among the United States, Europe, and East Asia, led by Japan and perhaps a resurgent China. East Asia is likely to be the most dynamic and unpredictable. If China continues to enjoy 6–8 percent annual economic growth while escaping major political upheaval, the Chinese economy of 2020 will be formidable indeed, particularly if allied with a strong Japanese economy.

Yet the salience of military power will diminish, and economic power will be decreasingly at the service of national governments. Beneath the level of these familiar yardsticks of global power and influence, there will be an increasing diffusion of power among supranational, transnational, and subnational actors. The United States is well placed along these dimensions of power to continue exerting substantial influence, but the emerging structure of power will make it difficult for the U.S. government, either alone or in concert with others, to exert decisive influence on many critical issues that bear on American security and prosperity.

## THE HINGE POINTS OF HISTORY

The new world order will be determined largely by developments in four regions. The key questions arising in each are not hard to forecast, even if the answers are elusive.

### *Europe*

Will a stable, more united Europe contribute to a wider transatlantic partnership that will be the cornerstone of a secure global order? Or will the forces of fragmentation now on the loose in the East overwhelm the self-confidence, cohesion, and ultimately the institutions binding the Western democracies? (Aside from the spillover of instability from the East, are the postindustrial democracies of the West up to the demands and expectations of their populaces?)

### *Russia*

Russia will remain the predominant European and Eurasian military power and, as it emerges from its present agonies, one capable of threatening U.S. interests across two continents or of becoming a genuine partner in those areas and beyond. Can Russia be brought into a cooperative and democratic international order, even if its internal character retains strong authoritarian elements?

### *East Asia*

Will China move, whether through revolution or evolution, toward greater openness (including to American trade and investment) and cooperative international conduct? How will Japan and China sort out their roles? Will Korea reunify, and if so, on what basis and with what consequences? Can a stable regional balance be created and sustained?

## Middle East

Can a new structure of regional stability be created that secures unimpeded access to world oil supplies while also assuring Israel's security?

While questions of such magnitude are not ours to answer by ourselves, the U.S. role will be important, sometimes decisive. Without U.S. involvement, it is unlikely that these questions can be answered in ways consistent with U.S. interests. Regional dynamics alone cannot produce those preferred outcomes, nor is any other state or group of states capable of replacing us.

These considerations do not argue for a post–Cold War "Pax Americana" of unlimited burdens and responsibilities. Some favorable trends are likely to continue without American leadership; many unfavorable ones, notably in sub-Saharan Africa and parts of the former Soviet Union, will remain essentially beyond our influence. The challenge will be to engage in those areas and on those issues where important American interests are at stake and where a publicly sustainable level of commitment can make a decisive difference.

### TRANSNATIONAL TRENDS AND PROCESSES

Beyond these issues affecting relations among the major powers, several cross-cutting global trends and processes are at work that will decisively alter world politics over the next quarter century. Even those that are themselves benign will pose enormous challenges for the international system.

*The globalization of the economy* means that the basic factors of production—capital, labor, technology—are increasingly mobile, dispersed beyond national control, and subject to transitory calculations of profit. The capacity of governments to affect macroeconomic trends and solve fundamental social problems such as unemployment is weakened by the influence of outside forces on interest rates, foreign exchange markets, and capital flows. Firms are increasingly global and politically neutral, yet their entry into big emerging markets will pull national policies in unplanned directions.

*The telecommunications revolution*, among its many other ramifications, accelerates economic globalization, breaks down barriers between states, empowers nongovernmental actors, and reduces the government's control over information flow and its near monopoly over some forms of information. It globalizes local problems by giving local groups unfettered access to international networks, whereby they directly influence foreign publics, which, in turn, exert pressure on their own governments. The struggle waged by the Chiapas rebels in Mexico may be a model that future groups will follow in the sophisticated use of public diplomacy and advanced telecommunications technology.

*Ethnopolitics*, together with religious and other particularistic movements, will increasingly undermine the authority and integrity of states, especially in postcolonial Africa and the former Soviet empire. The telecommunications revolution and arms proliferation (from suppliers outside any system of controls) will give these groups a disruptive capacity far beyond their intrinsic power and importance.

*Environmental and demographic changes*, particularly among less-developed countries, will accentuate divisions between the haves and have-nots, both locally and internationally. Resource scarcities will make some regions uninhabitable, driving rapid urbanization, fierce competition for resources, and mass migration across increasingly permeable borders. China could become the focus of North-South conflicts over the environmental effects of aggressive industrialization.

These trends, to which others could be added, are leading, even more basically, to the *declining capacity of the state*. It is not that state power is being transferred to supranational institutions—in Europe, for example, the federalist impulse seems to have peaked—but that the capacity and authority of governments is eroding. This phenomenon, while global in scope, is not uniform. On the territory of collapsed empires, the very existence of states is at risk. This clearly is not the case for the industrialized democracies, which face instead diminished capacity to deal with urgent problems. Some states, particularly in Asia, may even gain authority, though they too will be affected by the transnational forces beyond their control.

The rise of nonstate actors with resources rivaling major countries—international financiers, multinational corporations, crime syndicates, and others—means that governments are unable to determine outcomes for which they are nonetheless held accountable by their publics. Yet even as public demands for state action are increasing, public willingness to cede authority to governments is declining absent the generally accepted exigencies of the Cold War.

## POWER AND POLICY IN THE NEW ERA

All this adds up to a world in which the greatest challenges are not to the basic (formal) structure of the international system, barring a dire turn of events in Russia. This system will continue to be driven by the interests and institutions of the Western industrial democracies, but it will have to accommodate other newly powerful states, principally in Asia, as well as confront the Four Horsemen of the Apocalypse now galloping through parts of Africa and Central Asia.

The modern state system will persist. Yet it will be a world increasingly ungovernable and unmanageable, in which the capacities of states acting singly or in concert risk being overwhelmed by intractable problems beyond their ability to control. The chief threats will come not from aggression by one state against another, the predominant threat to international security in the modern era, but from a complex of factors emerging within states.

Under such circumstances, the concern will be not so much with the locus of world power as with its effective exercise. Accruing power will continue to be a driving force for those outside the Western-dominated system, particularly in the Third World, but for those within it the focus will shift toward the patterns and institutions through which states can act collectively. The institutions binding the Western democracies—not only the North Atlantic Alliance but also the European Union, the United Nations, the international financial institutions, and others—will have to be transformed rapidly and fundamentally to meet the challenges that lie outside the Western community. The challenge is threefold:

—extending cooperation among the Western democracies into the new era;

—integrating Russia, Eastern Europe, and potentially China, that huge portion of the world largely excluded from its key institutions, into a new order; and

—creating, out of whole cloth, an institutional capacity for common action among traditional allies and former adversaries, particularly on newly urgent problems of environmental degradation, population pressures and migration, international crime, and terrorism.

## DARKER SCENARIOS

The current, relatively benign transitional period in world affairs could change abruptly to one of sharply increased threats to American security. Three dangers are paramount.

### Reversals in Russia

Russia, still in the midst of revolutionary upheaval, could enter a new "time of troubles" characterized by a severe economic decline and a chaotic breakdown of order. Such a scenario could lead in two broad directions. First would be a collapse of government authority and the proliferation of criminal organizations that gain control of nuclear, biological, and chemical weapons. Second would be the advent of a hard-line, revanchist regime bent on restoring authoritarian rule at home, reclaiming lost territories abroad, and reasserting itself as a hostile power in Europe, across Eurasia, and perhaps beyond. Even though Russia will be incapable for the foreseeable future of regenerating the military capacity of the former Soviet Union, either of these contingencies would produce threats to U.S. security more diverse, unpredictable, and potentially unmanageable than anything our country has faced since the earliest days of the Cold War.

### Explosion in China

China, on the threshold of major change, could follow similar paths—toward disintegration and civil conflict or an authoritarian restoration that took an aggressive turn internationally. Certainly China cannot continue much farther down the path of economic modernization without profound, regime-threatening political change. For example, the annexation of Hong Kong, though accomplished peacefully, may trigger profound developments. If permitted to remain an island of economic and political liberalism, it would surely become a focal point for dissent throughout China. By the same token, a crackdown would energize powerful interests on the mainland with vested interests in a more open China, and a massive human rights outrage in Hong Kong could mobilize the huge overseas Chinese community. Under such conditions, particularly if accompanied by major upheaval on the Korean peninsula, Japan might fundamentally reevaluate its security relationships for the sake of regional stability and its future role.

### "WMD Terrorism"

The collapse of the Soviet empire and the relaxation of Cold War constraints elsewhere creates an environment in which the barriers to acquisition of nuclear, biological, and chemical weapons have been lowered.

The theft or creation of these weapons of mass destruction by rogue groups, beyond the control of any government, is as yet a potential rather than an actual danger. But U.S. intelligence and law enforcement agencies will be expected to monitor and deter threats emanating from terrorist states or groups that may acquire a capacity to inflict significant damage to American lives and property. Indeed, because of the public outrage they evoke, terrorist acts acquire attention disproportionate to the actual damage they may inflict. No set of issues could more quickly put American lives at risk or undermine public confidence in the national security agencies.

### THE NEW FOREIGN POLICY ENVIRONMENT

During the Cold War, U.S. foreign policy priorities were set by an over-arching concentration on the Soviet threat. With Cold War constraints lifted, issues and problems that we could afford to treat as secondary, or to view solely through the U.S.-Soviet prism, now crowd onto the agenda.

Traditional security concerns will continue to dominate so long as Russia and China hover between liberalizing change and authoritarian reversion. At the same time, U.S. commercial interests call for greater attention to big emerging markets in countries that remain outside established international regimes for trade, investment, and technology transfer. And now a new foreign policy agenda may push itself to the fore, as it may no longer be possible to contain or compartmentalize intractable problems arising from environmental and population pressures in Third World countries traditionally seen as remote to U.S. interests.

It will be a less dangerous world but a more complex one. Those seeking to understand it will need to look back in time—Ukraine's problems cannot be understood on the basis of twentieth-century history—but also look ahead to anticipate newly emergent trends for which there are no adequate historical antecedents. The new foreign policy environment requires, for example, more than passing familiarity with Balkan history since the fourteenth century, but it also demands more acute understanding of the coming linkages among environmental scarcities, development, and conflict. How are the foreign policy agencies to develop the breadth of background and experience to deal with a world of such complexity?

The artificial rigidities of the Cold War produced among scholars and analysts of foreign affairs patterns of overspecialization and subdisciplinary inbreeding that will have to be overcome in a world where issues and problems cut across regions and categories. Academia is arguably better equipped than government to make these connections, but the transformation is not likely to happen quickly enough to inform foreign policy decision making. Meanwhile, thanks to the telecommunications revolution, scholars and policy makers are inundated with new information sources that they can neither monitor nor apprehend. Information is exploding, but human wisdom is not noticeably on the rise.

Moreover, there is a large new range of issues—highly operational microeconomic intelligence, environmental and nuclear safety concerns, crime, and others—about which the policy and intelligence agencies will be expected to acquire expertise, but without significant new resources. This calls for better coordination between traditional foreign policy departments and those with specialized expertise on trade, environmental, and many other issues. Making better use of nongovernmental sources of information will be indispensable. These burgeoning information sources, which cannot and need not be duplicated, are available—but in forms that are dispersed, disorganized, and often unusable. Here the problem will be not so much one of accessing this information as of harnessing it to the needs of policy makers—through sophisticated information retrieval systems, innovative techniques of modeling and pattern recognition, and others. Even approximating that capacity will be a monumental undertaking that is probably unrealizable in an age of budgetary stringency.

## AN ERA OF FOREIGN POLICY "FAILURES"?

In the coming era of complexity, no new paradigm or single organizing principle will be adequate. The Bush administration's "new world order" failed, in part, because it focused on aggression by one state against another and had no answer for the problem of conflict arising within states. The Clinton administration's stress on democratic enlargement failed to account for the wide variety of political systems lumped under the rubric democratic. The concept quickly ran up against the problem that democracy is not the only good, but a good that takes its place alongside security, stability, culture, spirituality, and many other values.

The new era will also present new pressures on the execution of foreign policy. It is now common to have three or four diplomatic exchanges, at the highest levels, in a single day. Russian President Boris Yeltsin may make a statement in the morning (Moscow time), to which President Clinton reacts at the start of his day several hours later. By early evening Moscow time but only mid-day in Washington, Yeltsin may have reacted to the president's remarks. CNN will be providing constant reporting in policy makers' offices. The way issues come to the fore is increasingly media-driven rather than policy-driven, and choices are framed even before the most senior policy officials have an opportunity to assess matters and define their own options.

More problems, greater complexity, less predictability, a post–Cold War agenda of topics outside existing capacities, an explosion of information, heightened pressures for immediate foreign policy action: this is a combination that calls for more resources that will not be forthcoming. Instead, the precipitous downsizing of foreign policy agencies is likely to continue.

No amount of strategic planning or governmental re-invention will be able to offset entirely the rising specter of foreign policy failures. The costs of failure will be lower than during the era of mutually assured destruction, but the number of lesser dangers will surely grow. Awareness of this inescapable reality may be the starting point for a foreign policy that is up to the challenges of the early twenty-first century. In a world of proliferating lower-level threats and problems, trying to meet every such contingency is a recipe for paralysis. Instead, foreign policy agencies will need to differentiate more sharply than in the past between those policy failures that are acceptable and those that are not, distinguishing threats that are merely problematic from those that impinge on vital American interests.

### NOTE

1. An earlier version of this chapter was presented by the author at the opening of the annual war game at the U.S. Naval War College, Newport, R.I., in May 1995.

# CHAPTER SIX

# An Anarchic World

ROBERT D. KAPLAN

*Robert Kaplan is a journalist and author whose influential books include* Balkan Ghosts: A Journey through History, The Arabists, *and, most recently,* The Ends of the Earth: A Journey at the Dawn of the 21st Century. *A contributing editor of the* Atlantic Monthly, *he has also written for the* New Republic *and the editorial pages of the* Washington Post *and the* New York Times, *among others. His* Balkan Ghosts *was named by the* New York Times Book Review *as one of the fourteen best books of 1993.*

Identifying a single paradigm to explain our increasingly interdependent and complex world is likely to remain elusive, but it is clear that certain trends will be fundamentally important in shaping the decades ahead. More children are being born into poor, resource-starved areas such as West Africa, casting a shadow over economic success stories in places like Japan and Singapore. Throughout the world, population growth and resource depletion—often accompanied by migration—are exacerbating regional tensions and severely straining the capacity of states to deliver essential goods to their citizens. Thus the politics of the twenty-first century increasingly will be shaped by the physical environment and demographic change.[1]

### THE MEXICAN SYNDROME[2]

Compared with other developing nations, Mexico at first glance seems to be in relatively good shape. It is not as backbreakingly poor as parts of sub-Saharan Africa, its bureaucratic system is not nearly as intractable and unwieldy as those of China or India, and its future is generally viewed optimistically in contrast to places like Pakistan—which is virtually imploding. But a closer look shows that the Mexican state is in trouble. Mirroring a trend underway in much of the developing world, Mexico is experiencing a dramatic decline in state capacity—that is, a reduction in the government's ability to project visible and unquestioned authority while providing citizens with basic services such as water in the sink taps, steady flows of electricity, and effective police forces. Mexico's precarious situation illustrates much graver problems that will beset many other developing countries in the decades ahead.

Uneven population growth rates have been the source of considerable social stress, since they have exacerbated economic divisions and further strained Mexico's cohesion. While northern Mexico has emulated a First World pattern of two children per family, the south is experiencing much higher population growth rates. The resulting poverty has prompted southern Mexico to loosen its connections to the rest of the country and begin slipping into the Central American morass. It has encouraged rural-to-urban migration, deepening already serious poverty in Mexico City and adding to the number of shanty towns and millions of inner-city slum dwellers. Meanwhile, the urban middle class is becoming increasingly disgruntled and harder to satisfy with increased exposure to living standards in the First World via global information networks.

A further danger is the inability of the economy to generate jobs for the rapidly increasing work force. The overall rate of population growth in Mexico is dropping slowly, and the staggering 25 percent real unemployment rate shows no sign of lessening. Mexican demographers say that if Mexico is to provide even menial jobs for new entrants into the work force, the economy must grow at 6 percent each year—an unlikely prospect, considering that annual growth rates have hovered around 3 percent in recent years. And if Mexico is to attain First World status, generating jobs that pay more than poverty-level wages, it will have to grow at the rate of Chile and some Pacific Rim countries—about 10 percent per capita each year. Because this degree of growth is infeasible, Mexico is going to become poorer each year. Precisely because the

Mexican decline is occurring slowly, optimists will deny the seriousness of the problems and defer remedial action.

To complicate the picture further there are what Argentinean Guillermo O'Donnell calls "brown zones"—places in which the state has no legitimacy because the police are in cahoots with drug lords and the drug economy. Drugs, after all, generate more money for the Mexican economy each year than oil; but as the government is powerless to control the drug economy, drug dealers are increasingly subverting the government itself.

A former foreign minister of Mexico has said that Mexico is reverting to a loosely governed Aztec tributary state system—the system that governed until the era of strong government emerged about sixty years ago. The Aztecs never ruled the entire Mexican landmass, which lent itself to divisions of peoples because of its mountainous terrain. Rather, they ruled what today is considered Mexico, loosely and weakly through a series of alliances with other major Indian tribes. All factors indicate that this pattern is reemerging. The central state is dying, and the population—one-third that of the United States—is once again becoming more divided. The Mexican state and its government are being assaulted from all sides.

The failure of central governments in Pakistan and India to provide a legitimizing infrastructure presents an even bleaker picture. Still more alarming are the trends in sub-Saharan Africa, where thirty-one of forty-six states have even lower indices of human development than Pakistan, according to the United Nations.[3]


## POPULATION PRESSURES AND
## RESOURCE SCARCITIES

Population trends in the developing world can be illustrated by two examples: Thailand and Rwanda. In Rwanda—a country of eight million people with a landmass no bigger than Vermont—the average woman gives birth about eight times over her adult lifetime. Imagine if, over the last thirty years, the average Rwandan woman had given birth only two or three times: one can conceive of entirely different patterns for Rwandan family life, social relations, and politics.

In contrast, the situation in Thailand—whose population patterns once closely resembled Rwanda's—is remarkably different today. In 1960, the average Thai woman gave birth about six times, yet Thailand's birth rate today is almost as low as the United States' or Canada's. Thailand's economic growth rates display an almost perfect correlation: as birthrates have declined, per capita growth has risen. The country's economic growth in the 1980s was about 11 percent per capita each year, as its annual fertility rate dropped from about 4 percent to 1 percent.

Japan and Taiwan, which have robust economies despite their extremely concentrated populations, are sometimes held out as models for other developing countries. An argument is often made that if places with extremely concentrated populations like Japan and Taiwan have robust economies, other countries could embark on similar paths with appropriate fiscal and political adjustments. What is often forgotten is that places like Japan did not start doing very well until their populations leveled off about twenty or thirty years ago. So while Taiwan and Rwanda may have the same population densities, Rwanda's continuing population expansion puts enormous pressure on the economic and natural resources of the entire nation.

Given these trends, one can begin to understand how these so-called nonpolitical issues like demographics and the environment shape the context in which politics is acted out. In sub-Saharan Africa, the pace and scale of population growth and natural resource depletion seriously aggravate already existing poverty and ethnic and regional divisions— thus putting more pressure on the state and diminishing prospects for success. South Africa offers an excellent example. At the current growth rate, South Africa's population is doubling every twenty-five years—with most births occurring in the poorest parts of the country. Meanwhile, the water table is getting lower each year, and a pattern common to developing countries is emerging: scarcity invites discontent, which can wear the mask of Islamic militancy in Egypt or township violence in South Africa. In many of these places, the work of even extremely talented political engineers—such as Nelson Mandela—gets harder and harder as all these problems grow. The margin of error for the government decreases, and the window of success becomes narrower.

As all of this is happening, the tendency for the United States, which is experiencing historically low growth, is to cut back on foreign assistance. With less investment and involvement in developing countries, the United States and the West will have waning influence on the trajectory of history in places like Rwanda. Even if the West were to increase its aid modestly, it would make little difference given that there will be more and more Africans, Indians, and Chinese. The success or failure of individual nations and regions will depend heavily on their ability to reach down into their own cultures and devise everyday solutions. The necessary human cultural ingenuity will be critical if countries are to manage situations in which there are more people to satisfy, less water to drink, and more crowded urban areas where unemployed or disgruntled youths tend to congregate.

Urbanization trends complicate solutions to many of these problems. People often have a romantic image of sub-Saharan Africa's villages, but those villages are dying. By the end of the century almost half of all Africans will live in crowded urban areas. Imagining a crowded city environment, where stoplights do not work and sanitation is scanty, provides a far better picture of what daily life is actually like below the Sahara than any picture of a rustic village.

Africa might be able to handle many of its stresses better if it were experiencing the kind of industrial revolution that every other major continental landmass has experienced or is experiencing. Any periodic economic growth spurts—like Uganda's 10 percent per capita growth rate in 1995 and Ghana's fairly good per capita growth—are driven by the rise in prices of agricultural commodities. For example, when the world price of cocoa shot up after a ten-year slump, places like the Ivory Coast—which had been experiencing zero economic growth—suddenly grew by 7 percent in 1995. But unlike on the Indian subcontinent, growth is not being driven by the acquisition of industrial and post-industrial skills.

Last, the increasingly global economy means that success or failure will be driven by the ability of countries to produce exportable goods for which the outside world is willing to pay hard currency. For this to happen, sub-Saharan Africa will need to generate the needed labor skills—but this is not occurring, and Africa is falling farther behind the second-poorest region of the world, the Indian subcontinent. As the situation in Africa gets worse, the United States will have reduced ability to effect change. The one potential African crisis before the end of the century that could really vex the West morally is Nigeria, where the regime is increasingly approaching a degree of ferocity that rivals Saddam Hussein. While the military government could not be much worse, there is no historical proof that democracy would make things much better. The last time Nigeria had four or five years of democracy under Shehu Shagari, the situation deteriorated.

In short, as states become more populous and more urbanized, dictators have to be that much more ruthless to exercise control. In that sense, the Nigerian regime may be the first example of an environmentally driven hard regime. Democrats (democratically elected civilians), when they get the chance, will have to be that much more brilliant and ingenious to succeed.

## RISING PRESSURES IN THE MIDDLE EAST

The same problems, in more subtle form, could arise in the Middle East. In the last thirty years, Tunisia, Egypt, the Gulf, and Morocco have all experienced social and economic revolutions. There has been a doubling of the number of Egyptians who live in cities. Many Egyptians now have access to television with news from around the world, and work in factories rather than villages. Despite these dramatic changes, there has been barely a scintilla of political reform in Egypt or elsewhere in the region. History warns us, however, that politics ultimately catches up with social, demographic and economic transformations. Jack Goldstone, in *Revolution and Rebellion in the Early Modern World*,[4] presents an impressive history of how revolutions in China, the Ottoman Empire, and throughout the world were precipitated by decades of population growth or other intense forms of social transformation. These changes—combined with political stasis—eventually created so much pressure that, like an earthquake, they exploded with sudden and dramatic power.

If the past is any guide, the next thirty years in the Middle East could be far more traumatic than the past thirty. Historians may come to view the period of Arab-Israeli confrontation as a relatively easy one, when the differences among elites were clear-cut and conflict was stabilized by having such a neat, bipolar rivalry between two ethnic groups. Many of these countries, such as Syria—whose population doubles every eighteen years—will face an exponential increase of job-aged youths who will never fit into any planned educational or employment system. These dramatic demographic shifts will determine the future of the Middle East, much more so than any agreement that may or may not be worked out between traditional Middle Eastern enemies. And as the Middle East's social and political landscape changes, America will have a tougher time determining its interests and making choices.

The question then follows, "What can we do about this?" Often one reads that the solutions lie in democracy, free markets, and technology. But democracy and elections rarely make states. States are created by geography, settlement patterns, migration, and various forms of population movements throughout history. Greece is a very stable democracy because the Greeks committed their "ethnic cleansing" early in this century when there was no mass media to provoke an international backlash. The Greeks created a basically monoethnic state with numerically manageable minorities, but stability did not come overnight: Greece experienced coups d'état, and needed several generations to develop a middle class. But once Greece had one ethnic group and some decades of middle-class life, democracy and stability emerged. The same kind of process can be seen happening—without the mild ethnic cleansing—in Chile and the Pacific Rim.

What does democracy do? It does not create middle classes. The record of history suggests that middle classes, which are in fact the prerequisite for stability in modern and postmodern societies, tend to emerge more easily under various kinds of authoritarian regimes—whether in East Asia or elsewhere. The values brought to America were often middle-class values or petty bourgeois values that were generated in Europe under some form of authoritarian regime. Democracy emerges best when it emerges last—after all the other prerequisites of order are in place. In other words, it is difficult for ethnically or regionally based parties to debate issues like budgets and gun control until they have settled more explosive topics.

The situation in Central and Eastern Europe bodes well for democracy because of a sufficient prewar tradition of bourgeois values and other strong indicators of social stability—including literacy rates of 99 percent and low birthrates. Yet in places such as Pakistan and sub-Saharan Africa, democracy will not be enough to guarantee a stable government: literacy is relatively low; parties, when they are formed, are often just masks for various regions or ethnic groups; and there is often no significant middle class and very little industrialization. One therefore should not place too much hope in the mere fact that elections are being held in many parts of the Third World.

As with democracy, technology is no panacea. Moreover, technological gains can be accompanied by many unintended negative consequences. Technology can magnify human capacity for evil: Hitler and Stalin, for example, emerged in the twentieth century because they were the perfect dictators for a mass-industrialized state. So the question arises, what particular evils may spring from the information age, and how will they interact with the twin challenges of runaway population growth and resource depletion? The real moral requisite is to try to get some idea of what they may be.

Someone a hundred years ago looking for new evils could have done worse than to look at how the power of states in Europe and Japan was being intensified by the Industrial Revolution. Maybe it is appropriate today to examine how corporate power is being intensified by the information age. In the current age of diminishing state authority, the principal dangers may be less likely to come from totalitarian regimes than from the growing, unregulated power of nonstate actors such as multinational corporations. It is not that corporations are immoral, but that they are amoral—driven, as has been expected of them, by calculations of profit. States have hardly been paragons of virtue, but most are susceptible to influences that increase incentives to act morally or at least in a manner that is responsive to social concerns. Corporations, as currently conceived and constituted, lack such an incentive structure—except on the relatively rare occasions when public pressures reverberate in their board rooms and influence corporate decision making.

If states are no longer capable of controlling these forces, and if corporations do not take over these responsibilities, the solutions to emerging problems may lie elsewhere. This assertion is not meant to be coy, but rather to suggest that the fundamental structure of world politics—the modern state system and its institutions—may no longer be adequate to sustaining and managing the international system. The open question is whether some new set of institutions and relationships, without historical precedent, will emerge that harnesses and regulates the multiple sources of power and authority, governmental and nongovernmental alike. Where and how such an order might be constituted is obscure, but knowing where to look may be the beginning of wisdom in an increasingly anarchic world.

## NOTES

1. See, for example, Robert D. Kaplan, *The Ends of the Earth: A Journey at the Dawn of the 21st Century* (New York: Random House, 1996).

2. This argument is developed further in Robert D. Kaplan, "History Moving North," *The Atlantic Monthly*, February 1997: 21–24.

3. Developmental data presented in this article are taken from United Nations Development Programme, *Human Development Report*, 1994 (New Delhi: Oxford University Press, 1994), and annual editions of *The World Factbook* (Washington, D.C.: Central Intelligence Agency, 1993–1996). See also the analyses in *The Ends of the Earth*.

4. Jack A. Goldstone, *Revolution and Rebellion in the Early Modern World* (Berkeley: University of California Press, 1991).

# CHAPTER SEVEN

# The United States in a
# Turbulent World

JAMES N. ROSENAU

*James N. Rosenau is university professor at the George Washington University,
a rank reserved for scholars whose works transcend the usual disciplinary boundaries. His scholarship in international political theory has focused on the dynamics of change in world politics and the overlap of domestic and foreign affairs,
resulting in more than 35 books and 150 articles. His most recent books include*
Thinking Theory Thoroughly: Coherent Approaches to an Incoherent
World, Global Voices, Governance without Government, Turbulence in
World Politics: A Theory of Change and Continuity, *and* Along the
Domestic–Foreign Frontier: Exploring Governance in a Turbulent World.

If one probes deep below the surface of the current scene, assessing
America's role in the world, its reality, and its potential, is no easy
task. One can compare data on American capabilities with those of
any other nation and readily conclude that the United States is the
world's only remaining superpower. Or, with equal ease, one can point
to data across the last four decades and demonstrate that American leadership is not nearly so commanding as it once was.[1] And whatever may
be the country's situation relative to other countries, it is not difficult to
make the case for the United States as having exercised its leadership
wisely through the construction of effective institutions that serve its

values or, alternatively, as being on the verge of squandering its leadership and undermining its values.[2]

Yet, it is precisely the ease with which such analysis can be offered that should give us pause. Surely, the question of American leadership in the years ahead is far more complicated than simply a matter of relative capabilities and institution building. With so much change unfolding at all levels of community in all parts of the world, and with the United States itself undergoing profound changes, surely one's assessment must allow for changes within the United States as well as in the world it may seek to lead. And surely that is an enormous challenge, as is any analysis that focuses on the interaction between systems that are simultaneously undergoing transformation.

In short, there is a need to step back, to look beneath immediate events, to treat observable phenomena as expressive of deep-seated processes. From such vantage points, both the changes and continuities at work in the world, and the pull that each exerts on the other, become more fully discernible.

## AN EMERGENT EPOCH

Let me begin with the presumption that the world is undergoing a profound transformation that is far deeper and far more pervasive than any of us appreciate, so much so that it amounts to the onset of a new epoch. And let me further presume that while people have difficulty articulating the transformation, there is a widespread awareness of it, a sense of underlying change that is spreading everywhere—in every country, through every walk of life, and across all the layers of class and community. Among elites the emergent epoch is intuitively understood; among masses it is grasped in bare outline. But whatever the level of comprehension, the central direction of the change is shared across cultures and all the other boundaries that differentiate communities and peoples.

And what are some of the main dimensions of the epochal transformation? At its root lies the premise that the order that sustains families, communities, countries, and the world through time rests on contradictions, ambiguities, and uncertainties. Where earlier epochs had their central tendencies and orderly patterns, the present epoch derives its order from contrary trends and episodic patterns. People now understand, emotionally as well as intellectually, that unexpected events are commonplace, that anomalies are normal occurrences, that minor incidents can mushroom into major outcomes, and that fundamental processes trigger opposing forces.

This is not to say that people have adjusted comfortably to these new circumstances. On the contrary, a high level of disquiet and uncertainty persists and will doubtless continue during the emerging epoch until such time as a new, at present unforeseeable one replaces it. Rather, it is only to assert that what once seemed transitional is now accepted as enduring, and that the complexities of modern life are so deeply rooted as to infuse ordinariness into the surprising development and the ambiguities and anxieties that attach to it.

Being complex, the new conditions that have evolved in recent decades cannot be explained by a single source. The features of what we sometimes call the "post–Cold War world" are not necessarily the consequences of the end of the Cold War.[3] Technological dynamics are major stimulants, but so is the breakdown of trust, the shrinking of distances, the globalization of economics, the explosive proliferation of organizations, the information revolution, the fragmentation of groups and the integration of regions, the surge of democratic practices and the spread of fundamentalism, the cessation of intense enmities and the revival of historic animosities—all of which in turn provoke further reactions that add to the complexity.

Not surprisingly, therefore, contradictions are pervasive: The international system is less commanding, but it is still powerful. States are changing, but they are not disappearing. State sovereignty has eroded, but it is still vigorously asserted. Governments are weaker, but they can still throw their weight around. Company profits are soaring, but wages are stagnant. Scenes of unspeakable horror and genocide flicker on our television screens even as humanitarian organizations mobilize and undertake heroic remedial actions. The United Nations is asked to take on more assignments but is not supplied with the funds to carry them out. Defense establishments acknowledge that their roles have drastically altered even as they continue to adhere to traditional strategies. At times publics are more demanding, but at other times they are more pliable. Citizens are both more active and more cynical.

### THE NEED FOR A NEW LEXICON

Attaching a label to the new epoch is no simple matter. In good part the huge gap between our sense of profound transformation and our ability to grasp it stems from a shortage of the tools needed to narrow the gap. A new lexicon is needed for this purpose. Notwithstanding the widespread recognition that vast changes are unfolding, our vocabulary and conceptual equipment for understanding the emergent world lag well behind the changes themselves. We still do not have ways of talking about the diminished role of states without at the same time privileging them as superior to all the other actors in the global arena.[4] We lack a means for treating the various contradictions as part and parcel of a more coherent order.[5] We find it hard to expand the concept of security beyond the military realm.[6] Aside from vague uses of the concept of interdependence, we are deficient in our capacity to work around and through the overlap of domestic and foreign affairs.[7] We are bereft of analytic equipment that allows us to treat the United States as both the world's most powerful country and one that shut down its government twice in 1995.

In short, the need for a new vocabulary derived from new conceptual equipment is not trivial. Labels matter. Without the rudiments of a new vocabulary, our descriptors reinforce our old ways of thinking. They confirm our understanding of who the key actors are, what motivates them, and the processes that sustain their interactions. They impel us to privilege states by taking a stand on whether states are primary or secondary actors, to insist that the international system is anarchical or that it is marked by an underlying order, to affirm the importance of sovereignty by presuming that it still reigns supreme or that it has eroded somewhat, and so on across a number of long-standing presumptions that reinforce our conceptual jails. It is difficult to accord status to new actors, motives, and processes unless one has a way of capturing their essential qualities through words that differentiate them from the prevailing conceptions.

There are signs that this need for new conceptual equipment has begun to be felt on the part of those who analyze world affairs. Or at least a vocabulary is evolving that departs from past practice as people seek new terms to account for phenomena that are no longer readily accommodated by the existing lexicon.

Three terms are particularly noteworthy in this regard. As powerful forces shrink the world, erode boundaries, and shift authority, observers now refer as much to the *international community* as to the United Nations, as much to *global governance* as to the leadership of great powers, and as much to *coalitions of the willing* as to formal alliances.

On the other hand, we still lack a lexicon that captures the mush-rooming tensions between the fragmenting consequences of conflict and the integrative effects of cooperation. Accordingly, emboldened by these signs of terminological adaptation, let me dare to carry the practice a step further by offering a label that may seem awkward but has the virtue of calling attention to the transformative dynamics that have given rise to a new common sense of a new epoch. The label is *fragmegration,* a term that juxtaposes the processes of fragmentation and integration occurring within and among organizations, communities, countries, and transnational systems.[8] From a fragmegrative perspective, the world is seen as short on clear-cut distinctions between domestic and foreign affairs, with the result that local problems can become transnational in scope even as global challenges can have repercussions for small com-munities.[9] Indeed, fragmegrative processes are so pervasive and generic that the emergent epoch calls for some label to capture them, even if this one is too grating ever to enter the general vocabulary. To speak of the Westphalian system—that is, the modern state system as it emerged after the peace of Westphalia in 1648—as having been replaced by the fragmegrative system runs counter to the need for historical landmarks as a basis for thinking about global structures.

## THE DYNAMICS OF FRAGMEGRATION

The close links between the integrative and disintegrative forces at work in communities are manifest at all levels. Industrialization unites soci-eties as well as divides them; civil wars disrupt states but unify nations; and so on. Sensitivity to these linkages is a major consequence of the diverse technologies—sometimes referred to as the communications or information revolution—that have collapsed time. Until recently, the importance of fragmegrative processes could not be readily grasped in a short time frame. Such a perspective tends to highlight globalization and localization as separate and unrelated dynamics. Only as the time frame was lengthened to allow for a full array of the impacts and conse-quences of each dynamic could the interactions between them be dis-cerned. And even then it was difficult to draw the connections. Their consequences for each other were obscured in the twentieth century by world wars and the Cold War (which focused attention on national con-cerns) and in earlier centuries by the slower pace at which life unfolded (thus making globalizing and localizing events seem independent of each other). But today, with the superpower rivalry over and with a wide array of technologies quickening the pace at which people and communities are becoming ever more interdependent, the interactions of globalizing and localizing dynamics and the tensions they foster are increasingly manifest.[10]

This is another way of saying that the large degree to which frag-megrative dynamics have become recognizable is a measure of the extent to which the information revolution has intruded complexity and inter-dependence into the course of events. In earlier times—that is, during that long stretch of history when the boundaries between national and international systems were less permeable and when it took weeks and months for ideas, people, and goods to move around the world—integrative developments such as the formation of states, the industrial-ization of societies, the evolution of empires, or the opening of new trade routes were not readily apparent as sources of fragmenting conse-quences. Nor did the onset of fragmenting processes such as civil wars or class conflicts lend themselves easily to tracing their integrative con-sequences. Doubtless both sets of causal links did exist and could be dis-cerned in retrospect if a time span of decades or generations was used. But only as technologies of communication advanced did the simultane-ity and interaction of fragmegrative dynamics became so readily evident. Now we can see how they produce tensions that career back and forth through systems at all levels of economic, social, and political organiza-tion.

Indeed, so interwoven are these contradictory processes that it is not far-fetched to conclude that every increment of fragmentation tends to give rise to a comparable increment of integration, that localizing and globalizing forces are products of each other.[11] Viewed in this way, it is hardly surprising that fragmegration constitutes the core of the emer-gent epoch. People have come to expect, to take for granted, that the advance of globalization poses threats to the long-standing ties of local and national communities, that some groups will contest, even violently fight, the intrusion of global norms even as others will seek to obtain goods or increased market shares beyond their communities.

It follows that the forces of fragmentation are rooted in the psychic comfort people derive from the familiar and close-at-hand values and practices of their neighborhoods and nations. Contrariwise, the forces of integration stem from the aspiration to share in the distant products of the global economy, to benefit from the efficiencies of regional unity, to avoid the dangers of environmental challenges such as global warming, and/or to yield to the implications of the pictures taken from outer space that depict the earth as a solitary entity in a huge universe. The tensions inherent in these conflicting impulses dominate the agendas of political systems at every level of community. They raise the crucial question of how both individuals and societies are going to adapt to the transformations, elusive and contradictory as they may be. How well, that is, will societies, groups, and individuals be able to keep their essential structures intact and move toward their goals in the face of dynamic changes that are giving birth to a new epoch? Or putting the question in terms of the concerns of this book, how well will the United States adapt to a fragmegrative epoch and find a role in the turbulent world that has emerged since the end of the Cold War?

## THE UNITED STATES IN A
## TURBULENT WORLD

While space does not allow for a full discussion of the last question, the outlines of how it might be framed can be discerned in Figure 7.1, which seeks to probe beneath the current scene through a characterization of the dynamics at work both in the world (the left-hand column) and in the United States (the right-hand column).[12] Here it can be seen that powerful as the United States may be relative to other countries, it is faced with enormous adaptive problems. Not only do challenges from abroad add up to an increasingly less stable environment in which the United States must seek to navigate its ship of state, but contradictory and incongruous trends on the domestic scene are also substantial and add up to an increasingly vulnerable society.

If the adaptation of any human system is conceived to involve keeping fluctuations in its essential structures within acceptable limits—else the system will begin to deteriorate and, as sociologists put it, disappear into its environment—Figure 7.1 makes clear that there are a host of fragmegrative dynamics currently unfolding that threaten to overwhelm the United States' capacity to adapt in a turbulent world.[13] The external challenges no longer loom as threats to physical security, but they are no less serious as factors that, by spinning beyond the control of U.S. policy, can undermine the country's adaptive capacities. Globalization, the communications revolution, the weakening of foreign governments, the growing tendency to question legitimacy, and the other dynamics listed in Figure 7.1 pose a more extensive set of challenges than was the case

**Figure 7.1**
The United States in a turbulent world

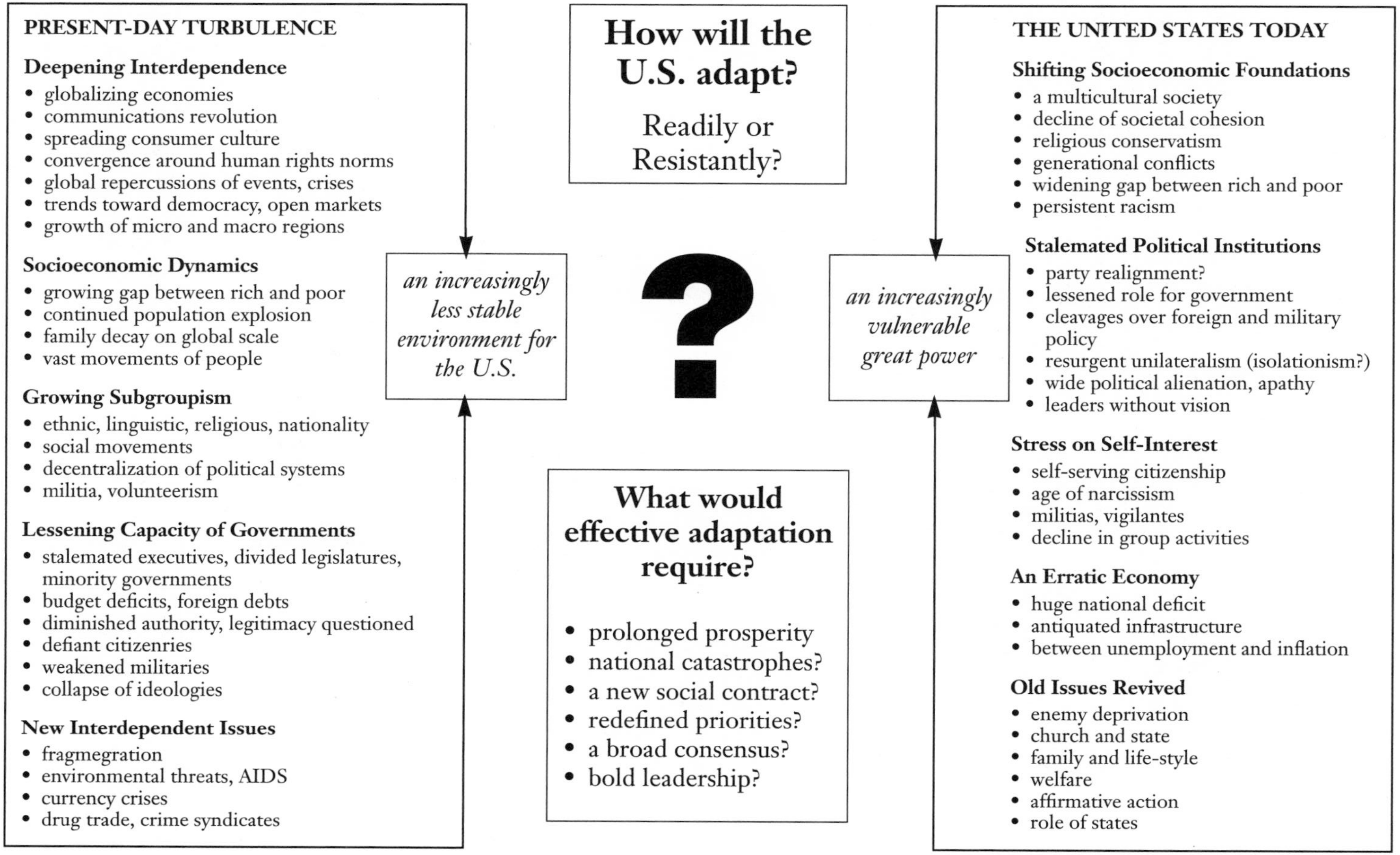

**THE UNITED STATES TODAY**

**Shifting Socioeconomic Foundations**
- a multicultural society
- decline of societal cohesion
- religious conservatism
- generational conflicts
- widening gap between rich and poor
- persistent racism

**Stalemated Political Institutions**
- party realignment?
- lessened role for government
- cleavages over foreign and military policy
- resurgent unilateralism (isolationism?)
- wide political alienation, apathy
- leaders without vision

**Stress on Self-Interest**
- self-serving citizenship
- age of narcissism
- militias, vigilantes
- decline in group activities

**An Erratic Economy**
- huge national deficit
- antiquated infrastructure
- between unemployment and inflation

**Old Issues Revived**
- enemy deprivation
- church and state
- family and life-style
- welfare
- affirmative action
- role of states

*an increasingly vulnerable great power*

**How will the U.S. adapt?**

Readily or Resistantly?

**?**

**What would effective adaptation require?**

- prolonged prosperity
- national catastrophes?
- a new social contract?
- redefined priorities?
- a broad consensus?
- bold leadership?

*an increasingly less stable environment for the U.S.*

**PRESENT-DAY TURBULENCE**

**Deepening Interdependence**
- globalizing economies
- communications revolution
- spreading consumer culture
- convergence around human rights norms
- global repercussions of events, crises
- trends toward democracy, open markets
- growth of micro and macro regions

**Socioeconomic Dynamics**
- growing gap between rich and poor
- continued population explosion
- family decay on global scale
- vast movements of people

**Growing Subgroupism**
- ethnic, linguistic, religious, nationality
- social movements
- decentralization of political systems
- militia, volunteerism

**Lessening Capacity of Governments**
- stalemated executives, divided legislatures, minority governments
- budget deficits, foreign debts
- diminished authority, legitimacy questioned
- defiant citizenries
- weakened militaries
- collapse of ideologies

**New Interdependent Issues**
- fragmegration
- environmental threats, AIDS
- currency crises
- drug trade, crime syndicates

during the Cold War period when the dangers were perceived largely in military terms and seen as offset by simplified notions of containment and deterrence.

The challenges of the emergent epoch are complex, elusive, deep-seated, and not readily reducible to simple propositions. Thus it is increasingly easy for the United States, or any country for that matter, to go off course and fail to adjust adequately to the changing world beyond its borders. Figure 7.1 also highlights the many ways in which the central tendencies unfolding within the American economy, society, and polity are lessening the coherence and consensus necessary to keep the country on an adaptive course.

Another kind of evidence is presented in Figure 7.2, which offers some data relevant to the extent of agreement among foreign policy elites on the country's proper role in world affairs.[14] Here it can be seen that the American leadership community is deeply divided over foreign policy orientations and that these cleavages have persisted without much

**Figure 7.2**

The distribution of hardliners, internationalists, isolationists, and accomodationists in the 1976 to 1996 F.P.L.P. surveys

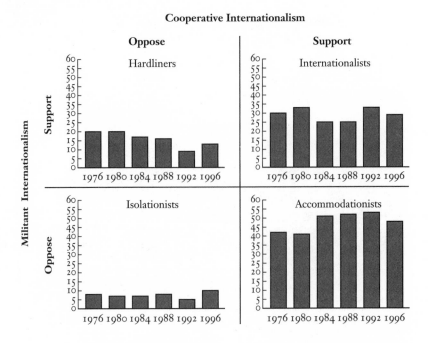

change since the Vietnam war.[15] Viewed in the context of these data, it is little wonder that American policies toward Bosnia, Haiti, NAFTA, and a host of other contemporary issues have proven highly contentious. To expect American foreign policy to rally around any one of these orientations is inconsistent with all the evidence of our recent past.

It seems clear, in sum, that the continued adaptation of the United States cannot be taken for granted. There are too many highly potent variables at home and abroad that can foster a diminution of this country's ability to keep its essential structures within acceptable limits. Indeed, as indicated by the large question mark in the center of Figure 7.1, there are good reasons to be concerned about what the future holds for the American people as a people. It is risky to presume that because the country has managed to muddle through more than two centuries, it will surely do the same throughout a third century.

To repeat, the world has moved into a new epoch, and the presumption of continuity seems ever more tenuous. Or, at least there is enough murkiness about what lies ahead to justify pondering what effective adaptation on the part of the United States would require. Will effective adaptation depend on prolonged prosperity, national catastrophes, a new social contract, redefined priorities, a broad consensus, and/or bold leadership? The six rhetorical questions listed toward the bottom of the center of Figure 7.1 suggest that stark, perhaps unrealizable, choices may confront society in the coming decades.

### NOTES

1. The literature debating whether the United States is in decline as a world power is too voluminous to cite here. Works by Samuel Huntington, Paul Kennedy, Henry Nau, Joseph Nye, Bruce Russett, and Susan Strange are among the more conspicuous features of the debate.

2. G. John Ikenberry, "The Myth of Post–Cold War Chaos," *Foreign Affairs* 75 (May/June 1996): 79–91; Charles A. Kupchan, "Reviving the West," *Foreign Affairs* 75 (May/June 1996): 92–104.

3. Since repercussions of the end of the Cold War were clearly evident at all levels of organization, it is tempting to treat this development as an epochal turning point. Such an interpretation, however, is misleading; it exaggerates the impact of a single historical moment and does not allow for the possibility that the end of the Cold War was the culmination of underlying and long-standing processes of change that, as stressed here, ushered in a common sense of dynamics and structures that amounted to a new epoch. For an analysis in which the Cold War is seen as having

"left so light an impact on the living memory of states and societies that it is already en route to oblivion," see Ian Gambles, "Lost Time—The Forgetting of the Cold War," *National Interest* 41 (Fall 1995): 35.

4. For a rare effort to come to terms with this problem, see Yale, Ferguson, and Richard Mansbach, *Polities: Authority, Identities, and Change* (Columbia: University of South Carolina Press, 1996).

5. Partial exceptions in this regard can be found in Hans-Henrik Holm and George Sorenson, eds., *Whose World Order? Uneven Globalization of the Cold War* (Boulder, Colo.: Westview Press, 1995).

6. Attempts to confront these difficulties are undertaken in Ronnie D. Lipschutz, ed., *On Security* (New York: Columbia University Press, 1995).

7. For an initial endeavor to focus on this overlap, see James N. Rosenau, *Along the Domestic-Foreign Frontier—Exploring Governance in a Turbulent World* (Cambridge: Cambridge University Press, forthcoming).

8. This concept was first developed in James N. Rosenau, "Fragmentative Challenges to National Security," in Terry Heyns, eds., *Understanding U.S. Strategy: A Reader* (Washington, D.C.: National Defence University, 1983), 65–82.

9. For a cogent example of the vast array of circumstances in which fragmetative dynamics are relevant, see Benjamin Barber, *Jihad vs. McWorld* (New York: Times Books, 1995).

10. For inquiries that explore the tensions and posit them as central to the course of events, see Joseph A. Camilleri and Jim Falk, *The End of Sovereignty? The Politics of a Shrinking and Fragmenting World* (Aldershot: Edward Elgar Publishing, 1992); Michael Zum, "The Challenge of Globalization and Individualization: A View from Europe," In Holm and Sorenson, eds., *New World Order? Uneven Globalization and the End of the Cold War,* 137–64; Antoni Kuklinski, ed., *Globality versus Locality* (Warsaw: Institute for Space Economy, University of Warsaw, 1990); and Zdravko Nflinar, ed., *Globalization and Territorial Identities* (Aldershot: Avebury, 1992).

11. Some analysts use the term "glocalization" to capture these casual links, but fragmegration is prefered here because it does not imply a territorial scale and broadens the focus to include tensions at work in organizations as well as those that pervade communities.

12. To a large extent the left-hand column of Figure 7.1 has been derived from the more abstract analysis presented in James N. Rosenau, *Turbulence in World Politics: A Theory of Change and Continuity* (Princeton: Princeton University Press, 1990).

13. For an elaboration of this formulation as it applies to national societies, see James N. Rosenau, *The Study of Political Adaptation* (London: Frances Pinter Publishers, Ltd., 1980).

14. The data presented in Figure 7.2 are drawn from the Foreign Policy Leadership Project that Ole R. Holsti and I have sustained since 1975. For the most recent articulation of our findings, see Ole R. Holsti and James N. Rosenau, "Liberals, Populists, Libertarians, and Conservatives: The Link Between Domestic

and International Affairs," *International Political Science Review* 17 (January 1996): 29–54.

15. The data in Figure 7.2 were generated by a mail questionnaire circulated to some four thousand elites in ten walks of American life ten months prior to the five presidential elections from 1976 to 1992. A preliminary and unsystematic examination of the results from the 1996 iteration of the survey suggests that the same patterns will be discernible yet another time.

# CHAPTER EIGHT

# Strategy and Ethics in World Politics

## J. BRYAN HEHIR

*J. Bryan Hehir is professor of the practice in religion and society, Harvard Divinity School, and a member of the executive committee of the Harvard Center for International Affairs. He also serves as counselor to Catholic Relief Services in Baltimore, Maryland. From 1973–92, Fr. Hehir served in Washington at the U.S. Catholic Conference of Bishops and was Joseph P. Kennedy Professor of Christian Ethics in the School of Foreign Service and at the Kennedy Institute of Ethics at Georgetown University. In 1991–92, he was associate vice president for church and university issues at Georgetown.*

The premise of this volume is the need to redefine U.S. foreign policy because the world confronting the United States has been transformed profoundly and lastingly. The United States itself has been a unique source of the change that has occurred, but this does not give it a privileged place in the new arena of world politics. Like all other actors the United States must redefine the threats and opportunities of this new moment and recast its foreign policy accordingly. The purpose of this chapter is to examine the dimensions of a changed international order from the perspective of how empirical (i.e., political and strategic) factors and normative (i.e., ethical) factors intersect today in a new setting. The significance of trying to grasp the interplay of empirical and normative aspects of world politics lies in the fact that only such an approach can capture the double transformation that characterizes the international system in the 1990s.[1] The transformation is empirical in the sense that it involves a dramatic and decisive change in the structure of power in the world; this dimension of international relations has been the abiding point of reference for the realist tradition. The debt any analyst owes to realism involves its insistence on the role of power in world politics. Redefining the American role in the world requires a clear-eyed view of the emerging structure of power. Clarity, however, may require that the debt owed to realism (paying attention to power) cannot be rendered in exclusively realist currency (the discourse of politics and war); to understand the changed *structure* of power involves a differentiated understanding of the *nature* of power. The debates of the 1990s, therefore, have taken both analysts and actors in world affairs back to basics.

The debate about the changing structure of power has been three-dimensional. At one level it has been about the nature of the post–Cold War system; at a second level about the capability of different theories of international relations to illuminate and interpret a changing international order; the third level of the debate, dependent upon the first two, is about the content of U.S. foreign policy in a changed world. In the systemic debate there is both striking consensus and persistent pluralism. The consensus affirms the end of the Cold War legacy—a bipolar structure with nuclear weapons at the core of the bipolar competition.[2] The pluralism arises from multiple proposals about the successor structure to bipolarity. The options, which are still being formulated, differ about *actors* (states alone or other forces shaping the system); *distribution* of power (unipolar and multipolar models); and definition of the *nature* of power (military versus economic versus other kinds of power).[3]

The pluralism evident in the description of the emerging structure of power arises in part from deeper theoretical differences about international relations. The debate preceded the collapse of the Cold War, but has been intensified by it. The Cold War system was user-friendly for the traditional realist theory, but even in the midst of Cold War politics, questions were raised about the scope of the realist lens when faced with the complexity of world politics in the 1970s and 1980s. Few argued for discarding realism; the real possibility was the need to complement its undoubted analytical capacities to assess the relationships of states and the persistent role of military power with a theoretical lens that captured the dynamic of power beyond military force and accounted for the role of nonstate actors or suprastate institutions. The collapse of the intense political-military competition of the Cold War, and the burgeoning importance of global economics, has sharpened the debate between realism and liberalism in assessing what order will replace the well-known pattern of the last fifty years.[4]

The implications for U.S. policy of how the emerging structure of power is defined are evident. Vigorous advocates of a unipolar definition of the world are questioned about how they define power; globalists, intent on giving new problems equal standing with issues of politics and war, are quizzed about the gamble it would be to underestimate the abiding role of force in world affairs. Even with these differences of theoretical perspective and policy priorities, some consensual conclusions can be sustained: militarily, the United States is the unipolar custodian of order; equally important, it is the only actor that makes the short list of leadership in both politics and war and politics and money. Finally, there are abiding questions about the consistency of the U.S. policy vision and about the degree of domestic support that exists to sustain the objective status the United States has in the new structure of power.[5]

The limits of this essay and its author preclude any effort to resolve the expansive debate of the 1990s seeking to define the emerging structure of power in the world with the clarity and consensus that marked the Cold War period of American foreign policy. The principal objective here is to argue that the wide-ranging debate over the structure of power is not sufficient to define the changed world confronting the United States today. The change is normative as well; it touches not only the structure of power but the principles of order of world politics. Those principles are older than the Cold War, more deeply rooted in the history and fabric of world politics than the conflicts of the twentieth century. To revert again to the theorists of international relations, these principles of order are the product of the Westphalian legacy of politics.

The legacy is identified with the Treaty of Westphalia, but there is not consensus on whether the treaty can bear the burden of such identification.[6] In a sense the legacy is broader than the treaty; it comprises three contributions to the way international relations and international law have been understood in the modern era. The first is the concept of sovereignty as the characteristic that legitimates political power in world politics; sovereign states have been the locus of legitimate power and the key to analytical understanding of international relations. The second is the correlative concept of nonintervention; sovereign states are expected to respect the principle of nonintervention. The role of the principle has been to reduce occasions of interstate conflict by focusing attention on actions taken against other states. To be sovereign was to be protected by the nonintervention principle; the theory was always clearer than the actual history of interstate relations,[7] but the theory served to identify violations even if it could not guarantee an effective response to them. Third, the Westphalian legacy sought to separate definitively the realm of religion and politics. The motivation was clear: Westphalia sought to end religious conflict in Europe; the objective was to separate religion from politics, to deny it public significance, at least as a *casus belli*.

The legacy of Westphalia, the way in which these three concepts of sovereignty, nonintervention, and the secularity of world politics have developed historically is a long and complex story. Without tracing its details, it is possible to make two limited assertions. On the one hand, the changes affecting the principles of order of world politics are at least as deep and as significant as those reshaping the structure of power. More precisely, each element of the Westphalian legacy (sovereignty, nonintervention, and secularity) is being eroded without prospect of being eliminated. On the other hand, it is the contention of this chapter that only by keeping in mind the framework of a changing structure of power *and* changing principles of order will it be possible to identify the kind of world that at the edge of a new century defines the challenge for American foreign policy.

In light of this background I seek to illustrate the intersection of empirical and normative dimensions of world politics by focusing on three cases of change within the arena of political-strategic discourse. Each is an example of how war, or the threat of war, continues to impact politics and how the ancient story of seeking to limit its impact continues today.

## THE RELATIVIZATION OF NUCLEAR WEAPONS

To understand the use of force in world politics in the 1990s, it is instructive to begin with the changed status and structure of the nuclear question. For the fifty years prior to this decade, nuclear weapons, in one way or another, were at the center of world politics. They have posed the ultimate danger in the always dangerous arena of international relations. Even to those accustomed to grappling with the intersection of war and politics, the advent of the nuclear age posed a qualitatively new intellectual, political, and moral challenge.

The depth of the challenge can be grasped by assessing nuclear weapons in light of two thinkers who shaped the way war, politics, and ethics have been related in the Western intellectual tradition.[8] The first, Carl von Clausewitz, argued that war is the extension of politics not its abolition. War, in this view, has a rational foundation, purpose, and method. To go to war is not to leave the world of rational political choice, but enter a uniquely demanding arena of political action.

For Clausewitz, war was a rationally defensible activity; long before he drew this conclusion as a strategist, St. Augustine made a parallel judgment as a Christian theologian. For Augustine, war was a morally defensible activity as long as it fit within a defined framework of ends and means. War could be an instrument of justice when it was constrained by moral calculus. Clausewitz and Augustine together—an unlikely combination of strategist and saint—provided a framework within which one could relate the political order, the strategic order, and the moral order. The essence of their combined arguments was that to be rational and moral—therefore justifiable—war had to be a last resort and be limited in ends and means.[9]

Nuclear weapons exploded the calculus of limits that made it possible to think of war as always humanly tragic but not always morally evil. Inherent in the nuclear age, if not in every weapon, lay the possibility of destruction without limit. This kind of war was neither rational nor moral; distinctions drawn from the past between civilian and combatants, between tactical and strategic objectives were obliterated. Yet, from 1945 on, nuclear weapons were an irreducible fact of international relations.

The response to the fact—both strategically and morally—is a well-known story. After some initial groping at the political-military level, an intellectual consensus began to take shape in the late 1950s rooted in the twin concepts of deterrence and arms control.[10] The strategic synthesis woven from these two ideas was foreshadowed in earlier writings of Bernard Brodie, then developed and refined by a corps of strategic thinkers: Thomas Schelling, Donald Brennan, Raymond Aron, Hedley Bull, Morton Halperin, Herman Kahn, and Henry Kissinger were the most visible architects of a theory and a strategy that recast traditional conceptions of military doctrine. By the mid–1960s these ideas were incorporated in U.S. strategy and then adopted (more hesitantly) by the Soviet Union. The goal of this strategy was to live with nuclear weapons without using them. Arms control's first objective was to serve these purposes by directing the strategic design of arsenals toward a stable nuclear relationship. For the next thirty years, in voluminous academic studies and in successive versions of official declarations and policies, the basic elements of the strategic consensus persisted.[11]

The moralists had an even more difficult task than the strategists, particularly if one held to the ancient idea that the only morally justifiable war was one that spared the civilian population from intentional attack. The traditional ethic had as much difficulty with nuclear weapons as the traditional strategy. In the past, the ethic of war was wholly concerned with how war was fought. The nuclear age, with its central feature of deterrence, required both an ethic of war and an ethic of peace. Deterrence was a much more problematical reality for the moralist than for the strategist. For the latter, the key question was effective deterrence—that is, one that restrained one's adversary.[12] For the moralist there were added questions: how did deterrence succeed, by nuclear threats, through what kind of targeting doctrine and governed by what intentions? The moral consensus that was developed to address the nuclear age was never as robust as the strategic synthesis. They both had dissenters, but the moral arguments manifested greater internal tension. Justifying any kind of killing strains the fabric of moral argument; seeking to assess the legitimacy of an arsenal designed to execute nuclear strategy frayed the fabric of moral discourse.[13] In the end the dominant position in the literature sought to rule out nuclear use, while tolerating specific forms of deterrence and pressing for both arms control and political change as a way out of an intolerable moral dilemma.

Change came with the collapse of the Cold War; nuclear danger remains, but the strategic and moral issues have shifted. The dominant change has been the relativization of nuclear weapons. For fifty years they dominated the center ring of global politics. Today they have been moved from the center toward the margin of world affairs. They still number in the thousands, and a credible case can be made that the danger of some use of nuclear weapons may be higher in the post–Cold War world than during the Cold War, but the significance of such use has dramatically changed. The dominant problem of the last fifty years, the possibility of a massive nuclear exchange, has been radically reduced. The daily impact of nuclear threats, nuclear politics, and nuclear arsenals is abidingly important, but less significant than it has been for most of a half-century. The relativization of nuclear weapons has not been the product primarily of arms control or disarmament but of political change. To say this is neither to denigrate the past role of arms control nor to diminish its importance for the future. It is simply to locate the nuclear reality in a new political context, one in which the superpower conflict of the Two yields to a revived form of Great Power politics of Five or Six; one in which internal conflict claims lives daily in a way that nuclear weapons, fortunately, never did.

In the new setting, the relativization of nuclear weapons has changed the priority of nuclear politics. In the past, primacy had to be accorded to the superpower relationship, while proliferation was an addendum. Today proliferation of Weapons of Mass Destruction (nuclear, biological, and chemical) constitutes the central danger, while U.S.-Russian relations have been essentially revised.[14] The threat today is not the one deterrence was designed to meet: to prevent a conscious, rational choice that could do catastrophic damage. Proliferation results from conscious choices, but the characteristic danger of proliferation is the accident, a miscalculation or mistake that is the product of regional political conflict or social chaos.

Relativization of nuclear arsenals and the rising salience of proliferation changes the political and moral fabric of the nuclear question. The scope of the problem shifts from the superpowers to a systemic issue: threats can arise from any quarter of the globe. No state can approximate superpower status, but many could contribute to nuclear chaos. The character of the problem shifts from strategic to political discourse; deterrence has a role in preventing or discouraging proliferation, but there is a primacy of political persuasion that is central to lessening the possibilities of proliferation. Why nations go nuclear is a tale rooted in conceptions of national interest, prestige, and position in world politics, as well as the dynamics of unresolved local or regional conflicts.

How does the moral question change as proliferation becomes the central nuclear question? Presuming that one takes prevention of proliferation as the basic moral goal, it is crucial to understand that analysis for the nuclear states begins with a compromised moral baseline. This is not a new reality; it permeated the negotiation of the Nonproliferation Treaty in the 1960s. The primary advocates of restraint are nuclear states that show little if any indication of forsaking the status they possess. Hence, the moral problem, described by Lawrence Freedman, "of drunkards demanding abstinence of others."[15] Yet, as Freedman and others have made clear, moving away from a compromised moral baseline involves both strategic and moral problems. Deterrence still shapes attitudes and actions; exactly to what degree is very difficult to assess, but there is a *prima facie* sense in which it clearly induces restraint through a guaranteed threat of reprisal. It is clear that a long-term conception of the problem must include a willingness by the nuclear states to take the obligations of Article VI of the NPT seriously, and we now have calls from the Canberra Commission and others that are bound to create new pressures on the idea that nuclear arsenals are a permanent fixture of world politics.

But the best of scenarios would involve a phased reduction of such arsenals, hence the persistence of a two-tiered nuclear world even if it serves as a framework for reductions (by the nuclear states) and restraint (by non-nuclear states). Can one sustain this as a moral position? Yes, with about the same sense of ambivalence as one had about deterrence between the superpowers. But the ambivalence generates specific demands: the effort to minimize the status that nuclear weapons provide in world politics; progressive goals for reductions that would provide a sense of reality to Article VI; primary urgency given to the process of "deep reductions" for the United States and Russia; a system of guarantees of protection for non-nuclear states. Such conditions do not dissolve the moral problem of the compromised baseline; they seek to find a middle way between simply accepting a two-tiered world as legitimate and recognizing that deterrence does play a role in nonproliferation, so it must be reshaped with care.

## THE RETURN OF CONVENTIONAL WAR

It was often said during the Cold War that successful nuclear disarmament would make the world "safe for conventional war again." The international system is still a long way from disarmament, but the collapse of the Cold War was quickly followed by the return of the classical version of conventional war in the Persian Gulf. Seeking to demonstrate a causal connection is more than this writer is prepared to do, but clearly some of the restraints that superpowers exercised over client or dependent states were absent when Saddam Hussein made his move into Kuwait. The Gulf War was classical in several senses: in its basic cause— aggression across an internationally recognized border; in its style—set-piece armies facing each other across defined lines in the desert; and in its instrumentalities—conventional air power (even if it was so-called smart technology) and massive deployments of ground troops; finally, it was classical in its outcome—clear winners and losers. This return of a classical conventional conflict put it at odds with most of the military threats of the Cold War, which involved the intricacies of nuclear strategy on the one hand and unconventional or insurgency warfare on the other. Both of them placed severe pressure on the traditional Just-War ethic of the use of force. The moralists, like the strategists, had to reconfigure inherited norms to relate them to deterrence on the one hand and revolutionary war on the other. The Gulf War was familiar territory for the traditional ethic. The twin legacy of Clausewitz and Augustine was designed to assess this kind of war.[16]

In retrospect, what are the consequences of the Gulf War experience? A basic consideration is whether it stands as a preview of other conflicts or whether it was an aberration—a throwback to earlier wars that is unlikely to be repeated. Joseph Nye has distinguished three possible forms of conflict in the post–Cold War era: Great Power wars (including the possible use of nuclear weapons), Regional Balance of Power wars (the Gulf War), and Communal Conflicts, usually within the boundaries of an existing state.[17] The likelihood of conflict, in his view, rises as one moves from global to regional to communal conflicts. In concurring with Nye's judgment, I would say that the Gulf War—particularly in the clarity of its character of open aggression, mobilization of the international community, and rapid termination—is not a phenomenon likely to be repeated. It remains a possibility in several regions of the world, but not a model that will be replicated.

At the same time, it has consequences that are relevant to other dimensions of world politics. First, the authorization process for the use of force embodied in the United Nations Charter was invoked and implemented with a clarity and consensus that the Cold War had made impossible. In spite of the specific characteristics of the Gulf War that facilitated this consensus and will not be quickly replicated, the example of how the U.N. system can work in collaboration with major states in the system provides a model for the future. From a normative perspective, the authorization process established the political-legal complement to the moral criterion of *Jus ad Bellum*. In brief, there was a consensus about "just cause," a legitimate process of legal authorization of force, and a collective response to the authorization.

From the perspective of military strategy the move from authorization to implementation was remarkably successful. The diverse coalition assembled under the leadership of the United States (an unlikely mixture of democratic and authoritarian states) held together long enough to eject the Iraqis from Kuwait. The implementation, viewed from a moral perspective, assessing the *Jus in Bello*, or the means of war, yielded a more complex judgment.[18] The principal means of coercion used against Iraq included sanctions (before and after the war), extensive use of air power, and ground forces in the hundred thousands.

Sanctions during the Cold War were often an attractive method of exercising coercion without risking war and the escalation that was always feared whenever the superpowers were involved. Both liberals and conservatives found uses for sanctions (the former in Rhodesia and South Africa, the latter against Cuba and other communist states). Since the end of the Cold War, the use of sanctions has come under closer moral scrutiny. Sanctions still have the saving grace of measures short of war and they were widely supported leading up to the Gulf War, but the cases of Iraq and Haiti have highlighted what was always true of sanctions but not often acknowledged: the principal target of sanctions (in fact if not in intention) is the civilian population. In the years since the defeat of Iraq, sanctions continue to be a disputed method of enforcing the terms of surrender upon Saddam Hussein, and civilians continue to bear the burden of a regime they did not elect and a punishment they do not merit. Neither the Iraqi nor the Haitian case constitutes a decisive moral argument against sanctions in principle, but both have made the moral calculus of choosing to impose them more problematical.

Air power during the Gulf War induced similar moral ambiguity to sanctions. There was, at the level of principle and practice, an effort to avoid direct attacks on the civilian population of Iraq, a notably different strategy from World War II or Korea. There also was a demonstrable short- and long-term impact on the civilian population from the scope and nature of the bombing campaign.[19] In brief, noncombatants were not targeted, but they have suffered substantially. As in the case of sanctions, a strategy undertaken to accomplish a selective and specific purpose has left unintended but real consequences, which makes future resort to massive air power suspect even when civilians are not targeted. There are no good weapons in modern war, only some less problematical than others.

In summary, the Gulf War is likely to be seen as a rare case, not as a standard model of conflict. Lawrence Freedman makes the point:

> Saddam was unfortunate to pick a unique period in international affairs. Had he invaded Kuwait a few years earlier such wide-ranging collaboration would have been inconceivable. . . . As things stood a regional superpower swallowing its small neighbor

in one of the world's most sensitive areas threatened both to reverse the Middle East's hesitant drift from war, make the world oil market virtually captive to the whims of a ruthless and unpredictable dictator *and* challenge a basic rule of international order.[20]

Seldom will the pattern of big-power cooperation, regional stakes, and international norms converge to create the dynamic of the Gulf War case. Yet there are themes (if not lessons) of this rare case that are useful for the future. The authorization achieved through the United Nations marks a new horizon of possibilities for using the UN as it was intended by its founders, but hardly ever employed because of the politics of the Cold War. This authorizing function has the potential to address what Nye calls communal conflicts. Whether the political role of the United Nations as a legitimating/authorizing body can be sustained without the hegemonic style of leadership the United States exercised in the Gulf War is not certain. The political paralysis of the United Nations caused by the Cold War is over, but its independent political capacity is still unproven.

The legacy of the Gulf War, from sanctions to high-tech warfare, does make it clear that modern war leaves no one with clean hands. Yet the memory of the Iraqi invasion and the pervasive intrastate violence of this decade demonstrate that, at times, force may be the only instrument capable of vindicating justice and restoring order. In terms of *Jus in Bello*, the ethical means of warfare, therefore, the lessons of the Gulf are the following. First, the efforts made to observe the principle of noncombatant immunity should be acknowledged and reinforced. The learning curve on this principle from World War II to the Gulf War is significant: directly intended attacks on civilian populations were part of policy in the former and were expressly excluded from the allied strategy in the latter. Second, the known consequences for the civilian population of repeated strikes on electrical grids and water supplies should be used to impose stricter restraints on future strategies of air power. In more technical terms, the principle of noncombatant immunity emerges from the Gulf War with new clarity and status, while its complementary principle of proportionality, which assesses combatant damage from a moral perspective, and, most important, the consequences for the civilian population even when it is not targeted, emerges from the Gulf War in need of refinement, strengthening, and a more significant role in planning and executing bombing strategies that are not only effective but morally acceptable.

## REVISING NORMS OF
## MILITARY INTERVENTION

Both the doctrines of the nuclear age and the strategy of the Gulf War were closely tied to the structure of power issues of world politics; the bipolar logic of nuclear politics and the response to Iraq in the name of defending territorial borders fitted nicely into realist conceptions of how to preserve the prevailing structure of power against threats to stability and safety. The intervention debates of the 1990s are related much more directly to the principles of order themes outlined above.[21] This makes them more complex in content and less clear in their resolution. In seeking to characterize and analyze these debates, it should be acknowledged at the outset that intervention has been a pervasive aspect of world politics since Thucydides, and it was a prominent aspect of the Cold War. The Cold War pattern of military intervention was three-dimensional. First, there was virtually no restraint on superpower *intrabloc* intervention: for example, the Soviets in Hungary, Czechoslovakia, East Germany, and Poland; the U.S. in Guatemala, the Dominican Republic, Panama, Grenada, and Nicaragua. Second, there were very effective constraints on *crossbloc* intervention: for example, the United States never seriously considered rollback as an option in Central Europe, and the Soviets understood where the lines were drawn in Europe and in the Western Hemisphere. Third, there were not well-defined limits, and, therefore, there were frequent dangers in the "gray areas" of the world: from the Middle East to Africa to Southeast and Southwest Asia. In these arenas the superpowers often pushed the envelope until either the threat of direct confrontation between them or effective resistance by local forces induced restraint or retreat.

This pattern of Cold War interventions, often reflecting Great Power politics of the nineteenth century, is not the subject of the intervention debates of the 1990s. During the Cold War, the Westphalian model of sovereignty and nonintervention coexisted with multiple violations of it by the superpowers (or their proxies). Interventions occurred; they also were recognized as contrary to international order. The prevailing normative code sought to rule out intervention in the internal affairs of states; the nonintervention rule, even if flouted in practice, was reasserted in principle; the UN system institutionalized the norm, even if the United Nations could not enforce it.

The striking change of the 1990s is not that interventions are part of world politics; it is that the dominant normative arguments seek not only to legitimize instances of intervention, but to redefine the norm itself. Rather than the Cold War concern of prohibiting intervention, the normative discourse of the 1990s focuses on whether intervention is obligatory for international institutions or major states.

It is, in part, the changes in the structure of power in the 1990s that have generated pressure on the accepted principles of order. The wisdom of Westphalia lay in its recognition that the collapse of the medieval order yielded states without allegiance to any higher power, hence the need to construct norms that would constrain actors who defined and enforced their own rules based on interest and reciprocity. Faced with this systemic change, the Westphalian tradition makes a conscious choice to give interstate peace clear legal and moral primacy over intrastate justice. The noninterventive norm, treated as virtually absolute, embodies this prior moral choice of peace over justice. The Cold War logic, with its Security Council objective of avoiding direct superpower confrontations and its General Assembly objective of restraining large states from dominating others, provided political reinforcement for the norm of nonintervention. Large and small states alike found it useful to affirm the norm, if not always to obey it.

The intervention debates and decisions of the 1990s cannot be understood by examining intervention apart from the wider political fabric of the international system. Quite distinct from the collapse of the Cold War, a broader process has been afoot in world politics that has eroded substantially each of the elements of the Westphalian legacy. Erosion but not elimination is the measured judgment that best captures the dynamic at work. Sovereignty epitomizes the process: it remains a visible and vibrant characteristic of world politics, but it does not retain its classical content. The converging influences of normative (e.g., human rights regimes) and empirical (e.g., economic interdependence) forces have eroded the capacities of sovereign states to act in ways their predecessors would have taken for granted.

While sovereignty was being eroded over the last forty years, its correlative concept of nonintervention remained unchallenged in principle if not in practice. It is the 1990s debate that now generates a challenge in principle to the adequacy of the nonintervention norm. The fundamental challenge is to dislodge the absolute status of nonintervention, which, in turn, means undermining the domestic jurisdiction claims of states. Once this moral-legal debate is initiated, several questions arise: (1) How interventionist an order should be legitimated? (2) Who are to be the guardians of legitimate intervention—in the classical phrase, what constitutes legitimate authority? (3) If the norm of nonintervention is diluted or overturned, how does one move from authorizing intervention to implementing it—whose forces, under which command, with what rules of engagement, and with what kind of firepower? (4) How does one build and/or sustain a consensus supporting interventions in the states called upon to participate and in the regions—for example, Africa, where intervention is likely to occur? (5) What happens ethically and politically when interventionist politics conflict with Great Power prerogatives (e.g., Chechnya)?

The politics of the 1990s have opened these questions, but the decade is unlikely to see a lasting resolution of them. Yet it is possible to outline the contents of a "new Westphalian bargain" mediating between the wisdom of Westphalia with its understanding of the centrality of sovereignty and the necessity of peace and the limits of Westphalia, both morally and politically, when faced with the kind of intrastate violence and injustice that Haiti, Somalia, Rwanda, the Sudan, and other failed or divided states can produce. The declining danger of superpower or even Great Power conflicts and the blurring of the distinction between internal/external dimensions of world politics highlight the possibility and the necessity of a more interventionist normative order.

The Westphalian legacy always had a vulnerable moral foundation, but the risk of changing its terms involved increasing the possibility of interstate conflict. That risk can never be eliminated, and it may return with new intensity at any time, but the current moment both allows for and calls for a recasting of the relationship between sovereignty and intervention. From a purely moral perspective, the political-legal legacy of the Westphalian tradition never erased the moral responsibility of individuals and states to address gross violations of injustice. The most that could be said morally for the Westphalian order was that the successful address of injustice was not feasible or raised disproportionate risks of greater violence and conflict. The recasting of a new Westphalian bargain would be an acknowledgment that contemporary patterns of world politics allow the international community an opportunity to assume in practice some of the responsibility that it always had in principle.

This would constitute a further erosion of sovereignty, but, as I have tried to argue in another context,[22] it would mean a revision of Westphalia, not its negation. In a new Westphalian order both sovereignty and nonintervention should be relativized by reducing them from absolute status to one in which a presumption against intervention exists, but can be overridden for specified reasons. Sovereignty would still characterize the status of states, but its claims would be relativized when confronted by issues of human rights violations and internal violence. The casuistry that would be needed to determine how to adjudicate claims of sovereign independence and interventionary interdependence would be substantial, but not unlike the moral decision making that accompanies any complex legal system. Both the rhetoric and the decisions of the 1990s have moved in the direction of relativizing the restraints of nonintervention. The next step is to gain greater clarity about authorization, actors, and implementation.

From Bosnia to Haiti to Somalia, the international community, after much hesitation, produced authorized interventions. In all three cases there was ambivalence about who should lead and what strategy would be successful. The policy of the United States exemplified the ambivalence about going beyond the revision of norms to effective design of strategy. After leading the coalition that reversed Iraq's challenge to the structure of power in the Middle East, the United States seemed both well positioned and ready to address the more complex problem of redesigning policy to fit new principles of order. President Bush's return to the United Nations for authorization to act in Somalia, and his decision to commit U.S. troops to the enterprise, seemed to many a logical step beyond the precedent established by the Gulf War. At the same time President-elect Clinton was expressing a stronger multilateral emphasis for U.S. policy in the 1990s.

Neither Bush nor Clinton was clear about a U.S. role in Bosnia beyond that of looking to European powers to take the lead. The experience of Somalia, in which the United States took casualties, the domestic support that had sustained the original commitment collapsed, and the Clinton administration took refuge in some very dubious definitions of U.N. responsibility for what was declared a failed policy, all led to a reconsideration of multilateralism and the demands of a revised Westphalian bargain for the major states in the international system.[23] Even though the United States did commit troops to Haiti and eventually espoused and participated in a more aggressive policy in Bosnia in support of the Dayton Accords, the impact of Somalia has left a gap between advocating a more expansive responsibility for intervention and implementing a policy that can sustain such a position.[24]

But, again, the broad lines of a strategy for joining authorization to implementation are visible. The need for regional or international authorization, modeled on the Gulf War, is a basic requirement. It is the best safeguard against an expanded justification of intervention being used by powerful states purely for their own interests. The safeguard is procedural but not insignificant. Implementation of a decision to intervene militarily would best reflect an international commitment if undertaken with multilateral forces, but this standard may not be achievable for several reasons. Factors as different as timing, the nature of the interventionary task, and the need for clear leadership by the major states could justify and call for a narrowly representative force, or even a single state.

Here again the U.S. experience has been problematical. In spite of his campaign position in support of multilateralism, President Clinton retreated quickly after Somalia to a position that makes U.S. participation in a multilateral force (unless under U.S. command) very difficult. Ensuring U.S. command, at least in major missions, is feasible, but the long-term need is for a standby UN force that has substantial resources and capabilities to act quickly and effectively. Short of this objective (not likely in the near term) it is wise not to have the major states—particularly the United States—in most situations of internal conflict. The U.S. role in the world tends to politicize the intervention more intensely than that of other actors.

Recognition of this fact points in the direction of a division of labor for interventionary forces: financed by major states but not manned by them. It is not clear such a bargain can be struck; such a force might not have the effectiveness to go beyond traditional peacekeeping missions; conversely, the resistance to the idea of major states expending treasure while others invest lives may be substantial. In the case of the United States, where domestic resistance to missions involving casualties is highest, a long-term approach may be to have a "double volunteer" military. Not only would the military be a volunteer force, but within that force an option would be offered to serve in a multilateral force. The experience of both Somalia and U.S. policy in Bosnia points to the utility of such a method for raising troops from the United States for humanitarian interventions.

It is evident that the debates and the decision making of the 1990s have resulted in an untidy outcome. Normatively, there is growing moral and legal consensus to support more interventionist policies to respond to intrastate violence. Politically, lack of policy consensus among the major states and fragile domestic support for an activist policy of intervention (most evident in the United States) have produced a series of ad hoc responses to intervention with a mixed record of success.

Militarily, the lack of political consensus has stymied any systematic approach for the international community to design an effective multi-lateral strategy. The means are clearly available, but strategic vision and political will are lacking. The experience of the first post–Cold War decade has produced a significant gap on intervention between moral conviction and political choice. The gap is costly in both human life and the legitimacy of prevailing norms of international order.

In all three cases examined in this chapter, the use of force or the threat of it remains as both a threat to order and a potential instrument of order. Neither changes in power nor principle that have accompanied the post–Cold War age have expunged the possibility of war as part of world politics. Because it is possible, war must continue to be thought about strategically; because it is never self-regulating, war also must continue to be conceived and restrained morally.

## NOTES

1. See also: J. B. Hehir, "Intervention: From Theories to Cases," *Ethics and International Affairs* 9 (1995): 1–13.

2. J. L. Gaddis, "The Cold War, the Long Peace and the Future," in M. J. Hogan, ed., *The End of the Cold War: Its Meaning and Implications* (Cambridge: Cambridge University Press, 1992), 21–38; also "Toward the Post–Cold War World," *Foreign Affairs* 70 (1991): 102–22; L. Freedman, "Order and Disorder in the New World," *Foreign Affairs* 71 (1992): 20–37.

3. A sampling of the arguments: S. Hoffmann, "A New World and Its Troubles," in N. X. Rizopoulos, ed., *Sea-Changes: American Foreign Policy* in a World Transformed (New York: Council on Foreign Relations, 1990), 274–92; J. Nye, "What New World Order?" *Foreign Affairs* 71 (1992): 83–96; H. A. Kissinger, *Diplomacy* (New York: Simon and Schuster, 1994), 804–35.

4. Stages of the debate can be found in: R. O. Keohane, ed., *Neorealism and Its Critics* (New York: Columbia University Press, 1986); D. A. Baldwin, ed., *Neorealism and Neoliberalism: The Contemporary Debate* (New York: Columbia University Press, 1993); C. W. Kegley, Jr., ed., *Controversies in International Relations Theory: Realism and the Neoliberal Challenge* (New York: St. Martin's Press, 1995).

5. See also G. John Ikenberry, "The Myth of Post–Cold War Chaos," *Foreign Affairs* 75 (May–June 1996): 79–91; J. Mearsheimer, "Back to the Future," *International Security* (1990): 5–56; J. Joffe, "'Bismarck' or 'Britain'? Toward an American Grand Strategy after Bipolarity," *International Security* 19 (1995): 94–117; J. G. Ruggie, "The Past as Prologue? Interests, Identity, and American Foreign Policy," *International Security* 21 (1997): 89–125.

6. The poles of the debate about the significance of Westphalia are: L. Gross, "The Peace of Westphalia 1648–1948," *American Journal of International Law* 42 (1948): 20–41; and S. Krasner, "Westphalia and All That," in J. Goldstein and R. O. Keohane, eds., *Ideas and Foreign Policy: Beliefs, Institutions and Political Change* (Ithaca, N.Y.: Cornell University Press, 1993), 235–64. Between the poles there remains much debate.

7. The best treatment of the history and doctrine is R. J. Vincent, *Nonintervention and International Order* (Princeton, N.J.: Princeton University Press, 1974).

8. For a sense of the history of ethics and war, see also: R. Bainton, *Christian Attitudes toward War and Peace* (New York: Abington Press, 1960); J. T. Johnson, *Ideology, Reason and the Limitation of War* 1200–1740 (Princeton, N.J.: Princeton University Press, 1975); M. Walzer, *Just and Unjust Wars: A Moral Argument with Historical Illustrations* (New York: Basic Books, Inc., 1977).

9. See also: P. Ramsey, *The Just War: Force and Political Responsibility* (New York: Charles Scribner's Sons, 1968); J. C. Murray, "Remarks on the Moral Problem of War," *Theological Studies* 20 (1959): 40–61.

10. The argument is traced in several places; see also: M. Mandelbaum, *The Nuclear Question: The United States and Nuclear Weapons* 1946–1976 (Cambridge: Cambridge University Press, 1979); L. Freedman, *The Evolution of Nuclear Strategy* (New York: St. Martin's Press, 1981); F. Kaplan, *The Wizards of Armageddon* (New York: Simon and Schuster, 1983).

11. The nuclear debate is treated with great analytical detail in Freedman, *The Evolution of Nuclear Strategy*, and in McG. Bundy, *Danger and Survival Choices about the Bomb in the First Fifty Years* (New York: Random House, 1988).

12. For the dialogue of strategy and morality, see also: J. B. Hehir, "Ethics and Strategy: The Views of Selected Strategists," in T. Whitmore, *Strategy, Religious Studies and the Churches* (Dallas: Southern Methodist University, 1989), 13–32.

13. Representative views of the moral argument can be found in Ramsey, *The Just War*, 211–58, 314–66; Walzer, *Just and Unjust Wars*, 269–83; J. S. Nye, *Nuclear Ethics* (New York: The Free Press, 1986); National Conference of Catholic Bishops, *The Challenge of Peace: God's Promise and Our Response* (Washington, D.C.: U.S. Catholic Conference, 1983).

14. See also McG. Bundy, W. J. Crowe, and S. Drell, *Reducing Nuclear Danger* (New York: Council on Foreign Relations, 1993) esp. 1–12.

15. L. Freedman, "Nuclear Weapons: From Marginalization to Elimination?" *Survival* 39 (1997): 188.

16. For moral assessment of the Gulf War, see: D. De Cosse, ed., *But Was It Just?* (New York: Doubleday, 1992); J. T. Johnson and G. Weigel, *Just War and the Gulf War* (Washington, D.C.: Ethics and the Public Policy Center, 1991). See also: J. B. Hehir, "The Just-War Ethic Revisited," in L. B. Miller and M. J. Smith, eds., *Ideas and Ideals: Essays on Politics in Honor of Stanley* Hoffmann (Boulder, Colo.: Westview Press, 1993); I have drawn from this essay in what follows here.

17. J. S. Nye, "International Conflicts after the Cold War," in *Managing Conflict in the Post–Cold War World: The Role of Intervention*, Report of the Aspen Institute Conference (Washington, D.C.: The Aspen Institute, 1996), 66–74.

18. Hehir, "The Just-War Ethic," 157–59.

19. J. G. Heidenrich, "The Gulf War: How Many Iraquis Died?" 90 (1993): 108–25.

20. L. Freedman and E. Karsh, *The Gulf Conflict* 1990–1991: *Diplomacy and War in the New World Order* (Princeton, N.J.: Princeton University Press, 1993), 438.

21. The literature on intervention in its various meanings increases by the month; a sampling includes S. Hoffmann, "Sovereignty and the Ethics of Intervention," in *The Ethics and Politics of Humanitarian Intervention* (Notre Dame, Ind.: University of Notre Dame Press, 1996), 12–37; J. Mayall, "Nonintervention, Self Determination and 'The New World Order,'" *International Affairs* 67 (1991): 421–29; S. J. Stedman, "The New Interventionists," *Foreign Affairs* 72 (1993): 1–16; M. Walzer, "The Politics of Rescue," *Social Research* 62 (1995): 53– 67. I draw here on two previous essays of mine: "Intervention: From Theories to Cases" and "Expanding Military Intervention: Promise or Peril?" *Social Research* 62 (1995): 41–52.

22. See also Hehir, "Intervention: From Theories to Cases," 7–11.

23. W. Clarke and J. Herbst, "Somalia and the Future of Humanitarian Intervention," *Foreign Affairs* 75 (1996): 70–85.

24. L. Korb, "The Use of Force," The Brookings Review 15 (1997): 16.

# PART THREE

# The United States
# in the
# Global Economy

# CHAPTER NINE

# A New International Economic Order?

## W. BOWMAN CUTTER

*W. Bowman Cutter has held senior positions in government, business, and the nonprofit sector. From 1993 to 1996, he was deputy assistant to the president for economic policy and deputy chair of the National Economic Council. He is currently managing director of the venture capital firm Warburg, Pincus and formerly served as senior partner at Coopers & Lybrand and as the firm's vice chair for strategy. He is a former board chair of Volunteers in Technical Assistance (VITA) and currently serves on the advisory board of the Woodrow Wilson School at Princeton University.*

During President Clinton's first term, the increasing centrality of two questions of enormous economic and foreign policy implications became more and more apparent to policy makers: What would be the structure, the order of nations in the emerging global economy? How would the major new emerging economies be integrated into this order? These questions suggest that the real debates over economic and foreign policy will be quite different from the nostalgic musings on muscularity—of how tough our foreign commercial policy should be—of the principal theorists among President Clinton's critics.

Indeed, these questions suggest a set of concerns raised first by President Bush in the months immediately following the collapse of the

Soviet Union and at the time of the Gulf War and summarized as "the new world order." In the years that followed, both the term and the concept fell out of favor: becoming vaguely disreputable, regarded derisively, or considered to have no relevance or meaning. Recent popular and scholarly writings have argued variously that the new order is one of unending chaos; or that the new order is simply the old order; or that (in the conspiratorial form of the previous argument) the new order is simply an extension of the last fifty-year effort by the United States to extend its economic hegemony.

But President Bush was more prescient than he knew. In the real world, the conditions driving both the destruction of the old order and the creation—whether purposeful or not—of something in its place continue and even accelerate.

There is clearly emerging a new and distinctively different international economy. The emergence of this economy will change American foreign policy, American international economic policy, the nature of relationships among nations, and the lives of billions of people on the planet.

The sum of its effects inevitably will be the creation of a new economic order—meaning, for now, only some different shape of economic relationships among nations. But there is very little inevitability to the actual shape of that order, or to the degree to which it will reflect American values, objectives, or interests. Nor, despite the growing concern of policy makers, has the nature of that future order been a matter of sufficiently high priority for American foreign policy or international economic policy to date.

This broad issue has not been accorded high priority for two main reasons. First, policy makers are inevitably subject to the tyranny of the day to day. Second, and even more important, it is hard to come to grips with change. The fact of truly fundamental change—basic and permanent alterations in the structure, relationships, and context of their environment—is probably the most difficult issue for institutions—corporations, public agencies, administrations, political parties—to recognize, accept, and act upon. Indeed, most of the time institutional leaders find elaborate rationales to deny such change, or to argue that whatever change cannot be denied is really not much of a change after all. As a consequence, change catches most institutions and decision makers by surprise while they are in the midst of this act of denial. And fundamental change always alters the accepted arrangements of the day.

This article considers the old economic order, which has served the United States exceptionally well for the last fifty years, and argues that its foundation and basis have changed in fundamental ways. It then discusses the emerging world economy, which is the primary cause of those changes. Finally, it argues that a long-term focus upon the shaping of a new economic community must be at the center of American foreign policy over the next decade.

The core premise of this article is that we live today in the early stages of as profound a transformation in the world's economy as we have ever seen. The extent of those changes—and their implications for U.S. interests—is at least as great as those faced by the men and women who after World War II forged the world order that prevailed for fifty years. And the policy makers who must grapple with these changes must be as conscious of underlying realities, as purposeful, as creative, and as steadfast as were those policy makers of fifty years ago. We have the opportunity and face the inevitability of being present at another creation.

## THE OLD ORDER

As President Clinton has said in a number of his speeches, the architecture of the economic order of the West emerged from a crucial contrast the victors of World War II drew between the world of the 1930s as they understood it and the world they wished to create. They saw in the 1930s a depression that enveloped Europe and the United States. They concluded that the depression was exacerbated by a prevailing tendency for nations to look inward, to behave autarkically, and to undertake shortsighted economic and financial decisions such as competitive devaluations that prolonged the economic situation they were intended to remedy.

The leaders of these nations then made the crucial decision to turn outward, to create an economic community—and the multilateral institutions required by such a community—that recognized our mutual interdependence and the new realities of an increasingly international economy. They built concretely on this broad perception by establishing the United Nations and its subsidiary institutions.

In particular, they built an economic architecture composed of the Bretton Woods financial institutions: the World Bank and the IMF, the General Agreement on Tariffs and Trade (GATT), and the Organization for Economic Cooperation and Development (OECD). From this seminal starting point flowed the creation of dozens of companion institutions; the evolution of a trade negotiation process based upon a predefined negotiation "round," which over forty years completely redefined the trading relations among the member nations of the GATT; the rapid development of financial institutions that defined the rules for international financial markets; and the origination of a major leadership institution—the annual G-7 meetings of the leaders of the largest economies of the world.

The creation of this architecture was perhaps the most successful and sustained effort to create a community of cooperating nations in the recent history of the world. It produced a rapid postwar reconstruction in Europe and the subsequent flourishing of the economies of the West. It was sufficiently flexible to incorporate very recent World War II enemies, Germany and Japan. It made possible a vast improvement in the lives of the hundreds of millions of citizens of all these nations. And it played a crucial role in strengthening the Western democracies, enabling them to sustain successfully a fifty-year confrontation with the Soviet Union.

Thus, the creation of this community was also a significant foreign policy strategy of the United States. While this point is obvious, it deserves underlining and a brief digression. Perhaps because of the prolonged nature of the Soviet threat and consequent security concerns (which have been the central preoccupation and full careers of two generations of American policy makers), in our standard vocabulary, "high policy," true foreign policy, has come to be understood as being concerned with security and conflict.

International economic policy has simultaneously taken on a "low policy" character. As a policy area it has been consistently out of favor and relegated to the backwaters of the Department of State and the White House until the Clinton presidency. And it has been balkanized within the responsible agencies of the U.S. government. As a result, international economic policy came to mean either monetary policy or some form of mercantilism.

But the economic and architectural strategy of the postwar years was of a different order altogether. It saw the United States and its economy as depending critically and immediately upon economic recovery after the war, and in the longer term upon a stable international economic order within which an economy of our scale could function. Even more fundamentally, as John Ikenberry has written, the strategy focused upon basic emergent principles of Western industrial capitalism: the simultaneous requirement for economic openness; multinational management of the political-economic order; clear, organized rules and institutions for the Western world economy; and the anchoring of rules and commitments in binding mechanisms.[1]

This was strategy of the highest order. It was not mercantilistic in any meaningful sense. It did not focus simply upon American business interests. It was not a sophisticated way to do deals.

Rather, it focused upon the fundamental and long-run, not the transitory, interests of the United States. It sought to structure relationships among a large number of significant and independent nations over a long period of time. And it created major institutions to focus upon problems that the strategy defined as both big and of long duration.

But in the effort to think through where we go from here, it is important to understand also that the extraordinary success of this strategy depended upon three basic aspects of the postwar order that came together coincidentally and that are difficult, if not impossible, to replicate.

- First, there was a significant pre-existent cultural affinity among the nations of the new community. This was a community among the victors of World War II, nations that already had, in Ikenberry's terms, dense interstate connections, and among economies that were quite similar. There were no significant differences, other than those caused by the destruction of war, between the levels of development, the science and technology, the industrial processes, the degree of education, of these economies. And the policy makers of these nations already comprised an informal community.
- Second, the postwar economy—almost uniquely—allowed such a community to come into existence. The U.S. economy of these years constituted over half of the world economy, albeit artificially and temporarily, and was dominant in most critical sectors. As a result the merits of a stable and broader field of play were apparent to managements, to workers, and to consumers. The problems of international competition were very far in the future. Therefore, the United States was able politically and financially to support the creation of a community. At the same time, there were willing recipients of that support. The economies of Europe were flat on their backs, and there was an easily recognizable and uncomplicated

need for institutions like the Marshall Plan—which provided an enormous transfer of resources—and the World Bank.

- Third, the emerging Cold War, and the sense of a common threat it engendered, provided both energy and unity to the new economic order and architecture. This sense of a common threat encouraged compromise, and allowed trade-offs to be made in the name of mutual security that probably never would have been made otherwise, particularly in later years. The same common threat provided a sense of urgency. Only the immediate reconstruction of their economies and the development of a strong economic community would enable the Western democracies to counter the Soviet threat.

The first of these three factors provided the underlying understanding and sense of trust without which the construction of a complex community is impossible. The second and third factors, together, enabled the United States to provide throughout much of this period both the energy and the grease needed for the development of the community. For example, throughout most of this period, broad trade agreements were reached not only because of the admirable theory of the negotiating round but also because the United States was willing to make many specific compromises—compromises in procedure or in specific sectoral areas that might not be to its immediate benefit—because the overall agreements were overwhelmingly in American interests.

In the years immediately after World War II, then, all of the factors required to create a new economic order came together. A clear need for such an order or community of nations existed. The leaders of the prime-mover nations perceived the need in similar terms and drew the same lessons from the world economy of the 1930s. And circumstances were uniquely favorable for one nation— the United States—to provide the driving energy.


TODAY'S CHANGED CIRCUMSTANCES

Almost every crucial feature of that foundation underpinning the economic order of the last fifty years has changed. First, the energy and the unity of the Cold War is gone. This statement is not intended as a moment of nostalgia for the Cold War. We are vastly better off because that fifty-year era is over, because policy makers do not have to act with warlike urgency and because American citizens no longer live under the nuclear shadow. But it is at the same time undeniable that the disappearance of the Soviet threat has removed a fifty-year requirement that the nations of the West act more or less in concert, or attempt to see the world situation from the same perspective, or attempt to act in terms of some definition of long-run strategies. The removal of the threat has made coalition building vastly more difficult and has lowered the odds on any particular issue that the major developed nations of the world will act in concert.

On the economic plane, the result has been an increasing tendency toward trade friction, a difficulty in defining the basis for the next steps in economic integration, and a pronounced tendency—particularly in Europe—toward mercantilism. The United States is not immune from these developments, but they have placed American policy makers in particularly difficult circumstances. As the world's only superpower (a hackneyed but nevertheless true observation) the United States is often required to play the world economic game—to be part of the growing competition, but also to rise above the fray and attempt to define the rules of the game. American politics and concerns of immediate commercial advantage require the first; considerations of our long-term interest require the second. But increasingly, our former allies are not cooperating. In circumstance after circumstance, Japan or European nations have taken advantage of American policies intended to serve international interests in order to pursue entirely mercantilistic policies. The U.S. response has been an increased use of its own leverage to pursue, successfully, similar policies. In policy discussions within the U.S. government, multilateral solutions to economic problems are increasingly seen as unproductive areas to explore.

In anything but the shortest run, this does not suggest a successful model for the relationships among the developed democracies as they face the circumstances of the new global economy. It is a model that runs precisely counter to the conditions policy makers were able to count on after World War II.

Second, the relevant community of nations is vastly larger than the community that was formed after World War II. More important, this new community is not characterized by anything remotely close to the density of interstate connections that was so characteristic of the post–World War II order. That earlier community was essentially North America and a small group of northern European nations. This grouping was soon expanded to include Germany, which in cultural terms did not change the postwar community, and then Japan, whose incorporation represented a significant change and challenge. (Indeed, the difficulties attending Japan's absorption were harbingers of the greater difficulties we face today.)

The world economy of that period and most of the last fifty years did not include most of the world's other large or potentially large economies. The Soviet bloc and China were excluded for obvious geopolitical and economic reasons. The large developing nations were just becoming independent and were too poor to count for much in the world economy. They were, in any case, pursuing statist-oriented, dead-end economic policies that offered few attractions to the market-oriented economies of the developed community.

The future will be different. All of these "new" regions and nations are part of the relevant community. It is impossible to imagine an economic order that does not include them from the start. But at the same time there is nothing among these nations or between them and the former economic community of developed nations that resembles the network of professional, business, academic, and policy relationships that are the defining aspects of community.

An underlying sense of familiarity and trust is essential in the building of any community or maintenance of any set of policies based upon shared considerations of long-term mutual interest. This underlying community of interests is only built layer by layer as all different elements of civil society transcend boundaries. What policy makers do is act on the basis of the existence of these layers of trust. They do not create them. The policy makers of the future have to act in the knowledge that the density of relationships does not even approximate those of the past.

Third, and finally, the underlying economy presents a totally different set of circumstances. The United States, after a natural catching-up by the rest of the world, now constitutes about 21 percent of the world economy, rather than more than 50 percent. The United States is not, and the U.S. political and business communities do not feel themselves to be, in the same circumstances, or able to function with the same degree of economic freedom, as twenty-five or forty years ago. At the same time, the changes that are occurring in the world economy (which will be discussed in some detail below) have caused substantial turmoil in all of the developed economies. In today's world economy, policy makers are not able to make the same kinds of decisions that were possible decades ago. Neither in the United States nor in other developed nations do policy makers have much latitude to make the long-run trade-offs that are necessary in the building of any order.

These changes matter a great deal for how to think about the notion of an economic order. They mean, for example, that it is not very useful to insist that the task of shaping a new economic community under today's circumstances is simply a matter of returning to the principles of the old order. The task is vastly more complex and difficult today. Those undertaking the task will face such a different underlying economy, such different actors on the world scene, and such significant new difficulties of implementation that to maintain that it is the same task obscures its meaning.

If our heirs look back fifty years from now and see the establishment of a community even remotely as successful as the one established fifty years ago, functioning under principles as valid as those that gave rise to this economic order, then the work of policy makers today will have been spectacularly successful. But the first necessity is to recognize the scale of the changes we are living through for what they are, and to see the task of creation of a new economic community as a strategic effort of the highest order and difficulty.

### SOURCES OF CHANGE: NEW TECHNOLOGIES, NEW ECONOMIC POWERS

Two sets of changes are shaping the global economy. Each represents a major change in its own right, but it is the interaction between the two that is creating a fundamentally different world economy.

First, the shape and structure of economies and markets are changing. At the most fundamental level, these shifts in shape and structure are being driven by deep processes of change occurring in information technology and financial markets.

The emergence of information and telecommunications technology as the characteristic technology of our era is the most fundamental and pervasive force changing the modern developed economy. It changes the goods and services developed economies produce; even the most familiar products of these economies are often altered completely by these new technologies. It changes the costs of virtually every process of production. It alters the speed with which any change occurs or any idea diffuses or any market functions. It makes all boundaries and political authority less relevant in terms of market competition. It alters the structure of all institutions and allows the creation of new kinds of institutions that could not have existed twenty years ago. It changes most of the sources of productivity in developed economies.

Simultaneously, world financial markets—in large measure because of modern information technology—operate very differently from in the past. Immensely larger sums of money flow through the markets. Financial markets are more global, encompassing many more economies of greater diversity. They offer far more varied forms of savings instruments, of means to mobilize savings. And they make possible much more and much different investment from what they did even ten years ago.

The evolution of the world's financial markets has begun to change completely the way resources are allocated in the world. Two or three decades ago, a high percentage of the allocative decisions were made administratively—by state decision makers, by corporate planning departments, by the bureaucracies of international financial institutions, or by major money center banks. Today, those decisions are made more and more through financial markets.

These two changes and their interactions have altered virtually every aspect of what a modern developed economy is and does. They have changed what developed economies produce and exchange. For example, a far higher proportion of output and trade in developed economies is made up of services, and a growing proportion of services consists significantly of information. Even in largely manufacturing sectors, services make up a higher proportion of costs than does pure manufacturing assembly work.

As a consequence of these changes in what developed economies produce, there have been equally dramatic changes in how the citizens and workers of these economies earn their living. The typical worker in a developed economy is not a farmworker, or a manual laborer, or a factory line worker. To a greater degree every year, that typical worker is a technician, a service worker, or an information handler. And more and more, that worker spends his career in smaller companies. In 1975, companies in the Fortune 500 employed 15 percent of the total American work force; by 1993 that share had fallen to 9 percent. More starkly, between 1975 and 1990 firms with fewer than five hundred employees created twenty million jobs. The Fortune 500, during the same period, lost slightly more than 700,000.[2] To a considerable degree it has been the inability of public policy in Europe to cope with the changes in technology, financial markets, and labor markets faced by all developed economies that has led to a failure of the economies of Europe to create employment, leading to unemployment rates two and a half times those of the United States.

These same forces are also changing the shape of trade. Thirty years ago, most trade consisted of the exchange of finished goods through arms-length transactions between unaffiliated companies. Today, as production chains have become worldwide, most trade now consists of semifinished goods moving between affiliated companies from one point to another in the production process.

All of these changes have led to major institutional innovations. Companies are more decentralized, more disaggregated, and flatter. Jobs are more project- and team-focused. Most dramatically, we are seeing the rise of the network-based economy. More and more of the critical functions of corporations—purchasing, logistics, manufacturing management, inventory control, distribution, intercompany payments, financial control—are carried out via electronic networks. The networks are substituting electronic commerce for the previous administrative functions of corporations and are leading to the evolution of the virtual or the plug-and-play company that can be assembled and disassembled as needs arise. To these networks, distance and geography are irrelevant.

These changes, taken together, alter almost completely the issues and concerns presented to policy makers within developed economies. By themselves they would alter the nature of the existing developed international economic order. But the interaction of these changes with another major economic transformation occurring today is reshaping the world.

The second transformation is the arrival of major new economic powers on the world stage. This arrival presents a set of circumstances we have never encountered before. Over the next twenty years, five nations—China, India, Indonesia, Brazil, and maybe Russia—each larger geographically and each plausibly approaching (although only China will actually reach) the economic size of Western Europe, will become economic powers of significance. Another ten nations of more mid-size potential will arrive simultaneously. This process, this series of arrivals, will change the world completely. Considering the policy energy devoted to and the conflict created by the arrival of two major new players—Germany and Japan—on the world stage over the last one hundred years, it is clear that a vastly larger set of arrivals will preoccupy our policy concerns, no matter what we might wish to focus upon.

This point is often trivialized by displaying the arithmetic showing that the sheer weight of economic activity is still with the big three: the United States, Japan, and Germany. But the center of economic growth is shifting to these newer markets. As a group they are growing more rapidly than the developed economies. They are already the drivers for most of our growth in trade and trade-related investment. It is, for example, quite true that the trade and investment relationship between the United States and Europe is the largest in the world. But it is also true that since 1990 for every one dollar of increased exports between developed economies, there have been three dollars of new growth in exports from developed to developing economies. About half of all the world's growth over the next twenty years will come from a "new Big 7" of these emerging markets in China, India, Indonesia, Brazil, South Korea, Thailand, and Russia. The current Big 7[3] will account for less than a quarter of the increase. By that time, the same "new Big 7" will have a combined GDP larger than the current Big 7.[4]

The developing economies are becoming equally important in investment and in world financial markets. Over the last ten years, since 1985, portfolio investment—investment in publicly traded securities by institutions acting as intermediaries—and foreign direct investment from developed to developing economies has grown from $11.4 billion to $112 billion, an annual growth of 25 percent. Further, as an indicator of great importance in a world economy driven by capital allocation through equity markets, the developing economies are increasingly important in the those markets. Fifteen years ago, the equity markets of the developing economies were of no importance whatsoever, amounting to less than 1 percent of the equity markets of developed economies. Today, they are 15 percent of developed economy equity markets. In ten years, they will be close to 40 percent of those markets.[5] Put another way, in ten years the equity markets of the emerging economies will be approximately equal to the size of developed-economy equity markets at the beginning of this decade. No one—no foreign policy scholar, no policy maker, no financial market observer—would have predicted this five years ago.

The point here is not that these emerging economies have discovered a distinctly different path to growth and that this growth in emerging economies is a permanent phenomenon. Their growth is not very different from what other nations experienced. It is not permanent; they will make mistakes. But they will grow, and this growth will matter. Growth of this kind, and the scale it implies, will have effects and will create dislocations. Virtually every aspect of the economic relations between the old and the new economic powers—from the governing of trade and investment among nations, to the regulation of markets, to the allocation of power within economic institutions—will be affected whether we like it or not, or choose to admit and anticipate it or not.

## THE EMERGING GLOBAL ECONOMY

I have described two sets of changes occurring in the world economy today: fundamental changes in the overall shape and structure of markets, and the entry of major new economic powers. It is the combination of these two sets of changes—their interactions—that presents us with a completely new underlying world economy.

The market changes described as the first factor would by themselves force substantial changes in existing economic relationships and arrangements. One effect of these changes is to force increased globalization and integration upon us whether we like it or not. Financial markets allocate capital worldwide on the basis of perceived differences in national productivity and the willingness and capability of regimes to maintain stable economic policies. Production and distribution chains are now worldwide. Equity ownership is widely distributed. The question of what is an American, a European, or even a Japanese company is more and more a real policy issue than a cute conundrum. Nations have decreasing ability to affect cross-border data flows, and those flows themselves are becoming more integral to the modern economy.

Another effect of these changes is to make policy issues more internationally intrusive and, therefore, more difficult to resolve. Financial markets and distribution and production chains are entangled. Trade issues are inseparable from investment issues and both are inseparable from such questions as market and antitrust regulation. Trade in international services is an almost completely new phenomenon; it raises issues of competition among groups in societies that always thought themselves to be protected. Information and intellectual property questions are equally complex. In all of these cases, which are now characteristic of developed-economy relationships, the issues are vastly more difficult today and less clear-cut than simple questions of zero-for-zero tariff negotiations—which took us forty years to resolve. Most new international economic issues involve questions that nations have always considered previously to be issues of basic sovereignty.

Finally, these changes in the shape and structure of markets have effects on the lives of the workers and families of our societies. They have changed what we produce. They have altered the nature of our jobs and our places of work. They have subjected us to competition we had never previously experienced. They have raised the level of education required to achieve the good life. They have altered distributions of income.

Most of these changes are probably transitory, the result of a shift from one kind of economy to another. But such shifts take decades, and private expectations and public policy adjust slowly. From the point of view of one middle-aged worker, one married couple, or one family, these shifts are seen as permanent change. This change is unsettling and unwelcome and has proven to provide fertile ground for nativistic political reactions. The rise of opposition to these changes, to their perceived sources, and to the policies attempting to cope with them is inevitable. Yet, all of these changes—and their effects—are almost certainly due to changes in the structures of and interactions among largely developed economies. When to this factor is added the arrival of the emerging economies, the global economy changes completely. The emerging economies are the key.

All of the consequences of change described above will be intensified. Existing institutions, and the existing order of things, will have to cope simultaneously with major change in how markets function, in where they function, and with much larger differences among markets. It is, for example, one thing for public policy to cope with the implications of open and competitive financial markets that search relentlessly for the smallest differences in costs and returns when the differences are themselves small—as they are, in general, between developed economies. It is quite another thing when the cost and return differences are an order of magnitude larger, as they often are between developed and developing economies.

At the same time, the new emerging economies themselves are faced with all of the changes and pressures imposed by market change, information technology, and global financial markets. And they are, in almost every instance, simultaneously going through a shift from statist economies—characterized by high levels of state ownership, state-protected monopolies, and heavy state regulation and administration of the economy—to market-based economies. The economic transitions of these nations are decades away from completion, but they are necessarily becoming part of increasingly complex world decision-making processes. These are nations with which we simply do not have the density of interaction that made creation of the order of the last fifty years possible. But these nations are inevitably and rapidly requiring that they be part of the world political and economic order.

None of these changes will happen immediately. Economic eras do not begin or end with sharp edges. Much that characterized the economy of the decades immediately after World War II will remain. On any given morning it will be possible to wake up and see elements of the world economy that has existed for the last fifty years. And many will choose to wake up in that frame of mind. But if we persist in that posture, if we do not acknowledge in intellectual and, ultimately, in policy terms how different the underlying economic context is, then we will never be able to summon the capacity to create the institutions and the community the next era's economy will demand.

### SCENARIOS FOR CHANGE: VICIOUS AND VIRTUOUS CIRCLES

There is no inevitable trend to the current set of changes. Because of the deep underlying changes occurring in the world economy, it is more true than was the case for much of the last five decades that the world can turn out differently, depending upon the policies we develop and pursue. And the crux of the problem is going to be whether we are able to develop stable, long-term working relationships—a new economic community—between the currently developed and developing economies.

We operate on the implicit assumption that progress in the development of such a community is natural. We have, after all, experienced an almost fifty-year record of success. But those successes were built upon the unique circumstances outlined in this chapter: the galvanizing power of a threat; the pre-existence of extensive economic, political, educational, and other relationships; the small size and homogeneity of the initial postwar economic community; and the relatively unobtrusive nature of international economic transactions.

The next fifty years will be very different from the last. There is little or no natural momentum toward the building of a new community. All of the unique circumstances have changed. There are forces working both to build and to thwart a new economic community.

Acting against the natural development of a new community is the current state of disarray of international economic relationships. Since the completion of the Uruguay Round in 1993, there has been no further progress in liberalizing world trade. No new round is in sight, and the new sectoral efforts—in finance and in telecommunications—have failed. In both cases, the failures were most directly linked to the inability of developed and developing nations to agree.

Every one of the existing multilateral international economic and financial institutions is in the midst of difficult and uncertain change. The evolution and future importance of the G-7 is unclear: so long as it is a rich (and formerly rich) boys' club with no involvement of the about-to-be significant economies, it will continually lose influence. It is hard to imagine a set of circumstances in which the emerging major economies will allow world economic policy to be made in a forum from which they are absent. But as in all such clubs, it is equally hard to imagine the circumstances of a graceful evolution.

All of the existing regional economic unions or processes of integration seem to be losing steam. What should be the easiest processes of integration—among developed regions—do not exist at all. None of the major developing nations has, even rhetorically, displayed any leadership, and each of the developed regions has problems of its own. Europe seems determined to turn inward and protectionist. When (or whether) Japan will become a more open, less managed economy is not a question one can easily be optimistic about. Within the United States there is enough opposition to open and liberal economic change that we may not be able to muster the political will to lead. Even with the requisite will, it is not clear that any set of forces can muster the political power to lead.

But at the same time, there are forces moving in more hopeful directions. The forces underlying the emerging world all point in the direction of integration. The world economy, viewed as a whole, is considerably more stable and less volatile than it was thirty years ago. The Mexican rescue effort of 1995 provided a successful example of how one of the kinds of economic crises we are likely to experience in the next decades can be dealt with. Virtually all of the developing economies are, to a greater or lesser degree, pursuing internal economic policies of openness, liberalization, and competition. The multilateral institutions are changing, albeit in fits and starts. And most of the world's political leaders argue—strongly, mildly, or wistfully—in favor of openness.

Across the board there is a generalized and intellectualized commitment to the development of the next economic community, although certainly not stated that way. But at the same time, many if not most of the specific circumstances we face and policy choices we are making argue the opposite case. Under these circumstances, it is easy to visualize both vicious and virtuous circles.

A sequence of vicious circles, leading inexorably away from the possibility of a new economic community, will develop if over the next ten years the relations between developed and developing nations become progressively more strained in more of the regional groupings and forums of the world. This could easily occur.

If the three developed regions of the world do not display a greater tendency toward open policies of integration, they will inevitably act more mercantilistically and will be unable to create the joint policies and politics that might accommodate the developing economies. If one or more of the major developing economies does not take on a more active leadership role, it will be impossible to build new coalitions, new bridges between the developed and emerging economies. If steady momentum does not develop either in the Americas or in Asia toward meaningful economic liberalization, then the regional approach—the region as stepping-stone to global change—will be politely abandoned.

If the G-7 does not in some way include some of the most obvious major economies—China, India, Indonesia, Brazil—it will matter less and less, and the world will gradually lose a forum and occasion through which major issues can be approached. If the World Trade Organization does not come up with mechanisms that can begin again to make progress on world trade and investment liberalization, then it will become increasingly discredited.

In these kinds of circumstances, it is likely that the major emerging economies will develop institutions of their own. It is easy, for example, to envision an annual meeting of the major developing powers; or a southern trade organization. Such a pattern of development could move us toward a world in which there was much more explicit and important confrontation between the developing nations and institutions of the South and the developed nations and institutions of the North.

Virtuous circles will develop if important progress is made in at least one regional grouping that includes developed and developing economies. Such progress would serve an important demonstration effect. If, simultaneously, the developed economies begin their own progress of integration, there will be less of a tendency toward competitive mercantilism and more of a capacity to accommodate a broader view of economic change.

If economic disputes are more frequently settled multilaterally in rule-based ways, the World Trade Organization will be strengthened, and both developed and developing nations will be more likely to define and commit to common principles of economic action. If the G-7 becomes something more like the G-11 and includes the most obvious emerging economies, there will be a yearly need to confront and deal with the different perspectives of the developed and developing economies. Incremental progress on these issues will be made for the same reason it is today: the leaders dislike going to meetings and not having visible successes. In such a world, we are more likely to see viable global and regional institutions that include both the current developed and developing nations. We are also more likely, over time, to see the domestic politics of both kinds of nations develop in ways that permit change.

One point here is that very different outcomes can emerge from the facts of today. And these differences make a difference. If we are fortunate enough to see (or to create the conditions allowing) the development of virtuous circles, our citizens will be better off. Economic growth as a whole is likely to be higher; financial markets, investment, and trade are likely to be more open; the capacity of the world to cope with economic and financial crises, or with the endemic and more chronic problems Robert Kaplan underlines, is likely to be greater.[6] And we would be far better able to deal with the noneconomic global problems we know we will face in the future: population, environmental issues, world health, and global crime.

But another point is that these different outcomes (and different economic orders) involve different levels of effort. Achieving the best outcomes—establishing the virtuous circles—probably requires more than allowing events to take their course. Explicit strategies, careful sequencing of decisions, conscious exercises of will, and acceptance of political risk will all be necessary. On the other hand, the natural momentum of events is probably more toward the vicious circles—the less favorable outcomes.

A CHOICE OF FUTURES: AMERICA'S
INTERNATIONAL ECONOMIC STRATEGY

The international economic strategy we build today will shape the future. And the structural economic issues we face today are analogous to those faced immediately after World War II.

Now, as then, the questions U.S. policy makers must ask are broad and structural. What kind of international economy provides the greatest scope and the most hospitable environment for the economy the United States is becoming? What promotes the most favorable long-run stability and best prevents potentially significant threats from emerging? What institutions, more broadly what community, is required to bring such an economy into being? What policy strategy, in other words, provides the most fertile ground for virtuous circles and is most likely to eliminate the possibilities of vicious circles?

After World War II the answer to those questions saw the recovery of Europe and Japan and the creation of institutions that would more tightly integrate the relevant nations of the world into a common order in the interests of the United States. Today, the answer is similar but necessarily far broader in concept. A principal objective of American foreign policy should be the creation of a global economic community designed to encompass increasingly both developed and emerging economies, and to eliminate the chance of a serious gulf between them

For all of the reasons argued in this chapter, accomplishing this objective will be enormously difficult. Neither domestic nor global circumstances make likely the kind of major step forward that Bretton Woods represented fifty-odd years ago. In today's circumstances progress must be made through steady, purposeful incremental change. Yet at the same time, visible progress must be achieved across a broad spectrum of policy areas. No one policy stroke will be sufficient.

Despite these caveats, the United States can raise the probabilities of a successful outcome by building short- and long-run policies along the following lines:

1. *A clear statement of direction.* Within the U.S. system of government nothing of any import happens unless the president makes clear that it matters to him. Likewise, it is still the case that on the international stage, while the other nations of the world may not do what the United States desires, they will almost certainly do nothing at all in a concerted manner unless the United States points the way.

The first requirement then, in order to begin defining and achieving a new global economic community, is that the president of the United States must say clearly that he intends to focus upon it as a major priority. He must say it in an important forum and he must repeat it often. Only through repetition can a president make clear domestically and internationally that this is a strategy; only then can the mechanisms of government and diplomacy begin to fall in line behind the president and the process of public education proceed.

2. *An increase in the day-to-day priority given to the emerging economies.* While President Clinton has done more to change these day-to-day priorities than any previous president, it is still the case that our governmental machinery operates on a Eurocentric basis. We may talk conceptually about a new economic orientation to our foreign policy; the Department of Commerce may host countless seminars on the "big emerging markets." But on a day-to-day basis, we continue to allocate more diplomatic resources, and more attention and energy, to the developed economies than to the developing ones.

The U.S. ambassador to any of the G-7 nations is more important in the U.S. scheme of things than are the U.S. ambassadors to China, India, Indonesia, Turkey, or Brazil. The same is true of the regional assistant secretaries in Washington. Prestige in our foreign policy establishment still comes from work on developed-nation issues. The day-to-day stuff of foreign policy—the notes, the visits, the phone calls—all occurs more quickly and more comfortably between the United States and Europe or Japan than between the United States and the principal developing nations. It is relatively easy to arrange a presidential phone call to the United Kingdom or to Germany. It is virtually impossible, or at least it becomes a matter of very high policy, to arrange a similar call to Brazil.

All of these attitudes and practices have to change. The president's national security and national economic advisers should ensure that he speaks regularly with the leaders of the major emerging economies. Presidential trips to these nations should be seen as substantively and politically of high priority. A particular effort should be made by the president, and followed up on by his cabinet, to enlist the leadership of one or more of the emerging economies to take a principal role in the effort to define the new economic community. Within the White House, the president should underline to the National Security Council and the National Economic Council that this policy is of long-run importance, that he wishes to see it expressed repeatedly in actions by the government, and that he wants it to be the topic of the first, or an early, presidential decision memorandum. The big three—the secretaries of state, treasury, and defense—should travel regularly to Asia, Latin America, and Africa to create the network of relationships we already have with Europe and Japan.

The first practical step—after providing a direction—that the president can take is to invoke the Woody Allen principle that 85 percent of success consists of showing up. What is required as a start is a reorientation, a focusing, of our policy machinery toward what is important now.

3. *A focus upon the architecture of the world.* None of the existing international economic and financial institutions is well adapted to the emerging world economy. All are making efforts to evolve. But for every one of these institutions, this evolution must be accelerated and must focus simultaneously upon the need for substantive policies that better reflect the changes now occurring in the world economy, for significant improvements in the efficiency of these institutions, and for reform in their structures of governance.

Reform in the structure of governance is probably the most urgent of these requirements for reform, and the G-7 represents the most obvious example. To put it bluntly, the G-7 must evolve or it will become almost completely irrelevant to our long-run concerns. The G-7 annual summits are often criticized for dullness or a failure to arrive at major decisions. However, such criticisms miss the point entirely. Of course the meetings rarely are the occasion for major and dramatic change. The leaders are all elected heads of the governments of large-scale democracies; their steps inevitably will be cautious, careful. Every one of the leaders has to convince an electorate that is normally skeptical of any international agreement to go along with each step.

But there is a value in the meetings by themselves. It is highly useful for the leaders to develop a sense of each other and to be able to have at least one weekend of conversation in a relatively small group. At the same time, the corridor conversations and business done on the side are often as valuable as the formal agenda. And if there is rarely a single dramatic moment, sets of decisions made over the span of several summits are highly useful.

But all of this is valid only if the right leaders are at the meeting. Increasingly, this is not the case. And if the G-7 does not either change or enlarge itself sufficiently within the next decade—to include China, India, Indonesia, and Brazil—it will lose stature and meaning unrecoverably.

### AN AGENDA FOR AMERICAN LEADERSHIP

The first two years of President Clinton's first term were the most successful two years in terms of international economic accomplishments since the creation of the original postwar economic community in the years immediately following World War II. But the growing hostility in both parties to international economic agreements, and the election of Republican majorities in both houses of congress in 1994 meant that little additional progress could be made thereafter.

Yet it is vitally important that the United States regain the initiative and provide a set of visions and strategies for the nation. Defining and making the first concrete steps toward a new global economy, bringing together the developed and emerging economies of the world, should be one of our highest priorities.

- First, relationships between the developed economies and regions should be pushed beyond bilateral and sectoral trade disputes toward a more integrated economy in the developed world. While neither Europe nor Japan seems ready for such movement, unless they are both part of any overall economic strategy, success is extremely unlikely. Indeed if they are not part of the answer, they will be part of the problem, and it is more likely that we will see a strong tendency toward the development of mercantilist blocs than anything else.
- Second, progress must be accelerated in at least one of the two regional communities—APEC or the Free Trade Area of the Americas—that President Clinton did so much to create during his first term. A logical starting point would be to move aggressively with the inclusion of Chile in NAFTA or with the conclusion of a separate free trade agreement with Chile.
- Third and last, the role of global agreements and of the WTO must be better defined. Nothing of any significance has been accomplished on a global basis since the completion of the Uruguay Round in 1994.

It is simpler to list such an agenda than accomplish it. But even to make a start requires, more than anything else, that this vision—of creating the foundations for the global economic community of the twenty-first century—be presented to the American people in a way that defines the nation's place in the emerging global economy, gives Americans an understanding of how their domestic well-being is linked to the success of the nation's international economic strategy, and provides a sense of confidence and direction.

Conceiving and implementing such a vision will never be done by governments in the normal course of events, in the midst of the normal cut and thrust of daily politics. Governments are inevitably captives of the crises of the moment, or the policies they have already developed, or the turf instincts of government agencies. This is uniquely a task of agenda-setting and of inspiration that only a president can accomplish.

## NOTES

1. G. John Ikenberry, "The Myth of Post–Cold War Chaos," *Foreign Affairs* 75 (May–June 1996): 79–91.

2. U.S. Department of Commerce figures.

3. Canada, France, Germany, Great Britain, Italy, Japan, and the United States.

4. Figures from the office of the U.S. Trade Representative.

5. World Bank figures.

6. See, e.g., Robert D. Kaplan, *The Ends of the Earth: A Journey at the Dawn of the 21st Century* (New York: Random House, 1996), as well as Kaplan's "An Anarchic World Order" in this volume.

# CHAPTER TEN

# The New Mercantilism: Where Is Business Leading Our Foreign Policy?

MICHAEL F. OPPENHEIMER

*Michael F. Oppenheimer is a consultant on foreign economic policy and national security to several government agencies, specializing in models and scenarios for thinking about the future. He is currently a principal with Multinational Strategies, having served from 1975 to 1993 as executive vice president and director of the Futures Group. An adjunct fellow with the Center for Naval Analyses and the Rand Corporation, he is also a member of the Council on Foreign Relations and the American Council on Germany. He is author of* Nontariff Barriers, *among other works.*

This deliberately provocative question is a useful entrée into a broader, more fundamental issue—namely, the commercialization of U.S. foreign policy, its origins, its extent, and its consequences. By the commercialization of foreign policy I mean the elevation of economic/commercial interests over more traditional, political/military concerns about the stability of the international system, the use of force to deter or prevail over adversaries, and the maintenance of key diplomatic relationships. It conveys a sense that the interest groups that influence the process, the intelligence relevant to policy, the priorities that animate U.S. foreign policy, the key relationships with countries that require nurturing, the links between domestic and foreign policy, all revolve to a greater extent than they used to around a commercial agenda. This new agenda entails accessing markets for U.S. traders and investors, stimulating economic growth and job creation, encouraging economic reform in emerging markets, and sustaining the momentum toward liberalization in the global trade and payments system.

This agenda is based not on clear, explicit principles but on emerging and still uncertain practice. In the post–Cold War environment, policy is made less from doctrine than from impulse when confronted by events. Policy has an ad hoc, improvised quality that indeed suggests a broader conclusion—that foreign policy itself is generically less important than heretofore, that diminished government operational capacity, the ascendancy of domestic issues, and a highly networked and resilient global economy have marginalized what used to be high politics. In this sense, the triumph of improvisation in foreign policy is simply a manifestation of how little it commands in attention or resources, and not a conceptual confusion about U.S. interests and the direction of the international system that will clarify as we free our thinking from Cold War rigidities. Foreign policy, including foreign economic policy, has become the residual, deserving our attention only after we have exhausted our political capital on issues that are more proximate—taxes, spending, health care, values. This is not something to be applauded, but those who understand the dependence of our prosperity on our global leadership now face a hugely more difficult political task.

## WHAT'S NEW ABOUT OUR COMMERCIAL DIPLOMACY?

Part of this shift toward a commercial focus is the consequence of the increased role of business in the policy process, although this has evolved gradually during the postwar period. More significant is the fundamentally altered foreign policy agenda in the wake of Soviet collapse and a pretty well spent multilateral trade negotiating process that has shifted attention toward regional and bilateral opportunities. It is also an accurate expression of the Clinton administration's strong domestic priorities, the increasing sense that the returns to foreign policy need to be proximate and easily demonstrated in terms of job creation, growth, and export market shares.

Several things stand out as distinctive in post–Cold War foreign commercial policy. First is its pragmatism, its determination to seek opportunities for market openings wherever they exist, regardless of the dictates of trade policy orthodoxy (with its emphasis on multilateral negotiations, the play of market forces, and avoidance of any corporate or sectoral bias). This emerging policy is not consistently mercantilist, nor is it focused exclusively on regional arrangements, although this is where much of the energy has gone recently. It is opportunistic and has produced or contributed to several achievements:

- an ambitious and partly successful multilateral round of negotiations through the General Agreement on Tariffs and Trade (GATT) and now in the World Trade Organization (WTO);
- a series of regional negotiations that are essential to maintaining the momentum toward trade liberalization in light of diminishing returns from the multilateral process;
- bilateral negotiations with countries either historically outside the postwar liberalization process (the big emerging markets) or, like Japan, in violation of broad liberalization norms; and
- several commercial transactions where American leaders have intervened selectively to influence contract negotiations for large infrastructure projects in emerging markets.

So far this multilayered approach does not appear to have damaged the global free trade and investment regime; indeed, it appears to have reinforced it in some respects. First, the regional activities, and NAFTA in particular, have served as models for where global negotiations ought to go if and when political will can be mustered at the global level. Second, regional negotiations for the most part have been done in a way that minimizes trade distortion, and have thus provided the key source of forward movement toward increased liberalization. This approach also offers the possibility of achieving global harmonization in a different way from how it was done historically, by knitting together successful regional efforts instead of going for broke in heterogeneous, complex global negotiations. Furthermore, both regional and bilateral efforts—within APEC (Asia-Pacific Economic Cooperation) and with Japan and China—have been consciously used to reinforce global free trade. For example, our APEC initiatives were used to leverage greater flexibility during the final stages of the Uruguay Round of the GATT negotiations. In the Chinese case, we used bilateral negotiations to set the conditions for Chinese WTO membership; in the case of Japan, we negotiated on the basis of most favored nation (MFN) status. In addition, the deal-level discussions do not violate global free trade norms, so long as they adhere to OECD (Organization for Economic Cooperation and Development) guidelines on export credit subsidies and other forms of government support.

Second, this increased pragmatism has been pursued with bare knuckles, without the usual diplomatic niceties and deference to our traditional allies. This has been true at the deal level, where we have slugged it out with Europe and Japan over big infrastructure projects in the emerging markets, where the president has become directly involved in trying to tip the scales toward American bidders, and where intelligence about foreign corporate bribery has been used effectively to increase U.S. leverage. This has also been the case at the multilateral level, where the United States told its trading partners to try again on a telecommunications services agreement as a follow-up to the Uruguay Round and in which U.S. demands for reciprocal market access were made quite explicit. This represents a big change from our historic role in guaranteeing favorable outcomes in trade negotiations by making any necessary last-minute concessions. It has become clear that U.S. tolerance for anything less than equivalent market access, particularly in areas of our competitive advantage, has been exhausted. And the willingness of the president to invest the prestige of his office and exercise personal leverage is an extraordinarily visible sign of the shift toward commerce in American foreign policy.

Third, there is a clear shift toward a country focus in our commercial policy, particularly with respect to the big emerging markets as designated by the Commerce Department (to include the Chinese economic area, South Korea, Indonesia, India, Turkey, South Africa, Poland, Mexico, Brazil, and Argentina). This is an obvious departure from the historic emphasis on multilateral negotiations, and involves a more strategic and focused market promotion effort directed at countries that have large and growing populations, high economic growth rates, and substantial barriers to entry that maximize the potential government contribution to market access. They also happen to be the countries that pose the greatest problems for new foreign policy issues such as environmental degradation, violation of human rights, the diffusion of weapons of mass destruction and their technology, communal violence and the threat it poses to stability, and population/immigration. This fact has enabled the current administration to defend commercial engagement on the basis of anticipated benefits in these other policy domains, a claim that is likely to prove extravagant.

The fourth characteristic of this emerging commercial policy is its effort to define a forward-looking agenda, one that tries to stay even with commercial practice and is targeted at measures whose impact on market access is heightened as more traditional forms of protection diminish. Of particular concern are measures that block access for investors or distort the investment process by treating American investors less favorably than domestically domiciled firms, as well as measures that interfere with the right of establishment for service companies, distort the flow of services across borders, weaken intellectual property rights (IPR), or permit anticompetitive behavior that limits the ability of U.S. firms to do business on a roughly equivalent basis with local firms. While the Clinton administration has been slow to embrace this agenda at the global level, it has made significant progress in more tractable regional and bilateral settings.

With our leverage diminished by the erosion of the Cold War consensus among OECD countries, competing against these same countries for the big emerging markets and with this very demanding trade and investment negotiating agenda, the development and execution of U.S. international economic policy will absorb much of our diplomatic energy over the next decade. This leads to the fifth and perhaps most distinctive feature, the sense that foreign commercial policy is where diplomatic capital gets spent, where proximate interests are perceived to be most clearly at stake, where the public is most involved, and where the potential domestic political rewards are the greatest. The most obvious way to validate this conclusion is to consider U.S. policy toward China. It is with respect to this most gigantic and fastest-growing of the big emerging markets that many U.S. foreign policy interests are at stake and in sharpest relief. Our policy toward China is the test of our convictions and our priorities, and in the absence of a clear and explicit policy, the accumulation of cases points toward commercial engagement as the centerpiece. These cases suggest not indifference toward Chinese misbehavior, but a sense that the issues worth fighting for are commercial issues (IPR protection, WTO membership, major infrastructure projects). Given our limited leverage with the Chinese, these priorities pretty well dictate a tolerance for Chinese missile and nuclear technology sales as well as violations of human rights.

## WHY THE ENLARGED EMPHASIS ON COMMERCE IN OUR FOREIGN POLICY?

Several forces are at work here. A rapidly globalizing economy has made us more dependent on foreign economic conditions and the accessibility of foreign markets for our economic growth and job creation, acquisition of new technology, the profitability of our firms, and our overall prosperity. Our borders are more porous—to goods and services, to capital, to immigrants seeking a better life, to terrorists—and the closing of borders has become far more difficult and costly. We are more vulnerable to external shocks and more dependent on foreign capital to finance official deficits. These factors have raised the visibility and importance of commercial policy, since it can now be argued that such policy directly affects proximate interests, thus the role of trade issues in the recent presidential and congressional elections.

This is but a delayed reaction to a global reality that has gained momentum over the last two decades, but whose salience was obscured by the central role of the Soviet threat in our foreign policy. The end of the Cold War has had two effects on commercial policy. One has been to increase the importance attached to our commercial interests relative to security. The other effect has been to shift the negative strategic consequences associated with a more assertive commercial strategy, which had been seen as increasing the vulnerability to Soviet power, but now involves a more subtle and elusive weakening of global institutions. This more commercially driven posture represents global economic policy detached from a necessarily broader political framework—a fact most economists are loath to admit.

The centrality of China in our diplomacy, commercial and otherwise, and the now open conflict between us and our trading partners over how hard to press the Chinese on IPR protection and conformance to WTO norms, is a case in point. Competition with the Soviet Union unified us and our allies. China, on the other hand, has had a deeply divisive effect, partly because we are competing for the market, partly because the acrimony that results is perceived—wrongly, I believe—as having fewer negative consequences for American interests in such areas as nonproliferation and regional stability.

While globalization and Soviet collapse have raised the importance of commercial policy, the intractability of global trade negotiations has increased that policy's pragmatic, opportunistic character. The relatively easy reforms in trade practice have been made, in the form of near elimination of tariffs and quantitative restrictions (among developed countries). Beginning with the Kennedy Round but more prominently in the Tokyo and Uruguay rounds, the focus has shifted to trade-distorting measures that are often manifestations of domestic policy, are more subtle in their effects, and are often highly technical in the way they operate. This makes negotiations on so-called nontariff measures difficult, time-consuming, and often contentious. They have absorbed much energy and diplomatic capital with results that leave a great deal to subsequent monitoring and implementation. Furthermore, efforts to bring developing countries into the process have increased the diversity in interests, economic structure, and negotiating style, thus vastly complicating recent negotiations on services, IPR, and investment. As tremendous effort has been expended for relatively little gain, attention has naturally come to focus on regional trading arrangements, where the prevailing interdependencies are greater, where the political will exists to move forward, and where the heterogeneity associated with global negotiations is often less.

Parallel to the regional focus of recent negotiations is the shift in U.S. commercial priorities from developed to so-called big emerging markets (BEMs). This reflects not pre-existing levels of trade and investment, but rather a new push into high-population, high-growth markets where trade practice is often protectionist and where U.S. companies have much to gain from a more assertive government role. While Japan continues to resist market opening and Europe stagnates and focuses internally, the big emerging markets have received by far the greatest attention recently—both by marketers at the Commerce Department and by trade negotiators at State and USTR (office of the U.S. trade representative).

To reinforce this emphasis, it is argued that commercial engagement with this set of countries is an effective (and increasingly the only realistic) form of influence over their behavior on such issues as environmental protection, nonproliferation, and human rights. In a period of inevitably declining U.S. military presence and increased competition for these markets, we may have to settle for indirect forms of influence on their behavior as their economies become more integrated with the global economy, as their markets are frequented by Western companies, and as global competition for capital encourages more acceptable commercial practice. While these effects of increased interdependence with the BEMs may occur over the longer term, they would be the inadvertent consequences of these trends, and not the product of deliberate policy. We are, in fact, doing what comes naturally, and the other benefits from commercial engagement are afterthoughts.

While these factors have enabled a more pragmatic and assertive commercial policy to emerge, the role of business has been very important in several respects. For one thing, it is no accident that the opportunistic, nondoctrinaire approach to foreign economic policy that characterizes the current administration accurately reflects business style and culture. And the persistent business criticism of American foreign policy during the Cold War—that we were unnecessarily subordinating our commercial interests to Cold War diplomacy, while our allies sold more freely and benefited more—undoubtedly had a cumulative effect. More tangibly, the trade policy positions taken by major business associations and firms on international trade in services, intellectual property rights, competition policy, and tariff elimination by sectors has led the way in setting a forward-looking negotiating agenda and in generating support for these ambitious objectives. As we achieve formal agreements in these highly technical, complex, domestic issues, business will be critical in monitoring adherence and supporting their implementation.

## HOW IMPORTANT IS THE SHIFT TOWARD COMMERCIAL INTERESTS?

The role of business in the post–Cold War international economy is only marginally a matter of influencing government policy, and overwhelmingly a matter of shaping the global environment to which policy reacts. While business support is critical in advancing the trade and investment agenda, the heightened global competition for business investment is probably a more powerful incentive for trade liberalization than are threats of protection or government-to-government trade negotiations.

This raises a fundamental question: Are recent innovations worth much attention, as policy itself recedes as a determinant of the global economy?

- Is globalization irreversible? Is the global economy so intricately networked among such a multiplicity of players, with most governments committed to getting out of the way, that not much is foreseeable that could interrupt it? Is not the resiliency of this global system its most noteworthy character, having survived a global energy crisis, several wars, a staggering realignment of currency prices, several protectionist outbursts, the debt crisis among the less-developed countries, and the Mexican financial implosion?

- Is the so-called Washington consensus—open markets, privatization, fiscal tightening, price stability—already enforced by competition for capital, with official diplomacy playing at most a reinforcing function?
- Do the big emerging markets behave in a commercially responsible and rational way, regardless of what incentives are offered by competing suppliers? How much additionality is there in the Department of Commerce–led effort to exercise political leverage for contract awards?
- Do regional and global trade negotiations essentially ratify pre-existing trade and financial interdependencies, rather than (as in the early postwar period) create them?
- Is U.S. global competitiveness overwhelmingly a matter of productivity, levels of investment, technological innovation, labor skills, and the freedom our firms enjoy to adjust to shifting competitive conditions—and only at the margins a matter of official trade and investment policy?
- In other words, is the commercialization of our foreign policy tantamount to its marginalization?

POLICY MATTERS

These questions matter, not because the global economy is perfectly self-governing, but because increased precision is essential in defining where the added value lies in official policy as the amount of political capital available for international economic negotiations diminishes. The following are areas where our government can be useful in sustaining the movement toward international economic growth and reform.

First, the United States is justified in spotlighting the big emerging markets as areas of largest incremental increase in demand for foreign products, services, and capital; as the principal foci of global competition with other developed countries; as the principal threats to the multilateral trading system (because of their exclusion from most previous global trade negotiations); and as arenas in which major U.S. foreign policy interests are at stake. Current policy has the balance about right between aggressive selling (with its inevitably bilateral orientation) and a longer-term effort to liberalize the trade practices of these countries (with an emphasis on WTO membership and improvements in the treatment of services and intellectual property), although this balance is constantly in jeopardy of going awry. My criticisms would be of the administration's fondness for the illusion that commercial engagement will produce improved behavior in weapons proliferation, human rights, and the environment; a tendency to exaggerate the impact on U.S. sales; and a neglect of social and political problems that create market vulnerabilities.

Second, there is the critical function of establishing a forward-looking negotiating agenda, one that continuously redefines priorities in light of emerging commercial practice, the results of previous negotiations, and the interests of U.S. firms. While many of these priorities emerge from the private sector, and global firms are often able to mitigate the effects of trade distortions without recourse to government, the best solution combines corporate and government action to expand the global trade regime. Among other things, the formalization of more liberal practice is essential in minimizing backsliding during the inevitable periods of slower growth and protectionist pressures. Absent such efforts, we may still be able to pry open big emerging markets, but special deals will proliferate, competition will get destructive, and reversal of reform will become much easier.

Third is the increasingly important and difficult task of implementing agreements, important because the backlog of agreements is now very large, difficult because many of them cover highly technical measures that are the outgrowth of trade-distorting domestic policies. There is value in negotiators' reach slightly exceeding their grasp, but agreements with governments that cannot or will not take the necessary steps to implement can have a negative effect on the global system and absorb enormous diplomatic capital without commensurate returns. Implementation will be central to trade liberalization during the next decade, and again government-business collaboration—for intelligence collection, for exercising leverage on recalcitrant parties—is the best solution.

Fourth is the role our government must continue to play in organizing multilateral support for countries going through the often painful process of economic and political reform. The trade liberalization process is strongly reinforced by such reform in formerly centrally planned economies, developing countries, and the BEMs. There is no doubt that governments adhering to free market principles domestically are more cooperative negotiating partners. Yet the structure for supporting this reform process is very shaky (as demonstrated by the improvised response to the collapse of the Mexican peso and current uncertainties surrounding South Korea), and recent improvements in the safety net are untested, as are IMF oversight or surveillance measures. Since these kinds of currency implosions are bound to occur from time to time, a critical role for government in the future will be to create the right combination of transparency, domestic banking reform, and multilateral procedures that limit the damage and prevent contagion if an important currency collapses, but without removing the financial cost to countries that pursue bad policy.

As we work to improve the liberal system of trade and payments, we also need to keep in mind that a borderless world is not an unmitigated blessing for countries that are unattractive locations for investment, or for individuals within competitive economies who lack the training to benefit from globalization. The increasing integration of economies may be an inevitability—driven by official policy and rapid advances in technology—but a political reaction may also be inevitable should such a process continue to widen the gulf between rich and poor, creating a vast, global underclass attributing its ill fortune to these liberal policies. Provisions in U.S. and other countries' trade laws providing for temporary import protection in response to domestic injury acknowledge these realities; so do adjustment assistance provisions, though they are badly underfunded. But for the most part, we are haphazard in our reaction to the negative effects of globalization, and there will be a large political price to be paid for this.

American leadership is as key to sustaining the momentum toward global market reform as has been the case historically. Summoning the leverage to deal with new forms of protection, reconciling regionalism with multilateralism, effectively implementing agreements, preventing backsliding during periods of slow growth, integrating new actors into the global system, and sustaining the political consensus (especially in the Congress) behind globalization are all important to moving the process of globalization forward and maximizing its benefits. And it is a reasonable expectation, based on history, that others will not act without the push and the vision that only the United States can provide.

This suggests a close linkage between American power in the world and our success in achieving our international economic policy goals. Economists like to think of global trade and payment liberalization as the outgrowth of a natural process in which the laws of economics are progressively freed to operate. They see American policy as an instrument of these laws. American foreign policy experts are principally interested in America's military and diplomatic roles in the world, and tend not to pay much attention to the low politics of trade and finance.

Few understand the international economic system as a product of the exercise of American power on behalf of a uniquely American definition of how that system should work. And because of this, we have not yet addressed the central issue of how to maintain this leadership as our military presence diminishes, as our relationships with our allies become more competitive, as alternative forms of capitalism demonstrate their vitality, and as government sovereignty continues to erode. What this suggests, at a minimum, is a greater awareness of the effort required if we are to continue exercising a leadership role in global economics. And it may suggest, in both Europe and the Far East, a conscious decision to maintain our military and political presence as a precondition to exercising effective economic diplomacy.

These observations about the potential benefits of official policy prompt several questions about our post–Cold War approaches to global economics:

- Does the big emerging markets strategy work? How many important sales are made as a consequence of official leverage? Do these sales, as they accumulate, generate leverage that can be exercised on other issues, or do they absorb leverage and so make our representations on these other issues less effective? This empirical question is critical, since the acknowledged risks that bare-knuckle competition poses for the global trading system are not worth taking without significant commercial rewards. Experience suggests that there is some additionality, but that there are much greater benefits in effectively integrating the big emerging markets into the WTO system, and that aggressive, bilateral salesmanship and the necessarily collective defense of the multilateral regime are not easily made compatible.
- If the BEMs are to become central to our diplomacy and if we are to invest real political and diplomatic capital in their future, is our knowledge about them commensurate with the size of the bet we place on them? Policy uninformed by intelligence tends to bump up against unexpected obstacles. If commercial engagement with this relatively unfamiliar set of countries is to carry the weight of such issues as nonproliferation, human rights, and environmental protection, our understanding of these countries is in serious deficit. There is a myopia here that is a consequence of seeing the BEMs principally as markets, rather than as countries with severe problems of maldistri-

bution of income, overburdened urban centers, environmental scarcities, ethnic divisions, corruption, and weak governments. If these issues are not taken seriously in our policies toward these countries, they at least need to be factored into our expectations about how stable they are as commercial partners.

- What about the non-BEMs, those developing countries that are marginalized in a commercially motivated focus on the fastest-growing, largest markets? These are the countries that are the recipients of dwindling aid dollars, which we belatedly learn about when they explode in ethnic violence, generate huge numbers of refugees, and require outside intervention. Because these countries are demonstrably of some importance to us, we need to develop ways of addressing their population, environmental, ethnic, and other issues before they become crises.

- Does the Washington consensus generate the right policy advice for most developing countries and big emerging markets? In light of the Mexican and Asian currency/growth crises, we need to ask ourselves whether this orthodoxy really reflects experience and whether it can be sustained.

While these concerns are more or less specific to the current popularity of big emerging markets, the commercialization of foreign policy also raises several broader questions:

- How much stress can the multilateral system take before this hugely beneficial product of U.S. postwar policy begins to fray? As the leader in global trade and payment liberalization and the world's largest exporter, the United States has a huge stake in the strength and extension of a rule-based system. Our regional initiatives have so far been consistent with this fact, as have our more aggressive sales efforts. But the trend is disturbing. As we continue butting heads with allies over the Chinese market and focusing on our regional initiatives, there is a risk that new global negotiations will languish. There is additional risk that preoccupation with deal making and bilateral/regional initiatives will weaken an already shaky congressional consensus for trade liberalization. One real test will come on Chinese accession to the WTO, where the global trading system demands that we stand firm, while the dynamics of

U.S.-European-Japanese competition for the Chinese market
will create incentives to do otherwise.

- Does our leadership in global economic negotiations
  presuppose a broader American role in the world that will be
  very difficult to sustain given the absence of a clear threat? Is
  our leverage in international commerce more a consequence of
  our power than of being on the right side of the laws of
  economics? If so, the government's commercial preoccupation
  and its more improvised approach to international security are
  in conflict.

- How much low growth, high unemployment, wage stagnation,
  and income inequality can the countries that comprise the
  international economic system take, before the liberal system
  itself begins to implode? The ultimate test of the system
  remains the quality of life it is able to deliver, and while
  economists are fond of citing the dynamic returns to international trade, the adjustment agonies suffered by developed and
  developing countries alike are continuing to build. If we fail to
  respond effectively to these negative effects of economic
  liberalization, politics is bound to reassert itself with a
  vengeance—in the form of protectionism and a general
  disengagement from global problem solving. Although the
  global economy has demonstrated tremendous resilience, it has
  yet to face its greatest test: the simultaneous emergence of large
  impoverished minorities in the major trading countries,
  attributing their deprivation to the global economy and
  pressuring their governments, which are themselves less
  convinced of the benefits of collaboration and are in tough
  competition for emerging markets.

A mercantilist policy can take us only so far. Although it offers the tactical merit of transitory commercial advantage—a benefit not to be mini-
mized in an increasingly competitive world—it cannot deliver the strategic
goal of a sound global economy on which our long-term economic security
depends. Still less can it support our other national objectives—America's
business being more than business alone—or redress burgeoning global
problems that ultimately could overwhelm our own prosperity and well-
being. The challenge is not to resist these mercantilist tendencies, for they
are inevitable, but to steer them toward national goals and superimpose a
strategic design over the growing commercialization of our foreign policy.

# CHAPTER ELEVEN

# A New Protectionism?
# Tariffs versus Free Trade

ALFRED E. ECKES, JR.

*Alfred E. Eckes, Jr., is a historian, former senior trade official, and journalist. From 1981 to 1990 he was a commissioner (chair, 1982–84) of the U.S. International Trade Commission, a quasi-judicial agency responsible for administering import remedy laws and conducting investigations for Congress and the executive branch. Previously he served as executive director of the Republican Conference of the U.S. House of Representatives and as editorial page editor of the* Columbus Dispatch. *He is now Ohio Eminent Research Professor at Ohio University and author, most recently, of* Opening America's Market: U.S. Foreign Trade since 1776.

P ublisher Henry Luce first popularized "The American Century" in February 1941, when he exhorted *Life* readers to reject isolationism and to accept wholeheartedly America's opportunity for world leadership. "The vision of America . . . as the dynamic leader of world trade," Luce wrote, "has within it the possibilities of such enormous human progress as to stagger the imagination." He envisaged a hegemonic America acting as the "good Samaritan of the entire world."[1]

During the Cold War years American leaders pursued a commercial policy that mirrored these goals and supported the containment strategy. It was based on promoting free trade, on establishing an international trade organization to facilitate negotiations and resolve disputes, and on providing special concessions to assist war-devastated and developing countries grow through export expansion.

For some fifty years presidents from Harry Truman to Bill Clinton pursued this economic internationalist design with remarkable persistence and considerable success. In a series of multilateral tariff negotiations beginning in 1947, they reduced formal trade restrictions and opened the American market to global competition. This country rolled back tariffs from an average of 28 percent ad valorem equivalent on dutiable items in 1945 to about 5 percent today.[2] After two failed attempts, they also managed to create the World Trade Organization. Congress had been suspicious of such initiatives during the Truman and Eisenhower administrations, but during the Uruguay Round of the 1990s, economic internationalists finally prevailed.

As the leader in this effort to create an open, rules-based international economy, America also played the role of the good Samaritan, providing generous trading opportunities in the American market, while tolerating restrictions on U.S. exports from trading partners. During the long reconstruction period after World War II, Washington tolerated one-sided trade arrangements with former allies and adversaries, such as Great Britain, France, and Japan, among others. Later, during the 1970s, the U.S. government generously approved a similar program of unilateral free trade, the Generalized System of Preferences, to stimulate imports from developing nations. And to prevent import-sensitive industries from disrupting this strategy with trade-remedy complaints, the executive branch invoked discretionary executive authority regularly to deny and deflect protectionist pressures.

During much of the half-century after World War II, trade thus served as a vital instrument of Cold War policy. The issue today is whether that economic internationalist paradigm is appropriate for America in the twenty-first century. To address that question, it is important to understand the strengths and weaknesses of previous approaches, and to envisage future circumstances.

Unquestionably, American leadership and support for economic internationalism over the last half-century helped promote world prosperity and build a robust, liberal, democratic world order, especially in the North Atlantic region. As Henry Luce and other visionaries anticipated, trade expansion contributed to winning the peace and stimulating world economic growth.[3]

American consumers likewise derived many benefits from these import-promoting policies. Imports spurred domestic competition and presented new opportunities for Americans to buy low-cost shoes, apparel, electronics, and automobiles. However, it is important to keep consumer gains in perspective. Consumer greed is a good-times phenomenon. The unemployed consumer is an unreliable customer and can be a discontented voter. Accordingly, Congress, which has constitutional responsibility for regulating commerce, usually has assigned higher priority to domestic production and jobs than to consumer benefits.[4] In the future, when general unemployment rises, Congress can be expected to focus more intensely on trade-related job losses.

During the Cold War years, America's decision to open the domestic market also helped revive international investment flows. With lower import barriers, U.S. corporations took advantage of developments in transportation and communications and pushed overseas in search of new and cheaper sources of supply and new markets. The resulting globalization of business created many new opportunities for an educated elite of service providers, such as lawyers, management consultants, transportation specialists, and economists, among others.

To appreciate the anxieties and attitudes of ordinary Americans as we near the twenty-first century, it is important to understand that free trade has a second face, a grotesque one that frightens many working people. Along with recent presidential candidates like Jerry Brown, Pat Buchanan, and Ross Perot, many common people blame one-sided trade deals for job losses, plant closings, and dislocations of families and communities.

One of the first legislators to raise this issue was former Senate Finance Committee chair Russell Long (D-La.). Dissatisfied with the Kennedy Round agreement negotiated during the Johnson administration, Long complained that policy makers preoccupied with the stability of the world were making trade deals that over time placed in jeopardy import-sensitive domestic industries and unskilled workers, the parties least prepared to compete in an open global economy. The archival evidence suggests that Senator Long was right. During the Cold War years, trade negotiations frequently produced only sham reciprocity, and the United States made little serious effort until recently to monitor results. When American trade negotiators agreed to lower tariffs and bind the results, they frequently permitted others to defer obligations, devalue their currencies, or even ride free without making equivalent concessions.[5]

In effect, trade negotiators may have frittered away the bargaining power of the high 1930 tariff without gaining equivalent access to foreign markets. Extensive reliance on the unconditional most favored nation approach encouraged free riding by some trading partners, who benefited from our concessions but avoided parallel reductions. Thus, the post-1950 trade expansion that free traders celebrate became unbalanced and proved unnecessarily burdensome to domestic producers. U.S. imports rose rapidly while exports lagged. United Nations statistics show, for instance, that in the years since 1950, world exports rose 11.3 percent annually, but U.S. exports climbed only 9.8 percent, compared with 12 percent import growth. No other major developed market economy experienced such a wide gap between export and import performance or sustained such persistent merchandise trade deficits. In 1995, the United States experienced its twenty-first successive merchandise trade deficit, one approximating $175 billion. It is at least arguable that that figure signals a net loss of 2.5 million job opportunities to other nations, and has reduced the growth of U.S. gross domestic product 1.7 percent. Meanwhile, major trading partners like Canada, the European Community, and Japan all enjoyed export growth greater than import growth. Obviously, exchange rates, disparate savings rates, and a host of factors may help to explain this disparity. But trade discrimination is not an insignificant factor.[6]

Annual reports on *Foreign Trade Barriers*, submitted by the U.S. Trade Representative to Congress, provide a detailed record of such market-access problems. Among our top ten deficit countries, seven—Japan, China, Taiwan, Nigeria, Malaysia, Mexico, and Venezuela—pursue highly restrictive import policies that handicap access to their markets. In some instances, tariffs on U.S. exports still exceed 100 percent.[7]

Another factor contributing to popular disenchantment with trade negotiations has roots in Washington. To win public and congressional support, U.S. officials often exaggerate prospective gains from trade agreements and minimize losses. The North American Free Trade Agreement is the most conspicuous example. The Bush and Clinton administrations sold NAFTA with the claim that it would create some 170,000 jobs net by 1995. Ross Perot and other critics disagreed. Later, Jules Katz, one of the NAFTA negotiators, admitted the Bush administration used "totally phony [job] numbers, only because NAFTA's opponents were claiming NAFTA would be a job loser." After two years of experience with NAFTA, even government economists now concede that the results have not matched administration forecasts. One recent study, by a Labor Department economist, shows that for the first two years NAFTA boosted U.S. imports, and not exports. Attributing the peso crash to exaggerated expectations associated with NAFTA, the author concludes that exports to Mexico in the first two years would have been greater had NAFTA never passed.[8] The long-term assessment could be quite different, of course, but it is by no means clear that the extravagant claims for NAFTA will be vindicated.

Another fundamental concern relates to a paradox of free trade. Government policy makers preoccupied with promoting economic efficiency and global growth claim that trade liberalization reinforces American security interests by promoting international stability and prosperity. However, there is other evidence that trade liberalization may produce the opposite effect—that is, promoting chaos and instability. In the years ahead it is possible that the aggressive pursuit of free trade may magnify economic insecurity and thus jeopardize political support for a leadership role in foreign relationships.

Certainly this is the view of trade pessimists like Sir James Goldsmith, a member of the European Parliament and a former corporate raider. He has forecast that free trade agreements like the Uruguay Round would "impoverish and destabilize the industrialized world while . . . cruelly ravaging the third world." He anticipates that free trade may drive two billion people off the land worldwide and make it difficult for democracy to remain as the dominant structure.[9]

While Goldsmith and other trade pessimists may be unnecessarily gloomy, the notion that free trade promotes chaos has some foundation in history and economic theory. Karl Marx once embraced free trade, not because he thought it would produce peace and prosperity, but because he thought it would hasten the global social revolution. In 1848 Marx told a crowd in Brussels: "The protective system of our day is conservative, while the free trade system is destructive. It breaks up old nationalities and pushes the antagonism of the proletariat and the bourgeoisie to the extreme point. In a word, the free trade system hastens the social revolution. It is in this revolutionary sense alone, . . . that I vote in favor of free trade."[10]

In the nineteenth century many prominent persons associated free trade with chaos. Conservative Republicans like Abraham Lincoln and William McKinley propounded such theories. Lincoln, a high-tariff Republican, adhered to the view that "the abandonment of the protective policy . . . must result in the increase of both useless labour, and idleness; and so, in [proportion], must produce want and ruin among our people."[11] McKinley, the Ohio Republican elected president in 1896, delivered one famous speech that Marx might have authored. He asserted in 1892: "Free trade . . . will bring widespread discontent. It will revolutionize values. It will take away more than one half of the earning capacity of brain and brawn. Worse than all that, it will take away from the people of this country who work for a living . . . heart and home and hope. . . . Free trade results in giving our money, our manufactures, and our markets to other nations. Protection keeps money, markets, and manufactures at home."[12]

Until World War II, it was the conventional thinking among congressional Republicans that removal of the protective tariff would expose high-paid American workers to cheap foreign competition—and create enormous adjustment problems at home. Reed Smoot, chair of the Senate Finance Committee, warned that removal of the protective tariff barriers would force Americans "to slide back down to the economic level of the rest of the world."[13]

In light of such concerns, it is appropriate to take note of theoretical explanations. Economists have long postulated that because nations tend to export goods making use of the most intensive factors of production, free trade will tend to equalize factor costs. Stated in less technical language, there is some theoretical support for believing that the free movement of goods will narrow the gap between U.S. and foreign wages for unskilled workers, and perhaps widen the gap between the wages of skilled and unskilled workers within the United States.

A few years ago, Adrian Wood, an economist at the University of Sussex in Great Britain, stimulated debate with publication of book that claimed the removal of trade barriers in Northern Hemisphere countries had reduced demand for unskilled labor and aggravated "social corrosion." Crime, drug abuse, and racial tension he attributed in part to the surge in imports from low-labor cost countries. Wood is not alone. Even the London *Economist*, a journal founded by free traders, conceded that "low-skilled workers . . . are right to be worried." It warned that "some occupations higher up the earnings ladder will also feel the force" of Third World competition.[14]

When Pat Buchanan raised the economic insecurity issue in Republican primaries, the American establishment awakened. Soon the *New York Times* published a series on corporate downsizing and job dislocations, and *Foreign Affairs* featured a lead article, "Workers and the World Economy." Author Ethan Kapstein warned, "the world may be moving inexorably toward one of those tragic moments that will lead historians to ask, why was nothing done in time?" For globalization to proceed, he says, governments must give more attention to worker concerns. In every industrialized nation, he points out, "growing income inequality, job insecurity, and unemployment are widely seen as the flip side of globalization."[15]

Given such concerns, and the resulting debate among scholars, what American trade policy is appropriate for twenty-first-century circumstances? Many doctrinaire free traders urge more of the same; they urge more vigorous efforts to achieve the free trade millennium in the years ahead. To justify such an approach, economist C. Fred Bergsten invokes the bicycle theory. If one is not pedaling forward to reduce trade barriers, he asserts, one may fall off the bicycle as protectionism and nationalism revive. Thus, free traders propose to expand and intensify multilateral efforts to deregulate economies and promote increased competition in markets for services, like telecommunications and finance, and to reduce barriers to trade in agricultural products.[16]

Some economic internationalists stress the opportunities for concluding regional free trade agreements, such as an expanded NAFTA to include all of the Americas, an Asian-Pacific pact, and even a Trans-Atlantic Free Trade Agreement. Further trade liberalization, many of these crusaders think, can engage China and Russia and energize more and more developing countries, while promoting democracy and prosperity.[17]

The euphoric predictions of today's free trade enthusiasts bear a fascinating resemblance to the romantic prophecies of English anti-Corn Law crusaders like John Bright and Richard Cobden. They once touted commerce as the "grand panacea, which, like beneficent medical discovery, . . . serve[s] to inoculate with the healthy and saving taste for civilization all the nations of the world." Cobden forecast that free trade would act as a principle of gravitation, "drawing men together, thrusting aside the antagonism of race and creed, and language, and uniting us in the bonds of eternal peace." [18] Underestimating the residual appeal of nationalism, these romantics did not anticipate the two bloody world wars and the protracted Cold War that disrupted most of the 20th century.

Without question, free trade has yielded great benefits to the world economic system and to individuals. However, it is important to remember that in the non-Western world, many view these issues differently. In East Asia, for instance, the nationalistic economic teachings of Friedrich List have encouraged reliance on import substitution and export promotion as instruments of national development. This successful model, which many associate with Japanese development after World War II, actually had its roots in nineteenth-century American experiences. After World War II, Japanese officials fashioned policies that drew in part from America's protectionist past.

While Western economic theorists counsel free trade, a number of economic historians have concluded that no industrial nation has accomplished the difficult transformation from an agricultural society to an industrial one without a protectionist phase. Perhaps that is one of the reasons why protectionist measures enjoy strong support in remnants of the former Soviet empire.[19]

It is reasonable to expect developing nations to continue protecting domestic markets, under the guise of establishing infant industries, notwithstanding the preachings of fervent free traders. In the years ahead, China and much of the old Soviet empire may follow the Listian model, while seeking to attract outside investors and technology transfers. Economic nationalism is very much alive in the world, and ideologues and polemicists who ignore this point do so at their own peril.

It is not surprising that many in the business community remain confident that free trade and technology-driven internationalism will prevail. They foresee a prosperous and peaceful world order in which place becomes irrelevant and nation-states, like the United States, continue to lose sovereignty to rules-based international organizations. Echoing that confidence, WTO Director-General Renato Ruggiero recently warned that stopping globalization is "tantamount to trying to stop the rotation of the earth."[20]

Such thinking seems overly romantic. Yes, advances in communications and transportation have compressed time and space and made the world a smaller, and perhaps more tolerant, place. Yes, the mobility of capital, goods, and people has never been greater. But that does not mean that markets and international rules control nations. National governments are not impotent in the face of changing technologies and improved communications. With accelerating information flows, residents of high-income countries are exhibiting greater interest in such sensitive issues as job security, income integrity, labor standards, environmental regulations, and federalism. Future events may oblige public officials to balance the old dream of global free trade against other realities—particularly the enduring vitality of economic nationalism in the world and the popular yearning for local autonomy. Grassroots pressure may persuade officials to trade off some economic efficiency in order to promote other political and social priorities.

Given the disposition of many alienated voters to blame wage stagnation on open markets, U.S. policy makers will need to assign higher priority to devising programs providing income security to all Americans. While retraining, a familiar panacea, is necessary and important, it is not sufficient—particularly for many low-skilled workers averse to education. If current free trade arrangements do in fact bring about a harmonization of wages and incomes, government may need to consider ways to decouple the domestic labor market from the world market.

One approach is temporary import restraints. Such remedies can work without perpetuating the inefficiencies of permanent protection. The best example involves Harley Davidson, the motorcycle maker that nearly went broke in the early 1980s, but has made a complete turnaround. (As one who participated in many such decisions, I know from experience that trade-remedy laws, like Section 201, the escape clause, and our antidumping and countervailing duty laws can serve constructive purposes.)

Regarding China and much of Eastern Europe, there is no compelling reason to proffer the benefits of full WTO membership, until those nations demonstrate a sustained commitment to market-oriented regimes. Endemic corruption and the absence of open and impartial judicial systems further complicate commercial relations. It is desirable to engage these nations in mutually beneficial trading relationships—but not at the cost of persistent trade imbalances or loss of low-skilled manufacturing jobs to countries that restrict our exports.

In East Asia and other areas of the world, new technologies and enthusiasm for free markets appear to be producing impressive changes. But many of the emerging nations speak in the language of free trade while practicing protectionism. The recent failure of WTO negotiations to break down walls to trade in financial services, communications, and shipping is evidence that many emerging nations still think the United States is prepared to act like the Good Samaritan—opening our market to the world while tolerating restrictions on access to emerging markets. On these matters the Clinton administration deserves credit for resisting bad deals. Until a critical mass of nations is prepared to provide parallel access to their own domestic markets, it behooves the United States to move cautiously, to preserve its own bargaining power, and not to repeat mistakes of an earlier era.

Over the past decade we have undertaken ambitious trade liberalization commitments, including free trade pacts with Canada and Mexico, a Caribbean Basin Initiative, and the World Trade Organization. Also, our leaders have pledged to extend free trade to the Americas and the Pacific Basin. It is not at all clear that they appreciate the magnitude of these commitments, or the costs and burdens to the American people of implementation over the next decade.

In closing, let me suggest a modification to the bicycle theory. Rather than attempting to pedal faster and accelerate the pace of change, I believe that U.S. negotiators should put their feet on the ground and take a rest until the effects of current arrangements become known. Nations, like institutions and individuals, occasionally need to catch their breath and to assess the results of prior efforts. During the late twentieth century our trade liberalization strategy hinged on a missionary faith in the benefits of free trade and a belief in America's hegemonic responsibilities. Little attention was paid to monitoring and implementing those accords, or to cushioning domestic disruptions. If America is to continue on the path toward freer trade without igniting a populist revolt at the grassroots from the dislocated and the anxious, a more cautious approach is required. If leaders wish to promote free trade arrangements for the business community, perhaps they should encourage regional groupings among nations with similar income levels, as the late Sir James Goldsmith has suggested. Widening and deepening the U.S.-Canada relationship is a possible example. Meanwhile, the executive branch needs to focus on trade administration—on finding innovative ways to implement existing commitments consistent with the economic concerns of ordinary citizens, our sovereignty, and our international interests. That is challenge enough for the next decade.

NOTES

1. Henry Luce, "The American Century," *Life*, 17 February 1941.

2. U.S. Bureau of Census, *Historical Statistics of the United States: Colonial Times to 1970*, vol. 2 (Washington, D.C.: Government Printing Office, 1975), 888.

3. For a recent assessment, see G. John Ikenberry, "The Myth of Post–Cold War Chaos," *Foreign Affairs* 75 (May/June 1996): 79–91. Also, Henry C. Simon, "The U.S. Holds the Cards," *Fortune* 30 (September 1944): 156–9. Generally, Robert E. Herzstein, *Henry R. Luce: A Political Portrait of the Man Who Created the American Century* (New York: Charles Scribner's Sons, 1994).

4. On consumer greed, see Ambrose Bierce, *Enlarged Devil's Dictionary* (New York: Doubleday, 1967), 227.

5. Alfred E. Eckes, Jr., *Opening America's Market: U.S. Foreign Trade Policy since 1776* (Chapel Hill, N.C.: University of North Carolina Press, 1995). See also: Steve Dryden, *Trade Warriors: USTR and the American Crusade for Free Trade* (New York: Oxford, 1995), and Thomas Zeiler, *American Trade and Power in the 1960s* (New York: Columbia University Press, 1992).

6. United Nations Conference on Trade and Development, *Handbook of International Trade and Development Statistics, 1993* (New York: United Nations, 1994), 16–18; Charles W. McMillion, *Trading Away U.S. High Wages and Good Jobs* (Washington, D.C.: MBG Information Services, May 1996).

7. United States Trade Representative, *Foreign Trade Barriers, 1995* (Washington, D.C.: Government Printing Office, 1995). In the case of Japan, the barriers to market access are no longer official trade barriers, but a combination of private industry exclusionary practices and bureaucratic impediments.

8. On job creation, see Gary Clyde Hufbauer, *North American Free Trade: Issues and Recommendations* (Washington, D.C.: Institute for International Economics, 1992), and Thea Lee, *False Prophets: The Selling of NAFTA* (Washington, D.C.: Economic Policy Institute, July 1995). On Katz's comment, see Bob Davis, "NAFTA Is Key to Mexico's Rescue of Peso; U.S. Exporters May Not See Tariff Help," *Wall Street Journal*, 17 April 1995; Robert Shelburne, "U.S.-Mexico Trade Under NAFTA: Two Different Years, Two Different Stories," in *Proceedings of the International Trade and Finance Association*, vol. III, San Diego, 22–26 May 1996, 665–86, supplemented by oral presentation.

9. Sir James Goldsmith, *The Trap* (New York: Carroll and Graf, 1994), 25–31.

10. Karl Marx, *The Poverty of Philosophy* (Chicago: Charles H. Kerr, 1913), 227.

11. Cited in Eckes, *Opening America's Market*, 30.

12. Ibid., 30–3.

13. Ibid., 280.

14. Adrian Wood, *North-South Trade, Employment and Inequality: Changing Fortunes in a Skilled-Driven World* (New York: Oxford University Press, 1994), 1–26, 351–2; *Economist*, 1 October 1994; 70 ff. Also, George J. Borjas, Richard Freeman, and Lawrence F. Katz, "On the Labor Market Effects of Immigration and Trade," Working Paper 3761, National Bureau of Economic Research, Cambridge, Mass., June 1991; Ravi Batra and Daniel J. Slottje, "Trade Policy and Poverty in the United States: Theory and Evidence, 1947–1990," *Review of International Economics* 1 (1993): 189–208; Edward E. Leamer, "Wage Effects of a U.S. Mexican Free Trade Agreement," Working Paper 3991, National Bureau of Economic Research, Cambridge, Mass., February 1992; Jeffrey D. Sachs and Howard Shatz, "Trade and Jobs in U.S. Manufacturing," Paper prepared for the Brookings Panel on Economic Activity, Washington, D.C., 7–8 April 1994. See also: essays in Robert A. Blecker, ed., *U.S. Trade Policy and Global Growth: New Directions in the International Economy* (Economic Policy Institute) (Armonk, N.Y.: M.E. Sharpe, 1996).

15. Ethan B. Kapstein, "Workers and the World Economy," *Foreign Affairs* 75 (May/June 1996): 16–37.

16. C. Fred Bergsten, "Globalizing Free Trade," *Foreign Affairs* 75 (May/June 1996): 105– 20.

17. Ernest H. Preeg, "Transatlantic Free Trade," *Washington Quarterly* 19 (Spring 1996): 103 ff.

18. Cited in Eckes, *Opening America's Market*, 1.

19. On protectionism and national development, see for instance Paul Bairoch, *Economics and World History: Myths and Paradoxes* (Chicago: University of Chicago, 1993), and Eckes, *Opening America's Market*, 28–58, 170–2. On protectionism in East Asia, see James Fallows, *Looking at the Sun: The Rise of the New East Asian Economic and Political System* (New York: Pantheon, 1994); Tessa Morris-Suzuki, *A History of Japanese Economic Thought* (London: Routledge, 1989), 59–61; "On Russia," *New York Times*, 29 May 1996.

20. William Knoke, *Bold New World* (New York: Kodansha International, 1996); Kenichi Ohmae, *The Borderless World: Power & Strategy in the International Economy* (London: Collins, 1990); "No Return from Trade Globalization, Secretary General Ruggiero Warns," *International Trade Reporter* 13 (15 May 1996): 798.

# PART FOUR

# American Foreign Policy in the Post–Cold War Era

# CHAPTER TWELVE

# Challenges Approaching the
# Twenty-first Century

### SAMUEL R. BERGER

*Samuel R. Berger is assistant to the president for national security affairs. Before joining the Clinton administration, he was a partner in the Washington law firm of Hogan and Hartson and director of its international trade group. His prior government experience included service as special assistant to former New York City Mayor John Lindsay, legislative assistant to former Senator Harold Hughes, and, from 1977 to 1980, deputy director of the State Department's policy planning staff. A graduate of Cornell University and Harvard Law School, he is author of* Dollar Harvest, *a book on American rural politics.*

Between the end of the Cold War and the dawn of a new century, America is at a moment of historic opportunity. Not too many years ago, Americans were gripped by a television movie called *The Day After*, which portrayed in graphic and horrifying detail what actually would happen in the event of a nuclear war. The genuine possibility of a massive nuclear exchange was vivid and real and cast a giant shadow over most of the last fifty years.

---

This essay is based on remarks delivered by Samuel R. Berger at a Woodrow Wilson Center noon discussion on June 18, 1996, and disseminated that date by the Office of the Press Spokesman, The White House. The original version has been edited to eliminate now-dated references.

Today, the grinding burden of the Cold War has been lifted. Our nation is at peace. Our economy is strong. The tide of democracy and free markets is rising around the world. We have experienced the emergence of a global economy and a cultural and intellectual global village. These developments enrich our lives in countless ways every day.

Traveling in Pakistan, Azerbaijan, Korea, Japan, or Moscow, I can turn on CNN and be instantly plugged into events around the world. Remember that scarcely more than half a century ago, when Franklin Roosevelt gave the order to launch one million men across the English Channel on D-Day, he didn't find out the results for several days. I use CNN only as a visible symbol of the revolutionary advances of the information age, which has so increased the goods, services, and knowledge that are available to us—and made Americans the most fortunate inhabitants of the global village. But this promising new era is by no means risk-free.

Democracy may be on the march, but forward progress is not assured—and the gains are not irreversible. We know this is true in Russia and many of the other states of the former Soviet Union. It is also the case in our own hemisphere. Not long ago, the democratic government of Paraguay narrowly avoided a coup—and elsewhere in Latin America, the power of the drug cartels throws an ominous cloud over some national governments.

Global communism and fascism have exited stage left and stage right. But the forces of intolerance and hatred, ethnic strife, and regional conflict persist in brutal and dangerous forms, from Northern Ireland to the Balkans, from the Middle East to parts of Africa.

The threat of nuclear annihilation has receded, but the danger that weapons of mass destruction—biological, chemical, and nuclear—will spread into unreliable hands has grown as the technology becomes more widely accessible and can, in some cases, be called up on the Internet.

As the president has noted, the very openness and freedom of movement that enriches our lives also makes us more vulnerable to the forces of destruction—terrorism, drug cartels, and international criminal organizations. We have seen this in the bombing of the World Trade Center, in the sarin gas attacks in the Tokyo subway, and the gunning down of journalists, police officers, and government officials by drug lords in many countries.

Because this new era of possibility carries with it so many real threats as well as new opportunities, the United States cannot afford to sit on the sidelines. Instead, American engagement in the world today is more important than ever. We cannot and should not go it alone, or take full responsibility for combating the new dangers of our age. But at the same time, we know that without American leadership, more often than not, the job will not get done. One of the most striking facts of the last few years is the extent to which, after the end of the East-West rivalry, others look to us—whether it is Arabs and Israelis in the Middle East; Muslims, Serbs, and Croats in the Balkans; or even, grudgingly, the nations of Europe and Asia—as they seek to deal with the same threats that face us.

There is only one superpower now on earth—the United States. That leads to one inescapable fact—the United States must lead in the world if we are to maintain our security and increase our prosperity. We cannot hunker down if we want our children to live safely and thrive.

From the beginning of his administration, President Clinton has recognized America's responsibility to lead in today's world. Let me focus on four dimensions of this leadership for the future that have been at the center of our attention during this administration. They are the cornerstones of our efforts to build peace and prosperity for America in this promising but uncertain era.

The first dimension is our nation's strength—military and economic. America's military today is undergoing its most fundamental transformation in half a century. Our armed forces are simultaneously downsizing and upgrading. A military that was designed to stop a massive invasion across Central Europe today is prepared to deal not only with traditional warfighting contingencies, as in the Persian Gulf or on the Korean peninsula, but has the flexibility and training to deal with a range of new missions—restoring democracy in Haiti without firing a shot, keeping the peace in Bosnia, or delivering nearly 15,000 tons of food, medicine, and supplies to Rwanda's refugees. When you consider that only a few years after Vietnam an Army chief of staff described a "hollow army," this reshaping of capability and doctrine has been an extraordinary achievement. Today, our armed forces are smaller than they were at the height of the Cold War, but they are also better, more flexible, and more sophisticated than at any time in our nation's history.

Increasingly, our nation's international position rests on the strength of our economy. And that, in turn, depends on our competitiveness in the global economy. The president has spearheaded the most dynamic program of innovation in international trade in U.S. history. He has expanded our economy by expanding the global economy, completing the Uruguay Round, passing NAFTA, securing the APEC agreement for free trade in the Asia-Pacific region, and forging more than one hundred bilateral trade pacts. Today, exports are the fastest-growing part of the U.S. economy. We are, once again, the largest exporter in the world and the most competitive.

The second dimension of American leadership is to use our capacity to be a peacemaker effectively. We cannot be everywhere and do everything. But where our interests and values are at stake, the United States must take risks for peace.

The United States is using its unique capacity as peacemaker to try to establish a lasting settlement in Bosnia. We have undertaken this task because continued war in the Balkans threatens both our interests and values. The fire that has burned in the heart of Europe since 1991 would have spread and engulfed our friends and allies—and drawn us into a wider conflict on this continent for the third time in a century. And the unspeakable brutality we all witnessed was an affront to our humanity.

American leadership was essential to put out the fire and stop the slaughter. We strengthened NATO's response to the unrelenting Serb assaults on Sarajevo and other civilian areas. More effective use of that power enabled our diplomats to make vital breakthroughs and produce the Dayton peace agreement.

Today, the most dramatic fact in Bosnia is that the guns are silent. The war has ended. That change, from war to peace, is the single most important reality for the people of Bosnia. It means that killing fields are once again playgrounds. Cafes and marketplaces are full of life, not death. Running an errand doesn't mean running a death race against snipers and shells. Women are no longer prey to systematic campaigns of rape and terror. The water and lights are on, and there is shelter from the wind and the cold. Peace means all of these very basic things. As we work to make sure peace endures, we must not lose sight of its reality.

Now we must help the people of Bosnia build the enduring peace they so desperately want. The hard work of civilian reconstruction has begun. It must move faster. We must continue assisting refugees to return, continue the work of the war crimes tribunal, and help the Bosnians build the institutions of a national government.

The Middle East and Bosnia are just two of the regions where America is engaged in work for peace. We are at a pivotal point in history when real change is possible and consistent with our interests and our resources. We must seize this moment and make the most of it—in Northern Ireland, on the Korean peninsula, in Haiti, and other places around the world. We must not overreach. We must work with others. But at this moment in history—when turmoil, radicalism, and instability threaten—America is uniquely positioned to be a powerful force for peace.

The third imperative of American leadership in the post–Cold War era is to continue to reduce the nuclear threat. In recent years we have taken a giant step back from the nuclear precipice. Already, under START I, some nine thousand nuclear weapons are being removed from the arsenals of Russia and the United States. It is extraordinary to see a team of Russians sawing up a Backfire bomber or dismantling missile silos and turning those sites into wheat fields. With reductions agreed upon in Start II the cuts will go even deeper. The U.S. and Russian arsenals will be reduced by two-thirds of their Cold War levels.

Our efforts to diminish the nuclear threat go further. Because of President Clinton's agreement with President Yeltsin, Russian missiles no longer target American cities. Through determined diplomacy, we helped persuade Belarus, Kazakhstan, and Ukraine to give up the nuclear weapons left on their soil when the Soviet Union crumbled.

But even as we destroy the weapons of the Cold War, we must intensify our efforts to prevent the spread of the weapons of tomorrow. That is why we worked hard to secure the unconditional and indefinite extension of the Nonproliferation Treaty. We achieved an agreement with North Korea to freeze and dismantle its nuclear program—and that agreement is being complied with under international supervision. We are working with the Russians and Europeans to make it harder to smuggle nuclear material, to keep Iran from acquiring the materials it needs to build a bomb, and to curtail dangerous arms races like the one in Southern Asia. This is the most ambitious arms control and nonproliferation agenda ever set by an American administration. This is the best chance to reduce the nuclear threat that we are ever likely to see— and we are determined to seize it.

Finally, there is one more great challenge for American leadership in this new era—to construct new institutions and new arrangements that reinforce the growth of democracy and civil society where the iron fist of totalitarianism crushed freedom for decades. We see this imperative nowhere more clearly than in Russia, which is in the midst of a great decision.

The choice of Russia's leadership is for the Russian people to decide. It is not for us to tell them how to vote. But we still have an enormous stake in the outcome. We have made clear our unwavering support for reform and reformers.

We support reform because a democratic, market-oriented Russia is more likely to pursue goals that are compatible with our own; it is more likely to be a reliable partner and to respect the independence of its neighbors and live in peace with them—including those that were once part of the Soviet Union. A Russia that chooses to stay on the course of reform is one that will be more likely to continue to reduce the nuclear threat, to work with us to promote peace around the world, and to create new markets for our products and jobs for American workers.

We do not have a vote in Russian elections, and we do not have a crystal ball. But several points are clear for the United States. First, we must support not individuals but a direction—the direction of reform, democracy, and free markets. We must continue to build, in Central and Eastern Europe, new bridges to the West—through NATO expansion, Partnership for Peace, and EU membership. And, we must do that in a way that strengthens the relationship between NATO and Russia. We must proceed with steadiness and judgment; but the fact is, we have made good progress.

Let me leave you with a final thought. While the need for American leadership has never been greater, our willingness to lead is very much in debate. The threat today is not so much from traditional isolationism, although that still exists on the left and the right in our society. Today, the more dangerous threat to American engagement are those who "talk the talk" of internationalism but who "walk the walk" of isolationism.

These are the people who argue that we must lead—but say we must not spend. Already U.S. spending on international affairs has plummeted 40 percent in just a decade. As a result, the United States, the world's richest nation, now ranks last among industrial nations when it comes to the percentage of GNP devoted to development aid.

These are the people who say we must be engaged in the world, but never want us to do so where our engagement is needed. They say yes in the abstract, but then they say no to Bosnia, no to Haiti, and no to Russia. The United States cannot lead in the abstract. This new era demands concrete engagement—if we want to defeat the new threats we face and if we want to turn the opportunities of today into tangible benefits for the American people. We cannot do so on the cheap, or simply through rhetoric or by empty posturing. But if we grapple with the challenges before us honestly and directly, if we devote the resources needed, and if we are prepared to take risks for peace, then we can make the difference for America's security, America's prosperity, and America's future.

# CHAPTER THIRTEEN

The Internationalist Temptation

RONALD STEEL

*Ronald Steel is author of several books on American foreign policy, including* Pax Americana, The End of Alliance, *and, most recently,* Temptations of a Superpower, *as well as the biography,* Walter Lippmann and the American Century. *A regular contributor to leading journals, he has been a fellow of the Woodrow Wilson Center, the Carnegie Endowment for International Peace, the Guggenheim Foundation, and the Institute for Advanced Study in Berlin. He has taught at several American universities and is now professor of international relations at the University of Southern California.*

It has become a litany for politicians, policy makers, and pundits that the United States must unfailingly and unquestioningly exert leadership. Rarely is it demonstrated why this should invariably be so, or whether the benefits always outweigh the costs, or what the alternatives might be. Leadership is simply asserted as a given. It is to be neither questioned nor qualified. The end of the Cold War offers a good opportunity to take a less celebratory look at the notion of leadership and what we mean by it.

During that long conflict, leadership meant protecting a collection of usually compliant allies from the various military and political threats posed by what we compendiously described as international commu-nism. Although encumbering, costly, and often dangerous, this situation had its gratifications, and over the years we simply came to take it for granted. The role also reaches deep into our national subconscious. America, after all, has always been a country with a mission, and with missionaries to carry it out. In fact, one could say of the religious non-conformists who flocked to these shores to build their city on a hill, that theirs was a mission in search of a country.

Our notion of leadership contains, as it should, elements of self-interest. But it also strongly implies service. American power is justified, to a striking degree, not for its own sake, but in service to a higher cause. There is a sense of obligation, and even of religious inspiration, in our approach. This approach is, of course, central to the rhetoric of Woodrow Wilson, who eighty years ago took the nation to war "to make the world itself at last free." Much later, but in the same vein, Robert Kennedy spoke of the nation's right to the "moral leadership of the planet." The tradition continues. Our current envoy to the United Nations has declared that America's task is no less than "to build a peace-ful world and to terminate the abominable injustices and conditions that still plague civilization." Similarly, the president's former national secu-rity adviser explained that the United States must punish not only states that pose us harm, but also "extreme nationalists and tribalists, terrorists, organized criminals, coup plotters, rogue states, and all those who would return newly free societies to the intolerant ways of the past." This list seems to include just about everyone except ozone depleters and whale hunters.

This is not to suggest that such goals are unworthy. Quite the con-trary. But virtue is not always easy to identify. Victims sometimes have a way of turning into villains, tribalists into native peoples, and terrorists into freedom fighters. Well-meaning actions, such as trade embargoes, often hurt the innocent more than the guilty, as in the cases of Iraq and Cuba. And occasionally the erstwhile victims turn against their well-meaning benefactors, as in Somalia. Virtue is said to be its own reward precisely because it is so rarely rewarded by others.

It would, of course, be naive to maintain that the foreign policy of any nation is largely inspired by altruism. Governments do not work that way, and the public would consider its leaders irresponsible if they did. But what is special about American foreign policy is the degree to which altruism, or moralism, is an element. An amoral, let alone an immoral, diplomacy is anathema to many Americans. Henry Kissinger's openly cynical pursuit of realpolitik may have been impressively adroit, but it lost him the support of idealists on both the right and the left. Aggressive and ruthless may be terms of praise for an American businessman, but not for an American statesman.

During the Cold War we did not worry much about exerting leadership. We just did what we thought necessary to keep Russians and other communists in their place, and to orchestrate a congenial global economic and political system. Those on our side—allies, clients, protectorates—simply got in line. Some chipped in to help, others applauded from the sidelines, and many just held out their palms. Rather than demanding the role of leader, the United States had merely to exercise it. American leadership was not a problem, or even an issue, because it was fully supported at home (except when the Korean and Vietnam wars got out of hand), and largely unchallenged abroad except by our communist adversaries.

### BOUND TO LEAD?

Whereas in the past leadership was simply taken for granted, today it is a topic for debate. Nations self-confident about their leadership role do not fret about it; they simply exercise it. American leadership is an issue today precisely because many of the pillars sustaining it have weakened. With the collapse of the Soviet threat, Cold War allies have become less dependent and thus less acquiescent. The American public is not so willing to make the economic and military sacrifices it did in a time of danger. The old consensus has become a cacophony of voices. Some urge a return to the glory days of the Cold War, while others insist that new players and a new game require new rules. Although foreign policy elites, both within government and without, insist that the United States is bound to lead the diverse nations of the world, this ambition is clouded by a domestic society that is hesitant to pay the price, and by former allies and rivals that are willing to follow only when persuaded that it serves their interests to do so.

There are, I believe, four reasons why most policy makers—as distinct from the wider public—believe that the United States must organize and lead the world even though communism is gone and there is no serious challenger on the horizon. The first is the one discussed earlier: that America has a mission, perhaps divinely inspired, to help other nations achieve the goals that it has defined for itself. In this sense the United

States is viewed as the leader of a wagon train, where it is assumed that everyone wants to end up in the same place and defers to the strong and reliable guide who will guide them there. This approach poses some problems, as I have indicated and will explore a bit further on.

The second reason is that it is deeply gratifying to run the world. Although this may sound like a frivolous explanation, it is not. The gratification is both psychological and material. To be number one means that other nations pay tribute and obeisance. This confirms the leader's sense of self-worth and the rightfulness of its preeminent status. It also provides foreign policy elites—the people who orchestrate the security alliances, staff the embassies, negotiate the treaties, attend the innumerable conferences, churn out policy papers at think tanks, devise scenarios and compose theoretical essays at universities, and write dispatches for the media—not only with prestigious jobs, but also with the sense that they are doing important work. For the public at large, it stimulates pride, like winning all the gold medals at the Olympics. Even though the United States is also the world's number one debtor nation, it commands respect for its ability to get away with it.

The third reason why policy makers want to lead the world rests on the mechanics of power politics: that greater strength means both more influence over others and more security from potential foes. The leader will be free to intimidate any challengers and pursue its interests as it sees fit. In this formulation, what is called leadership is simply a more benign term for dominance. Other nations will follow the leader—that is, accede to its wishes and concur in its policies, because they will have accepted that the United States has the power, and presumably the right, to define their interests for them. Political scientists describe this policy as hegemony. So do those who resent being instructed to fall into line for their own good; Charles de Gaulle often used to complain of American hegemony—to the applause of his own countrymen and the consternation of Washington.

The fourth reason differs from the earlier ones because it rests on the bedrock of economics, although it is often described in terms of world order. This order has never been clearly defined, though a common term is a world of "market democracies." Behind the anodyne phrase lies a belief in how the international political economy works. Global prosperity, advocates of this view argue, depends upon world financial markets and the removal of all trade barriers. Ideally, this should lead to maximum economic efficiency. During the Cold War, the United States created such a system, breaking down the tariff walls of the old colonial empires and embracing most of the industrialized world. The removal of such barriers was a major purpose of the Marshall Plan in 1947, just as it was recently of the North American Free Trade Agreement and the World Trade Organization.

The Cold War served the economic unification of the West, an objective with the highest priority for American statesmen. Defeated Germany and Japan were integral parts of the strategy that required their democratization and integration into the world economy. The result was stunningly successful: the creation of a global market bringing unprecedented growth and prosperity to much of the noncommunist world. This effort also served to prevent the independent remilitarization of Germany and Japan. Washington was able to do this by providing what both countries needed most: protection from their enemies and unrestricted access to vital markets. American armies were sent to both Europe and Asia, and even fought two immensely costly land wars in Asia, to reassure these allies.

## CONTAINING DISORDER?

During the Cold War, U.S. foreign policy was described as that of the containment of communism. Now, with communism gone, it is called leadership or, sometimes, reassurance. The label has changed, but the policy remains essentially the same. The demise of the Soviet Union does not change the goal; it merely marginalizes a key troublemaker. As a Pentagon official explained shortly before the Politburo's collapse: "Were the Soviet presence to disappear tomorrow, our role as regional balancer and honest broker would, if anything, be more important than ever."

Playing the role of balancer and broker means protecting the interests of the major trading states, the most important of which are Germany and Japan, so that they do not feel obliged to acquire powerful independent military forces. Were they to do so, U.S. officials believe, it would upset the current political equilibrium and imperil the flow of trade and capital on which economic efficiency and growth rest. This is the reason why it is argued that America must protect the world. It helps us understand why President George Bush felt it necessary to repel Iraq's 1990 invasion of Kuwait, even though Europe and Japan are far more dependent on gulf oil than is the United States.[1] Were the United States to fail in its responsibility as protector, its partners might equip themselves to perform these tasks. This is also why President Clinton has pledged to keep 100,000 American troops in Europe and another 100,000 in Asia, mostly in South Korea and Japan, on what the Pentagon describes as a permanent basis. These deployments cost the United States an estimated $100 billion a year, which explains why there has been no peace dividend following the Cold War, or that the defense budget remains at about 85 percent of the average Cold War level.

During the Cold War, the United States had a single adversary: the Soviet Union. Our goal was the containment of communism and the protection of the United States and its major allies. Now, with the disappearance of any powerful adversary, the threat is said to be even greater: global instability. Thus the repression of disorder—or in the new terminology, the creation of a "stable international environment"— has replaced containment as the new foreign policy doctrine. Its objective is to discourage major states, like Germany and Japan, from acquiring powerful independent military forces, and to repress rogue states that could, in the phrase of Pentagon planners, "unsettle international relations." To cope with this vague, but enlarged, realm of dangers, planners have proposed an American military protectorate of both Europe and Asia. Thus the projected extension of NATO across Eastern Europe, the maintenance of U.S. military forces permanently in Japan and Korea, and the creation of mobile brigades for quick intervention in the world's trouble spots.

Though sweeping in scope, this project is modestly presented as merely an assumption of the nation's international responsibilities. It views any breakdown of order in the world as a crisis, and transforms every such event into a vital interest. Such a definition of security is deliberately vague yet expansive. This makes priorities hard to determine. If disorder is everywhere, when is it threatening, and where do we draw the line? If we send an army to Kuwait, why not to Bosnia? If we intervene in Somalia, why not Rwanda? If we support Taiwan's quest for independence, why not Chechnya's? A global power with a global conception of its interests has trouble defining limits.

This was the problem facing British imperialists as they expanded commitments through Africa in the nineteenth century. To protect their investments in India they needed compliant states on that country's frontiers. To supply these states they needed to protect the Suez Canal. This required bases and protectorates in the Middle East and East Africa. Soon they were deep into central Africa, creating ever more sweeping frontiers of insecurity (as historians of that experience termed it) in areas of little intrinsic importance. Rather than strengthening their vital interests, the policy weakened them. And, of course, it stimulated rivals concerned by the ever-greater expansion of the British empire. The search for absolute security led to absolute insecurity.

## UNIVERSAL PEACE OR PERPETUAL INTERVENTION?

Everyone agrees that interests have to be protected. The problem comes in defining them. The new globalists describe everyone's interests as America's, and thus everyone's problems as ours. This is the kind of logic that gives internationalism a bad name. It is a recipe for perpetual intervention in causes we only dimly understand, and for stakes we have no way of measuring. It is not a policy that a democratic society will supinely support with its blood and treasure, nor is it one that is workable in a world of sovereign nation-states.

The notion of a benevolent Pax Americana in which the United States ensures democracy, free trade capitalism, and peaceful political change for the world may be self-flattering, but hardly realistic. The problem is that other nations, even the most friendly ones, have different ideas about their interests. They may be part of a global economy, but they want that economy to work in a way favorable to them. Those that are strong enough will find ways of advancing their interests, even in ways that their erstwhile protector might not like. They have no objection to being defended by the United States, but they want the freedom to decide when and how they should be defended, and against whom. Other states will be allies only insofar as we make their interests ours. When we do not, they will balk. If we do, we will be sacrificing our interests to theirs. This is hardly a policy likely to win public support.

Major states will not be content to delegate even to the most well-meaning friendly superpower critical decisions over their economies, let alone over war and peace. Every state, insofar as possible, seeks the freedom of action to pursue its political goals as it defines them. Those with the potential power to do so—Japan, China, Russia, perhaps eventually a unified Europe—can be expected to challenge even the most benevolent American protectorate. Nor, of course, will such a protectorate be benevolent toward everyone. The protector will have to make choices. What pleases Russia may anger Japan. What pleases Taiwan will almost certainly irritate China. For the United States to enforce its will everywhere, it must not only have to be far more powerful than any other state or even combination of states, but will also inevitably make itself, to one degree or another, the enemy of every state. This is more a recipe for general war than for universal peace.

Rather than strengthening American security, the globalist strategy has the perverse effect of undermining it. The maximization of economic growth, corporate profits, and unrestricted investment opportunities may require a high degree of international stability (although the international economy worked very well during the tensions of the Cold War), particularly among the industrialized states. And such stability may be easier to achieve in a world ruled by a single powerful state— what political scientists call a global hegemony, benevolent or otherwise. But such a hegemonic state is beset by two problems. First, by sparing others the cost of defending themselves, it gives them an economic advantage that over time weakens the protector and makes increasingly difficult its ability to perform its superpower role. Second, its very dominance incites the envy and resentment of rising powers (as was the case with Britain and Germany beginning in the late nineteenth century) that refuse to defer to its authority. States, like individuals, do not generally like others to define their interests for them. Thus the globalist strategy falls of its own internal contradictions. The American economy cannot indefinitely sustain it; rising rival powers will not accept it; and the American public will not support its enormous costs. Although ostensibly a formula for global peace under an American military and political directorship, it is likely to have the perverse effect of stimulating the very rivalries and wars it seeks to avoid.

A central problem of the globalist strategy is that it focuses so narrowly on military power. It calls for vastly increased military budgets beyond Cold War levels to defeat any possible combination of threats and to intimidate potential rivals. But the kinds of threats it proposes to meet are not the kinds we are most likely to face. The fact that the most likely threats come not from military adversaries but from our own trading partners, from environmental forces, from hostile political or religious movements, from ethnic wars and the collapse of once-viable states, and even from the workings of the global economic system—all this requires us to redefine the very notion of security. In what way is security a problem for the United States today? Why should instability matter if it offers no opportunity for a major rival to threaten us?

During the foreseeable future, military force of the kind we marshaled during the Cold War will be less usable, and thus less meaningful. This is not only because war between major powers is less likely, but also because the stakes are smaller. The rising states are regional powers. They have neither the means nor the ambition to become global giants. Thus although the enormous military superiority the United States enjoys over all other states may inspire fear or respect, it is of limited utility as an instrument to enforce our political will. Indeed, the more resources we put into military power beyond the needs of national defense, the greater advantage we give to our economic competitors.

## REDEFINING THE "NATIONAL INTEREST"

What is required today is a new concept of national interest, one that will go beyond the rigid categories and stale polemics of that devised during the Cold War. Such a concept will rest on the recognition that for the foreseeable future the United States faces no military threat from any other major power, that the costly military alliances it forged to contain the Soviet Union have become an unnecessary drain on the economy that weakens its competitiveness, that foreign policy increasingly will be focused on the dampening of regional conflicts that do not directly affect American security, and that humanitarian efforts can be used to mediate civil strife.

The decades ahead promise a plethora of Bosnias, Rwandas, and Somalias: situations where the rights and wrongs are not always clear, where the remedies are only temporary, and where no direct American interests are involved. Even when they cannot be happily resolved, or even resolved at all, these distant quarrels cannot leave the United States unmoved. They will require an American response in many cases, but a response coordinated with, and perhaps even led by, other nations. This means that we must think of leadership in different terms from the way we have in the past: no longer assuming that every problem anywhere must have an American solution, but working with others to establish a consensus for joint action. In other words, we must stop assuming that we must either run the world or submit meekly to it. That is a legacy of Cold War thinking, and it has become as dangerous as it is outmoded. Our interests are to defend our society from attack, to temper violence and alleviate distress where we can, to join with others to combat the social and biological degradation of the planet, and to make real for all Americans the promise of the values we profess.

Those espousing an American imperium suggest that the United States today is in grave peril. In fact, nothing could be further from the truth. Never over the past sixty years has the nation enjoyed such freedom of action. Indisputably the world's greatest economic and military power, we are challenged only potentially and in the very long run. Indeed, the greatest threat we face is from ourselves: from an unwillingness to bring our widespread commitments into line with our resources, from a failure to deal adequately with our severe domestic problems, and from a lingering Cold War mentality that is both grandiose and paralyzing. The hardest problem for the United States today is not how to run the world, but rather to recognize that the old game is over and that a new one, with new rules, has begun.

NOTE

1. While Persian Gulf oil represents only 10 percent of American consumption, it comprises 25 percent of Europe's and half of Japan's.

CHAPTER FOURTEEN

# Searching for a
# New Domestic Consensus

MILTON MORRIS

*Milton Morris is senior vice president at the Joint Center for Political and Economic Studies. Previously, he served as senior fellow at the Brookings Institution and on the faculty of Southern Illinois University. A member of governing boards of the National Planning Association and of the University of Pittsburgh's School of Public and International Affairs, he is also founder and chair of MDM Office Systems, Inc. He is author of* The Politics of Black America, Curbing Illegal Immigration, *and a forthcoming book on the African diaspora in the twenty-first century.*

In these final years of the twentieth century, we are entering a new epoch in international affairs. That epoch has been described in a variety of ways in the other essays in this book, though it has not always been put in this fashion. The focus has been on the pivotal, dramatic change that occurred with the fall of the Berlin Wall and the collapse of communism it symbolized.

Of course, the end of the Cold War has profoundly changed the international system and our view of it. Yet there have been some other noteworthy developments that have combined with that particular pivotal change to usher in significant new conditions and challenges. For example, we have seen the end of apartheid in South Africa, which in a way caps an important era on one front. We have seen the collapse or implosion of some states, a development that many of us believe will be with us for some time and that will pose its own array of challenges and strains. We have seen the creation of significant new international trade regimes such as NAFTA. Together these developments seem to characterize the start of a new period in world affairs that poses a number of interesting and important challenges for the United States and the American public.

While this new epoch still lacks any clear definition or focus, a few things about it are clear. One is that we have moved from an era of relative clarity and order to one of hazy disorder. We are moving from an era in which we had a clear enemy, a clearly defined strategy for dealing with that enemy, and a clearly perceived threat around which much of our thinking about the world could be organized to one in which there is no clear enemy. We have also moved from an era in which we were poised on the brink of global destruction from nuclear weapons to one in which there is a pervasive sense of unease about our personal well-being, about our sense of personal security, about preserving a set of values and institutions to which we feel strong attachment. Escaping that Cold War condition is a liberating experience but a sometimes bewildering one.

Public opinion polling results of the last few years reflect the public uncertainty and confusion about the new era. Reviewing those polls gives one the feeling that Americans were let out of a dungeon somewhere: they feel good about their liberation, but their eyes are not yet in focus and they have trouble making sense of their surroundings. What we see over these last few years then is an American public that is beginning to respond to these epochal developments and to respond in a way that is not nearly as dramatic or drastic or as radical as one might have been tempted to expect.

This essay briefly reviews public attitudes toward selected issues in international affairs from several major public opinion polls conducted between 1993–95. The surveys probe public attitudes toward the role of the United States in the world, about helping other countries through foreign aid and peacekeeping activities, and U.S. involvement in collective security operations. In many instances the data are broken down among major racial and ethnic groups as well as between the public and foreign policy elites. Because the polls come from several polling organizations and they did not all use the same ethnic breakdowns, the comparisons do not all involve the same groups. Nonetheless, the broad trends involving the major racial-ethnic groups emerge fairly clearly.

What the polls suggest is what I will call a period of restrained internationalism, with an emphasis on domestic well-being rather than assertive global leadership. Surprisingly, there is no evidence of dramatic cleavages in society involving major segments of the society. Neither are there sharp divergences across ethnic lines, and the differences between political elites and the public at large are not as great as the pundits would have us believe.

## THE UNITED STATES
## AS WORLD LEADER

The first cluster of polls, (Figures 14.1–14.9), concerns the role of the United States as world leader. What is readily apparent is that the country overwhelmingly seeks a reduction in the U.S. leadership role in the world. The results are quite consistent across ethnic lines as well as the elite/public divide. When asked whether the United States should use its leadership position in the world to help settle international disputes and promote democracy, or whether the country should reduce its involvement in world politics in order to concentrate on problems at home (Figure 14.1), there is overwhelming agreement that the latter should be the course.

The public overwhelmingly agrees that the U.S. is playing a more important leadership role internationally today than it did a decade ago (Figure 14.2). It is from this basic premise that people seem inclined for the U.S. to pull back from what they see as a growing international role. Thus the remaining data in this section should be seen against the backdrop of an international role that the public assumes to be increasing.

We go from here to a set of separate kinds of events or activities, depicted in Figures 14.3–14.6, in which there are questions about what the U.S. role should be. With respect to settling international disputes or peacekeeping (depicted in Figure 14.3), there is clear uneasiness with the United States' taking "the leading role." This is particularly true among African Americans, perhaps because they are disproportionately represented in the military and so would bear the brunt of the burden. Figure 14.4 shows an overwhelming aversion to a U.S. leadership role in settling civil war, and this attitude holds across racial and ethnic groups.

**Figure 14.1**

The United States as world leader: "Do you think the United States should use its leadership position in the world to help settle international disputes and promote democracy or reduce its involvement in world politics in order to concentrate on problems at home?"

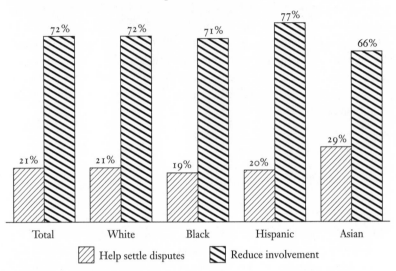

Source: Yankelovich Partners Inc., June 21–22, 1995.

**Figure 14.2**

The U.S. role as world leader: "Do you think the United States plays a more important and powerful role as a world leader today compared to 10 years ago, a less important role, or about as important a role?"

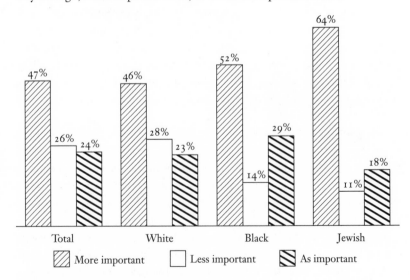

Source: Gallup Organization, October 7–25, 1994.

**Figure 14.3**
The U.S. role in settling international disputes: "Please tell me if you think the United States should or should not take the leading role in settling international disputes in general."

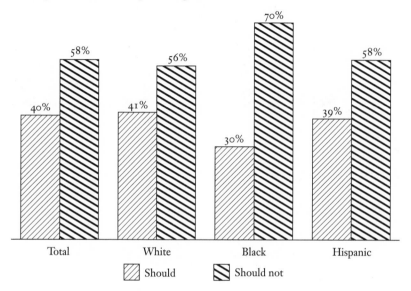

Source: ABC News/*Washington Post*, February 25–28, 1993.

In sharp contrast, (Figure 14.5) shows overwhelming public support for American leadership in "protecting friendly governments in countries that have been invaded." In short, the public seems to have said that settling disputes around the world or wars in foreign countries are activities that the U.S. should not be in the lead on, but we ought to be in the lead where our friends are concerned.

The area where one gets some mixed signals from public opinion involves our leadership in ensuring peacekeeping and humanitarian relief. Here, African Americans and Asian-Americans believe the United States ought to play a greater role, while the rest of the population thinks otherwise (Figure 14.6). The very high support among African Americans may be related to the aversion they showed in Figure 14.3 to U.S. leadership in settling international disputes: if the United States does not help keep the peace, they will be the ones fighting the wars.

**Figure 14.4**
The U.S. role in settling civil wars: "Please tell me if you think the United States should or should not take the leading role is settling civil wars in foreign countries."

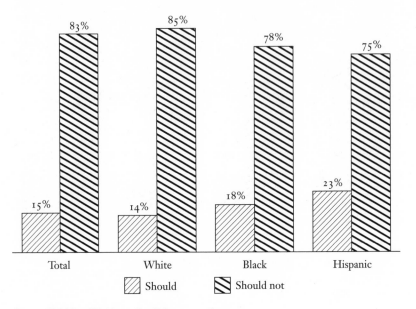

Source: ABC News/*Washington Post*, February 25–28, 1993.

## PUBLIC VERSUS ELITE ATTITUDES

Finally in this section, Figure 14.8 compares public attitudes with those of political leaders or elites on the question of an active role for the United States in world affairs. As we might have expected, political leaders tend to be significantly more internationalist than the public at large: 97 to 98 percent of the elites favor an active U.S. role and have done so consistently since these particular polls were first conducted in 1978, while public attitudes have averaged about 60 percent over the same period. (Some will find those figures worrying low; others may see them as impressively high.) Again, it is worth noting that the end of the Cold War caused not a ripple in these basic attitudes.

Figure 14.9 breaks the question down according to what the public and foreign policy leaders think should be the important foreign policy

**Figure 14.5**

The U.S. role in protecting friendly governments: "Please tell me if you think the United States should or should not take the leading role in protecting foreign governments in countries that have been invaded."

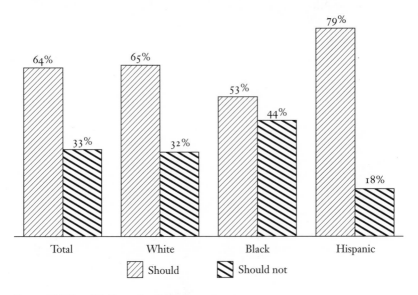

Source: ABC News/*Washington Post*, February 25–28, 1993.

goals of the United States. One dominant theme is the extent to which foreign policy priorities are driven by domestic concerns. The top priority for the public as far as U.S. foreign policy goes in this particular poll is to stop the flow of drugs. The second one is to protect American jobs. Skip one down and the next one is to reduce illegal immigration, and the next one after that is to secure energy supplies. In short, there is a strong focus on domestic well-being, on domestic concerns, as the primary interests of the American public—much more so than is the case with their leaders.

Much farther down the list are foreign policy goals that might be advanced as new points of emphasis or even new paradigms for post–Cold War American foreign policy. Take democratization, one of the strong initiatives of the Clinton administration. Many believe that the end of communism has created an environment in which

**Figure 14.6**
The United States as world leader to keep peace and assure humanitarian relief: "Do you think that the United States has a greater responsibility than other countries to keep peace around the world and assure humanitarian relief, or only the same responsibility as other countries?"

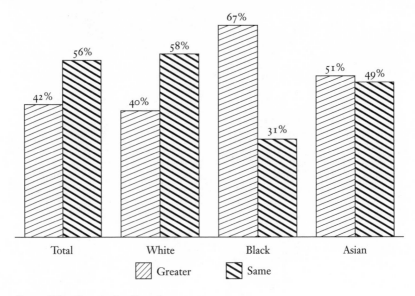

Source: Gallup Organization, December 3–4, 1992.

the U.S. can in fact democratize the world. Yet this objective ranks very, very close to the bottom in the public's priorities. And it ranks even lower for foreign policy leaders, despite the rhetoric of democratic enlargement and democracy building. The same pattern holds true with respect to defending human rights and protecting weaker nations: both rank low with the public and lower still for foreign policy leaders.

### AID TO OTHER COUNTRIES

The second cluster of polls (Figures 14.10–14.19) has to do with our role in helping others. Here we find that the public is somewhat ambiva-

**Figure 14.7**

The United States should go its own way: Agree versus disagree.

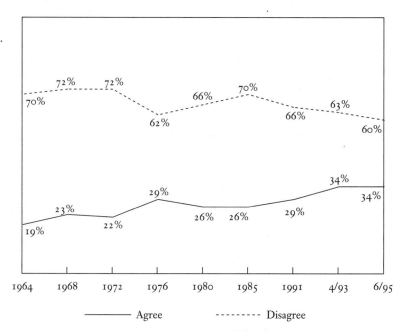

Source: Times Mirror Center for the People and the Press, June 1995.

lent and unclear about the appropriate American role. We also find here, significant differences in attitudes across racial and ethnic groups. When asked, "On the whole, do you favor or oppose our giving economic aid to other nations?" (Figure 14.10), the public was evenly divided. Among whites there was a slight plurality against while 50 percent of African Americans favored giving aid. Jewish Americans were the only population group who answered clearly (and overwhelmingly) in the affirmative.

Turning to the level of foreign aid, Figure 14.11 shows that the public overwhelming believes that the level of U.S. foreign aid should be reduced. Asian Americans were the only group supportive of current aid levels, though they are even less disposed than other groups to increase it. Of course, these findings should be seen against the background of the widespread public belief that we are spending vastly more

**Figure 14.8**
Preferred U.S. role: Respondents who favor an active role for the
United States in world affairs.

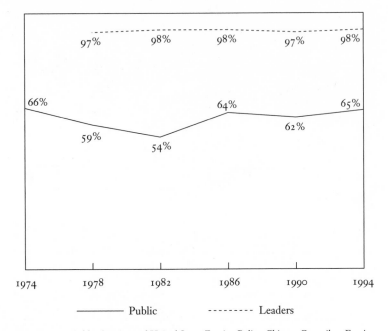

Source: American Public Opinion and United States Foreign Policy, Chicago Council on Foreign
Relations, 1995.

on foreign aid than we actually are. However, with 71 percent of the
public favoring reductions, Americans may be making a statement about
the degree of responsibility that the country should bear, rather than a
mere budgetary calculation. Even if the public knew the true levels of
our foreign aid, it is not clear that the polling results would be much
different.

When aid is broken down by region, there are differences among
ethnic groups, though probably not as great as might be expected. On
aid to Africa (Figure 14.13), African–Americans and Hispanics were
least supportive of decreased aid at 19 percent each, and were
overwhelmingly supportive of holding aid levels constant or increasing
it. On the other hand, nearly half of white respondents (48 percent)
wanted decreased aid to Africa. Finally, on aid to Latin America (Figure

**Figure 14.9**

United States foreign policy goals: The following should be a "very important" goal of the United States.

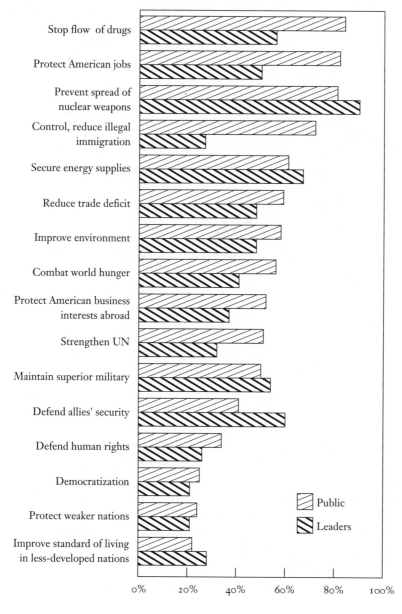

Source: Chicago Council on Foreign Relations, 1995.

**Figure 14.10**
Foreign aid: "On the whole, do you favor or oppose our giving economic aid to other nations?"

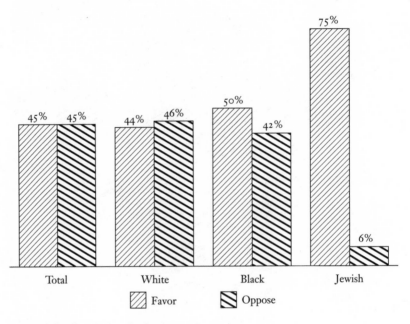

Source: Gallup Organization, October 7–25, 1994.

14.15), there was hardly a difference among ethnic groups, with the qualification that Hispanics were not broken out separately in this case.

As one probes deeper, one finds a public that is highly selective about what it wants to do with the aid. Figure 14.16, on the use of military force to provide humanitarian aid, shows impressively strong support across all groups, suggesting that the country may be ready to contemplate a changed role and mission for the armed forces, even in spite of bad experiences such as Somalia. The public also indicates substantial support for using the military to help combat drug trafficking (Figure 14.17). However, when it came to increasing economic aid to help combat drug trafficking, only African Americans were clearly supportive (Figures 14.18–14.19).

**Figure 14.11**
Level of U.S. foreign aid: "Do you feel that government spending in the form of aid to foreign nations should be increased, decreased, or kept where it is now?"

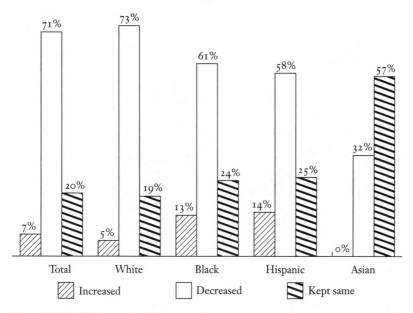

Source: Yankelovich Partners, Inc., January 25–26, 1995.

## THE UNITED STATES AND INTERNATIONAL ORGANIZATIONS

The third and final cluster of issues in international affairs concerns attitudes toward multinational institutions like the United Nations and the North Atlantic Treaty Organization (NATO). An important issue in recent years has been how the U.S. should relate to the UN with respect to collective peacekeeping operations. Figure 14.20 indicates that there is still fairly strong national support for United States cooperation with the UN in international peacekeeping efforts. This support crosses all racial and ethnic lines with an overwhelming majority of Hispanics and Jewish respondents affirming the U.S. role in assisting the UN in international peacekeeping.

**Figure 14.12**
Military aid to other countries: "As a taxpayer, please tell me whether you generally approve or disapprove of having your tax dollars used to help pay for military aid to other countries?"

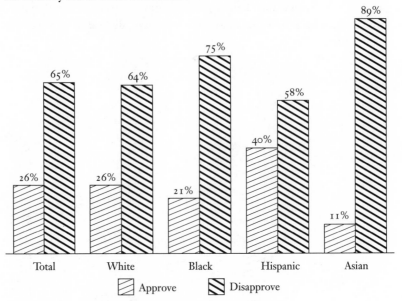

Source: Princeton Survey Research Associates, January 5–15, 1996.

**Figure 14.13**
Foreign aid to African countries: "Do you think the amount of foreign aid the United States gives to African countries should be increased, decreased, or remain the same?"

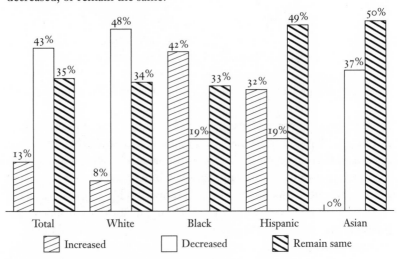

Source: Yankelovich Partners, Inc., June 2, 1995.

**Figure 14.14**
Foreign aid to Eastern Europe: "Do you think economic aid to newly independent countries in Eastern Europe should be increased, decreased, kept the same, or stopped altogether?"

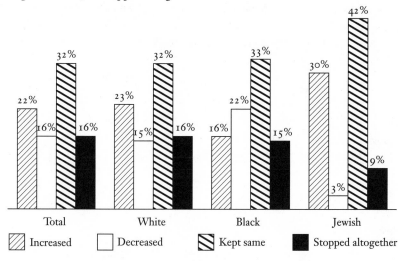

Source: Gallup Organization, October 7–25, 1994.

**Figure 14.15**
Foreign aid to Latin America: "Do you think economic aid to Latin American countries should be increased, decreased, kept the same, or stopped altogether?"

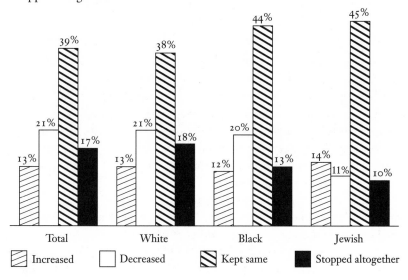

Source: Gallup Organization, October 7–25, 1994.

**Figure 14.16**

Military forces used to provide humanitarian aid: "Thinking about foreign policy issues, do you think the U.S. military forces should or should not be used to provide humanitarian aid when it is needed?"

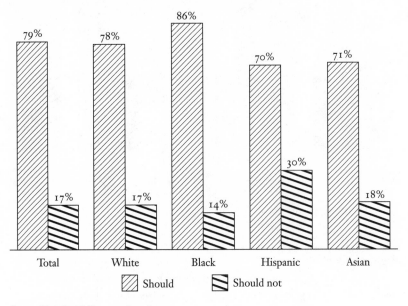

Source: Yankelovich Partners, Inc., August 4, 1994.

Looking more broadly at attitudes toward the UN over the past three decades, Figure 14.21 shows that there has been consistently strong public support, but with some noteworthy developments. The data shows that support and opposition to cooperation with the UN has fluctuated significantly over the three decades, reaching an all time low about 1971 of 46 percent support and a peak of 77 percent in 1991. It is notable that over the three decades there has been a substantial decline, suggesting a steady, gradual erosion in public support.

Finally, on the U.S. commitment to NATO (Figure 14.22), there is substantial agreement along ethnic lines on maintaining our present level of commitment, with some sentiment (20 percent) for decreasing it but almost none for increasing it. For NATO, identified almost entirely with the Cold War, that level of support reinforces the general findings

**Figure 14.17**

Use of military forces to help fight drug trafficking: "Do you favor or oppose the use of U.S. military and drug enforcement advisers in foreign countries to help fight and arrest drug traffickers?"

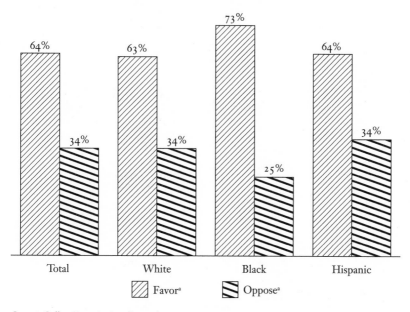

Favorª     Opposeª

Source: Gallup Organization, September 14–17, 1995.

a. Favor includes "strongly favor"; oppose includes "strongly oppose."

of continuity in public attitudes, albeit with a strong new emphasis on giving priority to domestic problems.

### CONCLUSIONS: IS THERE A NEW DOMESTIC CONSENSUS?

All of that suggests that there are no dramatic differences in how the public perceives or approaches international affairs. On balance, there is a rather restrained and pragmatic sense of the world and the American role in it. This itself is noteworthy in light of the ongoing debate in the academic literature. In his exhaustive review of that literature, Ole Holsti at Duke University observed that there have

**Figure 14.18**
Increased economic aid to help fight drug trafficking:
"Do you favor or oppose increased U.S. financial aid to foreign governments to help them fight or arrest drug traffickers?"

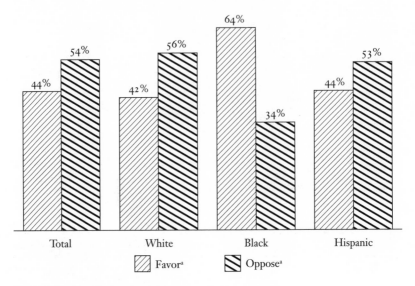

Source: Gallup Organization, September 14–17, 1995.

a. Favor includes "strongly favor"; oppose includes "strongly oppose."

been two schools of thought about the role of the public and public attitudes in international affairs. One holds that the public is rather emotional, volatile, and incoherent in its views of international affairs and, therefore, that public attitudes are poor guides for making foreign policy choices. A second school argues that if one looks closely, there is a rather strong consistency and pragmatism toward international affairs, so the public is much less volatile and emotional than some people believe.

In my view, what we are seeing in this transition period is a public that is rather reasoned and pragmatic in its view of the world and America's role in it. Is there a basis in any of this for some new kind of consensus? Does it matter how the public feels as we think about how the United States faces the world in the future? On the one hand, the absence of a widely perceived common threat will make consensus difficult to achieve. "Consensus about what?" the man in the street might well ask.

**Figure 14.19**

Increased aid to foreign farmers to help fight drug trafficking:
"Do you favor or oppose aid to farmers in foreign drug-producing
countries to make them grow crops other than drugs?"

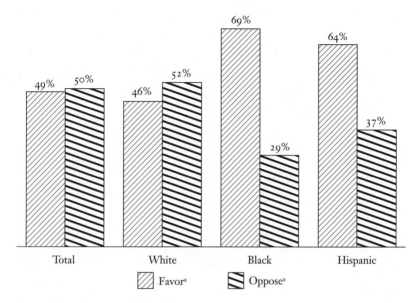

Source: Gallup Organization, September 14–17, 1995.

a. Favor includes "strongly favor"; oppose includes "strongly oppose."

My impression and expectation is that public attitudes will diverge
across a wide range of issues, becoming more partisan and contentious
in the absence of any enemy or threat to focus the mind. Yet there are
two themes around which the public might rally. One is trade and its
relationship to the economic well-being of the country. Our engagement with the world, in other words, should have prosperity as the pay-
off. The second theme is what I would call collective peace management. The public seems to be saying that the United States needs to
play a role, but that it should not play the leading role. In that sense, collective peace management is preferable to our playing the role of global
policeman or adopting a go-it-alone attitude toward the rest of the
world.

In the final analysis, coherence in American foreign policy is probably
not going to come to any great extent from the calculated choices of the

**Figure 14.20**
The United States and the United Nations: "Do you think the United States has a responsibility to contribute military troops to enforce peace plans in trouble spots around the world when it is asked by the UN?"

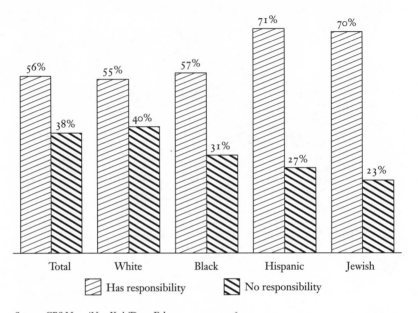

Source: CBS News/*New York Times*, February 22–24, 1996.

public or even of its leaders, but rather in response to international events. Events that are as yet unanticipated may serve to bring their own coherence to national thinking about international affairs. So when coherence comes or when some kind of new consensus about our role and behavior in the world comes about, it will be driven by changes in the larger international community.

Finally, what is the point in worrying about public attitudes to ward international affairs? Foreign policy traditionally has been the domain of a small elite within society. The public at large, most of the literature indicates, is rather poorly informed about international affairs and only intermittently engaged on foreign policy questions.

One is left wondering about what difference public attitudes make. Holsti concludes that this is one of the unresolved and unexplored issues in the understanding of foreign policy—that is, the relation-

**Figure 14.21**

The United States should cooperate with United Nations:
Agree versus disagree.

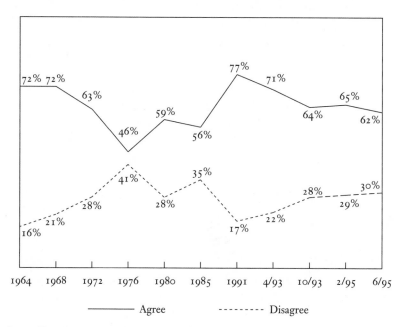

Source: Times Mirror Center for the People and the Press, June, 1995.

ship between public attitudes and foreign policy choices and behavior. There are a few instances in which we can see significant linkages between domestic pressure groups that pursue and agitate for particular foreign policy courses that are then pursued. One might take ending apartheid in South Africa—the final years of that effort—as an example. Another might be the decision regarding U.S. intervention in Haiti. But these are more exceptions to the general rule.

Of course, political leadership, especially presidential leadership, can be decisive in shaping public attitudes and leading foreign policy where it otherwise might not go. By the same token, the absence of effective political leadership can allow public opinion to exert a greater influence over policy than it otherwise might. Several other essays in this volume speak—descriptively as well as prescriptively—to that issue.

**Figure 14.22**

The U.S. commitment to NATO: "Do you feel that we should increase our commitment to NATO, keep our commitment what it is now, decrease our commitment, or withdraw entirely?"

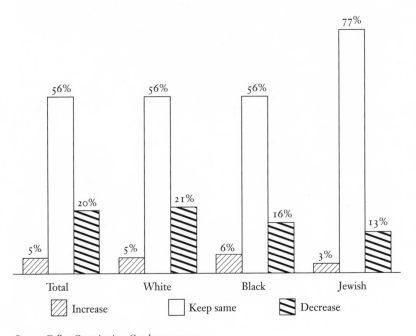

Source: Gallup Organization, October 7–25, 1994.

Where public opinion is crucial is in exerting a restraining effect on U.S. foreign policy behavior. What the public will support—what actions it ultimately finds reasonable—in the end will shape how America behaves in the world. It is a role that no president, no congress, can ignore. The polling data depicted in this essay suggest not so much a new consensus as a set of limits or constraints—sometimes ill-informed, perhaps, but on the whole reasonable—within which American foreign policy must find its way in the post–Cold War world.

# CHAPTER FIFTEEN

# Building Domestic Constituencies
# for Global Action

TIMOTHY E. WIRTH

*Timothy E. Wirth, former U.S. senator from Colorado, is president of the United Nations Foundation. From 1993 to 1997, he was undersecretary of state for global affairs, with responsibility for environment, population, human rights, refugee, and narcotics matters. In addition to his service in the Senate from 1986 to 1993, he represented Colorado's Second Congressional District for twelve years. He was deputy assistant secretary of education in 1969–70. He serves on the board of overseers of Harvard University.*

Recently, George Kennan, who has been engaged in U.S. foreign policy longer and more deeply than any other American public figure, said that the nation faces two great challenges ahead—the environmental crisis and the spread of weapons of mass destruction. He said that we should be organizing our foreign policy priorities and institutions to focus on those two issues. That is a very inexact quote of a much more eloquent statement, but it provides an important starting point for this discussion.

Annually, the U.S. government publishes a report to the Congress broadly portraying U.S. national security policies. It is largely an anesthetizing document about our goals around the world. The most recent report for the first time stated from the outset, not as an appendix, that our national security has to be redefined and that we in the United States must think about issues like the environment, pressures of population, and refugees. Slowly but surely our institutions are coming to understand that we have in fact gone very rapidly beyond our old priorities.

A few years ago, at the National Press Club, I stated that here in the United States and around the globe we are coming to understand the close connections among poverty, the environment, the economy, and security. This historic transformation demands that we now liberate ourselves—from outworn policies, from old assumptions, from fixed views that only yesterday seemed to be the dividing and defining lines of our policies.

## THE NEW FOREIGN POLICY ENVIRONMENT

Any agency, any bureaucracy, any political entity needs a constituency—that is its rationale for existence. It needs a constituency that will ring doorbells, get on the telephone, send faxes, and generally support what that agency does. Having been in politics for more than twenty years, I know that if something goes wrong in the Head Start program or education funding, then a lot of irate Head Start mothers, teachers, and lobbyists from the education institutions will be on Capitol Hill demanding a rapid response.

Unlike the Cold War era, foreign policy today lacks a broad coalition of constituencies. The Pentagon, with its domestic constituency of defense-related industries, used to be a significant source of support for the State Department and other foreign policy agencies. In times of trouble, that large establishment with its remarkably talented members and enormous wherewithal, both in terms of its own budget and the contracts it gave out across the country, was able to go to work very quickly generating support on Capitol Hill for various programs related to the Cold War and its threats. One could always count on that core constituency.

The fall of the Berlin Wall changed that situation dramatically. The State Department's mission is no longer very well understood by the public and is seen as less relevant to public concerns. The role of the Agency for International Development (AID) is no longer clear to the public. The U.S. Information Agency (USIA) does not have a constituency any more. The linkage between the foreign policy agencies and the interests of 260 million Americans is very fragile, if in fact it exists at all. The linkage used to be the Cold War. AID had funding because it was tied to U.S. security interests around the world. Similarly, USIA's mission of explaining American policy and values was justified in the Cold War terms of a global competition of ideologies.

Some of the traditional foreign policy constituencies have atrophied or are aging and have not brought in new blood. The age of many participants in the major foreign policy associations must be close to seventy. The World Affairs Councils' leaders are generally older than one would like to have them. There is a generation of Americans that grew up in the early Cold War with Harry Truman-FDR idealism pumping in its veins. This engagement was carried on and blessed by Eisenhower, and was given another shot of adrenaline by Kennedy. Then it stopped. Since then it has been hard to find a successor generation to that which was energized by Jack Kennedy. We have a big rebuilding job to do, and the World Affairs Councils and other organizations are working on that.

We in government must do more than simply ask such groups to come to Washington for briefings. That is what we used to do. Now we have got to go out there—to people's own backyards. The State Department now holds a series of town meetings, some better than others, around the country with the World Affairs Councils. The State Department has to understand this imperative of building public support, which is very difficult to do. It will not happen overnight.

There is another compelling reason to cultivate public participation: increasingly that is where the essential expertise resides. In the past, the issues of the State Department were defined by experts within the institution. Today, expertise on the issues that I will touch upon— population, environment, migration, and narcotics—is largely outside the State Department. The department therefore has to include those experts. That is a difficult thing to do in an institution accustomed to operating in a classified environment. What the State Department has said, in effect, is that "we have the expertise here, and everything is classified. Leave it to us, we'll take care of it." No longer is that adequate. Most of the information on these new agenda subjects is open data, meaning a very dramatic change in the way in which people within the State Department have to operate. For example, we have limited capability in the State Department to access the Internet. Electronic mail outside the system is impossible because our whole information system is designed for a closed, secure environment. This is as it must be, because there are many classified issues still to be discussed. But the adaptation to this new electronic world on the outside has not yet been made.

These are some of the needed changes in the culture within the department that have not yet been appreciated. There is reason for hope, however, that the department can tap into some of the latent constituencies behind its work. The American people are very concerned about terrorism. They are interested in counternarcotics programs. They are deeply committed to environmental protection. These are the natural constituencies behind our foreign policy agenda.

## BUILDING NEW CONSTITUENCIES

Foreign policy constituencies do exist, but they have to be cultivated. For example, when we were preparing all of the background work leading up to the Cairo Population Conference, we held a series of town meetings across the country. We did a twenty-four-hour concentrated blitz on major media centers—Minneapolis, Seattle, Denver, Los Angeles, San Francisco, Texas cities, Miami, Atlanta, Boston—where we could energize a serious discussion of the issues. It was important for public relations, but it was even more important because of the constituencies that we discovered. We found that the constituencies were much broader than Planned Parenthood of America and the Population Action Committees. The environmental groups were intensely engaged, as were the Garden Clubs of America.

Garden Clubs? The Garden Clubs had made population their number one issue for 1994. This was important because the Garden Clubs include a lot of relatively affluent, suburban, Republican women who could be engaged in these efforts and who are a huge constituency. They are some of the most exciting and interested groups of people, with discretionary time and income and an enormous amount of interest in pushing this issue. They are a constituency the State Department would not have imagined in the past.

As another example, I was invited to speak to a bank security conference in New York. I accepted as part of my duties. I truly thought that this would be one of the smallest and most obscure seminars imaginable. There were eighteen hundred people in the ballroom! They came because the bankers were very worried about the security of their offices around the world, and what we could do to protect the security of their employees in an increasingly international—and increasingly dangerous—financial environment. The major financial institutions and their related enterprises represent another constituency that had not previously been considered.

The environment has always been a powerful issue in American politics. This has been a constituency that has developed through very good bipartisan politics. There was the explosion of legislation in the 1970s: the Clean Air Act, the Clean Water Act, and the National Environmental Protection Act. In the 1980s the Republican party abandoned the issue; the constituency in part atrophied because it became captured entirely by the Democratic party. People grew alienated as the environment became a partisan issue, which should not be the case. Now the Republican party is beginning to understand this and is seeking part of the environmental constituency because the polls continuously show that one thing Americans expect of their government is protection of the environment. There is a huge constituency of people concerned about the environment.

In March 1996, Secretary of State Warren Christopher spoke on the environment and national security at Stanford University. The department followed up that speech with an analysis of how environmental issues relate to our national security. Each of our regional bureaus is engaged in meetings with the nongovernmental organizations (NGOs) that are concerned about the environment. We are bringing NGO representatives into bureau meetings to initiate discussions and to let people in the government know that NGOs are not threatening. Even though they may not always agree with government policy, NGOs constitute an extraordinarily smart group of people who have an enormous amount of talent and energy to offer to help carry out these new and complicated missions of the department.

## THE EMPOWERMENT OF WOMEN AND POPULATION ISSUES

A final note on this concerns the importance of women in the agenda and the huge gender gap that exists, not only in American politics but also among our State Department constituencies. Let me cite two examples.

The Cairo Population Conference highlighted a sense of urgency: "Population is exploding around the world. What are we going to do about it?" The Cairo plan of action is an extraordinary agreement that commits governments to provide family planning services and information, close the education gap between girls and boys, and focus on issues of reproductive health as a premier health care issue. The Cairo document held that abortion is not a matter of family planning but a medical and reproductive health problem. The document also focused on child survival. If babies survive, then their parents will have fewer children. Women need to be engaged economically and politically. The more engaged women are, the more opportunities they will have to make decisions about the size of their families and the spacing of their children.

This is a remarkable document that relates to the empowerment of women. It is also a very challenging and threatening document to many people because it talks about the transfer of power from men to women. I know of no time in world history when political or economic or any other power was transferred peacefully and easily. It will not occur easily with women's empowerment either. There are all kinds of tensions involved in the gender gap, and they affect our foreign policy because women are much more strongly supportive of the U.S. role around the world.

The second example was reinforced at the Beijing Conference on Women. It was impressive to see the involvement of nongovernmental organizations, not only from the United States (and we had the dominant numbers of people there), but from all over the world, and how the new electronic revolution makes possible a pattern of global communication and reinforcement. It is a very powerful agent for the kinds of change that many of us would like to see.

More than half of the people and voters in this country are women. How do we go organize their support for our foreign policy agenda? This will take a long while, but it is absolutely imperative to do so if we are going to meet the responsibilities that we have around the world, whether population stabilization, counternarcotics programs, or global climate change. If we do not take the lead, progressive actions will not happen around the world. If we really believe these are issues that must be met, then we must have the wherewithal and support to do so. We will not get support unless we organize the agenda and then assemble and work with the constituencies.

The population issue is one that could gain a great deal of public involvement. Environmental NGOs like the Sierra Club and Audubon

Society have been energetic supporters. Bipartisan public support exists across the country. Note also that the population issue was originally a Republican issue. In fact, the first head of the population caucus in the House of Representatives was George Bush.

Two things have happened that have complicated the issue. One is the right-to-life movement, through which the population issue has become entangled with the abortion issue. There is no debate that is more intensely felt by the right and by religious groups in the country than abortion. It is an extraordinarily powerful issue. There is nothing on the other side of the population debate that even comes close to it. Because of the power of the abortion issue and the need for many politicians to prove themselves to those constituencies, they use family planning as a way of demonstrating their bona fides on the abortion issue. In Cairo, we tried to separate family planning from abortion and address abortion as a health issue.

The second complicating factor is simply the awkwardness of talking about population. Discussing population issues means talking about two other concerns that people do not like to talk about in politics—sex and religion. Controlling population growth involves sexuality, and this impinges directly on religious values. Neither of those is a very comfortable issue to discuss in politics. But we have to find ways of continuing the dialogue on population growth. Our future depends on stabilizing the world's population.

## THE ROLE OF NONGOVERNMENTAL ORGANIZATIONS (NGOS)

The State Department now must link these constituencies with our policy agenda. We are just starting to learn that something has to be done. People in the State Department have not been trained to engage organized citizens groups and they are not particularly interested in doing so. It is not the job they were expecting to do when they came into the department, and the challenge is foreign to them. But the doors of the State Department are opening, slowly but surely.

Every American ambassador abroad now sees the promotion of U.S. commercial interests as absolutely integral to his or her portfolio. The sensitivity to U.S. commercial interests throughout the State Department is much greater than what it was just a decade ago. The next step may be to acquire sensitivity to another range of issues and another range of constituencies beyond purely commercial interests.

In foreign policy, the signature of this administration is going to be this kind of economic engagement by our foreign policy institutions. But the kinds of businesses that are engaged in this generally are not ones that are going to be vibrant political constituencies because what we do for them is mainly open doors. For the State Department, "business politics" is very different from the business politics of the Pentagon, where firms are competing directly for large contracts that mean jobs and profits.

There are a few places where the business constituencies can become deeply involved, sometimes negatively and sometimes positively. On the negative side, take climate change. If we are going to be serious about reacting to what now is pretty well-understood science—that man is having an impact on the temperature of the globe by carbon emissions and the greenhouse effect—the fossil fuel industry will be directly affected. And how will that industry respond? Predictably, it will feel threatened and respond negatively. This arose in the debate over acid rain, with which I was deeply involved in Congress. There is a lot of denial in this industry, which argues that there is no such thing as acid rain or climate change. That is not a good constituency for us because that particular part of the industry opposes our policies. But there are some other constituencies that could benefit from those policies. For example, there is a $400 billion environmental industry that may be supportive. There is an industry focused on environmental and energy control technologies that would have much to gain with an aggressive climate change program stressing more efficient burning of fossil fuels.

There are some other opportunities in the area of biological diversity. It is very important that we ratify the Biological Diversity Treaty; if we do not, a series of international protocols could be passed over which we have no control. There are discussions now about an international biosafety protocol that could be very damaging to many of our industries. There are threats of what I call "gene wars," of denying access by U.S. companies to the genetic pool that exists around the world. So there are some very real threats to our pharmaceutical industry, our biotechnology industry, and others. We have to educate them about the fact that they ought to be helping us get the treaty passed. Will they be a long-term constituency? Probably not. It is more likely that environmental NGOs and others with an ongoing interest will be the more steady constituency. Nevertheless, we need to communicate and cooperate with these supportive industries whenever possible.

There are nongovernmental constituencies on other issues as well. Organized labor, for example, has been a major focus around the world for the expression by individuals of their own sense of opportunity and search for dignity and well-being. We are a democracy with fundamental American values; we have a lot of ideological and practical reasons to promote democracy and we do. One of our jobs is to try to export what we think are good, sound values that lead to more stable societies, with viable economic frameworks, working legal systems, and a transparent financial system. These measures also work to our advantage in terms of trade priorities.

Regarding foreign assistance, there is an assumption that nothing can be done without great expense. I do not believe that. Through the remarkable expertise of our AID missions, U.S. NGOs, and U.S. business and industry, a huge amount can be done at low cost. For example, in Russia, our effective funding of NGOs and citizens' networks, together with personal computers and communications systems, deserves a larger premium. In the long term, that approach would yield a return that is greater for us substantively in terms of what we want to accomplish and certainly better for us in terms of building a network of citizen institutions.

We have to learn how to spend our money better and leverage our resources. We have many different tools. One bilateral tool, the bully pulpit of the American embassy in a country, is vital. We need to use international communications more aggressively. America dominates the culture of the world. We need to revitalize our educational exchange activities that have such widespread benefit for the national interest.

We also have a great deal of leverage in the international financial institutions. The flow of funds now is much more significant from the World Bank and Inter-American Development Bank than through our bilateral programs. In Brazil, for example, we have a tiny remaining AID program of what was once a huge mission. The Inter-American Development Bank alone has a program of two billion dollars a year. We are responsible for 60 percent of the capital in the Inter-American Development Bank's program, and have a significant impact on how it spends its money. That is real leverage.

The private sector now accounts for twice as much as the public sector in funding development and development-related activities, and that gap is growing bigger all the time. The flow of funds from private sources overtook public sources a few years ago and is now rocketing ahead as formal aid programs are declining around the world. There are a few government-funded programs that seem to me to be irreplaceable—such as the global environment facility—but not many. Most of them demand a cooperative effort and a lot of private sector input to support traditional development projects that we will not be able to fund through public sources.

## BILATERALISM VERSUS MULTILATERALISM

The United States is accustomed to operating bilaterally, using its financial and military leverage to achieve desirable outcomes in international affairs. While strong bilateral relationships will remain integral to America's leadership, the United States must increasingly adopt regional and multilateral strategies to address many serious global issues. In so doing, the United States must be perceived as a partner, not a bully. If this occurs, U.S. leverage will increase on global issues, and several bilateral relations will be enhanced.

In Asia, for example, the United States is engaged both regionally and bilaterally in addressing global concerns. In early 1993, the United States inaugurated a highly successful Common Agenda with Japan, which has helped reduce trade frictions and enhance cooperation on global issues. Through Common Agenda discussions, the United States, which spends about $600 million a year on population efforts, encouraged the Japanese to increase their contribution from $40 million to $400 million a year on population and HIV/AIDS research. In addition, the Common Agenda has prompted cooperation on technology exchange, earthquake detection and prevention, natural disaster assistance, transportation issues, and an infectious disease initiative. Furthermore, America's involvement in the Asia-Pacific Economic Community (APEC) has provided opportunities to promote U.S. trade interests while addressing global problems such as AIDS and environmental degradation.

In Latin America, the United States must work regionally to address issues like narcotics trade. We are perceived as being a big user, which we are, and therefore are held accountable for much of the problem. We are also seen as the enforcer because we intervene in Colombia, Bolivia, Nigeria, Burma, and elsewhere. Thus we have two strikes against us operating bilaterally. So we are working to try to regionalize our approaches, and I have been spending a good deal of time with Brazil, Venezuela, Paraguay, and the Andean countries trying to build a sense of shared responsibility on narcotics. This approach is progressing gradually as countries see their own narcotics use growing. Any time a country is a transit or production country, addiction spreads. We want to build on this growing awareness. Our bilateral relations are helping to make this happen. We have a sharply improved relationship with Brazil in part because of policies within the United States and in larger part because of the new government in Brazil, which is undertaking impressive changes. This in turn facilitates a regional strategy.

Secretary Christopher talked a lot about this multitrack approach in his Stanford speech, emphasizing not only what we have to do bilaterally, but what we have to do regionally, what we have to do internationally with the UN, and what we have to do with nongovernmental organizations. It is a new way of thinking, a new kind of governance, and that is bewildering to people. It is another part of the current transition to a post–Cold War foreign policy. It will take the country a while to understand these new ways of conducting foreign policy, but it is a transition that must be made.

# A New Paradigm of
# Shared Prosperity through Partnership

CAROL MOSELEY-BRAUN

*Carol Moseley-Braun is the first African American woman ever elected to the U.S. Senate. She is the first permanent woman member of the Finance Committee and also serves on the Banking, Housing, and Urban Affairs Committee, and on the Special Committee on Aging. Her legislative initiatives have included education reform, women's and children's rights, and community development. A graduate of the University of Illinois and the University of Chicago Law School, she served in the Illinois state legislature and state and county government before her election representing Illinois to the U.S. Senate in 1992.*

> I this infer,
> That many things, having full reference
> To one consent, may work contrariously.
> As many arrows loosed several ways
> Come to one mark,
> As many ways meet in one town,
> As many fresh streams meet in one salt sea,
> As many lines close in the dial's center,

---

Concluding address by Senator Carol Moseley-Braun to the conference on *End of the American Century? Searching for America's Role in the Post–Cold War World,* Woodrow Wilson International Center for Scholars, 4 June 1996.

So may a thousand actions once afoot
End in one purpose, and be
All well borne
Without defeat.

      (Archbishop of Canterbury, *Henry V*)

Shakespeare gives us guidance in these post–Cold War times, as the debate once again engages concerning the proper role and posture of United States policy in world affairs. On the one hand, the suggestion is made that we retrench to policies predicated on George Washington's famous prescription that this nation avoid foreign entanglements. On the other hand, important voices urge us toward a neomercantilist foreign policy, suggesting that trade alone be our beacon in world affairs.

Late Secretary of Commerce Ron Brown, to his great credit, focused the business community on the linkages between trade and our national security. We have had an economic foreign policy for fifty years, but the point is now made that with the collapse of communism, new opportunities for capitalism should be pursued with the active involvement and support of our government.

However, trade alone cannot guide the whole of our relations with the rest of the world, and indeed, cannot be the touchstone for a post–Cold War ideology, if for no other reason than the ancient warning that all wars start with trade.

Nor can our excitement about the collapse of communism make the exporting of democracy the sole theme of our policy. The development of free market democracies may be historically inevitable, but the fact is that we have a long way yet to go to get there, and concerns other than markets and politics command our attention in these times.

Like it or not, we must expand the discussion, and examine a set of policies for the twenty-first century. I submit, as I have since my campaign for the U.S. Senate, that our policies must follow our values, and that as we define the "one consent" Shakespeare refers to, our specific policies will better serve the interests of the American people, and will be capable of engendering their support. The architecture of our policy may "work contrariously," but so long as we have a clear view of the purposes of that architecture; so long as there is consensus that our approaches will be value-driven; and so long as the application of our espoused values is consistent, clear, and cogent, I believe the American people will support our engagement in world affairs as an expression and extension of our concern for our national, and our individual, well-being.

To the extent that our policies have "full reference" to our national character and are an expression of community, they will succeed. To the extent that they fail to reach that mark, we will inevitably be that much more subject to the siren song of the isolationists.

The collapse of the Soviet Union took the world by as much surprise as no doubt did the revolution that gave it birth. Although the end of the Cold War left the West victors of one of the great ideological struggles of world history, the United States was largely unprepared to grapple with the economic, strategic, and political demands of a new, emerging world order. But then, neither was anyone else. Negative objectives such as the containment of communism and superpower rivalry are no longer the centerpiece of American foreign policy and U.S. foreign assistance programs. The framework presented by the post–Cold War world is decidedly different.

In his seminal—albeit depressing—work, Robert Kaplan described what he called "The Coming Anarchy." He concluded that scarcity, crime, overpopulation, tribalism, and disease are rapidly destroying the social fabric of our planet. Essentially, Kaplan's case is that current trends lead ineluctably to a contagious disintegration of social order worldwide. I recommend it for those who would suggest that our interests can be confined and defined in terms of national borders. The fact is, many of the issues facing our country—international drug trade and international environmental degradation—by definition cannot be addressed at the local or national level.

What then is the architecture of our defense against the potential future anarchy? Can we define our interests in such simple terms as to address comprehensively the many-headed hydra of the new world order? Instead of viewing relations from a bipolar and unidimensional perspective, we are called upon to adjust to the challenge of a kaleidoscope of interests in this information age. These interests are interrelated if not interdependent, and American prosperity and security may well depend upon the facility with which we embrace and master change.

The first step is recognizing that we are required to do so. The traditional debates and responses simply do not address the changed realities of this new era. While it may be a tremendous letdown for those who specialized in the complexities of competing weapon systems, the fact is, that as the only superpower, the United States is confronted with new challenges and issues that do not lend themselves to the same analytical framework. The issues we confront today are as different from Cold War issues as the horse-drawn carriage was from the automobile.

Jean Claude Paye, former secretary general of the Organization for Economic Cooperation and Development, stated it eloquently when he said: "So leaders worried about their economies need to focus on society's fraying fabric. If the warp of societal well-being is economic growth, the weft is people who embrace and anticipate momentous change."

The next step is to recognize that we have inherent advantages that enable us to face the new challenges of the emerging world order. Budget deficits notwithstanding, we still have the largest, most advanced, and wealthiest economy on the planet. We are, however, witnessing growing instabilities in our economy that threaten our future capacity for economic growth. The widening gap between the haves and have-nots is a by-product of the momentous change we face, not the cause of it. Our workforce is challenged to keep up with the technological change science has given us. Wage stagnation is in part a glimpse of employment maladjustment. It now often takes two wage earners to maintain the standard of living one worker could achieve a generation ago. What corporate balance sheets now show as productivity gains more often than not has the human face of a downsized or wage-stagnant employee. The development of an underclass, people who are trapped in poverty without the skills or opportunity to achieve the traditional American success story, represents the growing marginalization of people for whom inadequate economic options exist.

During the raucous public debate over NAFTA, I told a group of laborers in Chicago that I favored the trade agreement because, and I quote, "in the history of the world, the lowering of trade barriers increased trade, and the increase of trade creates jobs." I was taken aback, however, by one man's quiet response after the speech, when he said to me, "but we don't want to have to compete with two dollar-an-hour Mexican labor." He was in no small part right, of course; the challenges of opening up trade with nonindustrialized and emerging markets in part lies in the differences of labor forces. Our mission therefore must be to secure for American workers, and for our people as a whole, that part of the world market that will support the standard of living that characterizes the American dream.

In the face of the globalized economy, the technological revolution, and the information age, American workers will need to be more skilled, not less. We meet the trends Kaplan and others describe by providing the foundations for economic revitalization in the context of this global market. The environmentalists touched succinctly on the formula in their prescription that we "think globally, act locally."

Our domestic well-being influences directly our ability to lead in the relations with the rest of the world. As such, our willingness to make the sacrifices and to take the initiative in revitalizing our economy and our workforce is a determinant of our capacity for leadership. The pressures toward economic, political, and social breakdown mandate a new look at the fundamentals of growth.

First and foremost among those fundamentals in these times is education. Whether one calls it the information age or the technology age or the millennium of markets, the fact is that only an educated workforce can hope to hold its own in a global competition. The alternative is the race to the bottom the worker in Chicago suggested. It is estimated by the year 2000, over half the new jobs will require more than a high school education. The private sector, particularly high-tech industries, is already beginning to feel the crunch of a lack of adequately trained American workers.

It is significant to note that, during the immigration debate, it was the business community that was most forcefully agitating for open immigration for trained workers. The business community also has had to make up, in costs associated with remedial training, for the failings of our public elementary and secondary schools. The General Accounting Office (GAO) recently completed a study I requested that documented the need for $112 billion in investment in facilities and infrastructure, just to bring our nation's schools up to health and safety standards—and that does not count the additional investments needed to make computers and other technologies available to students.

Investment in education is more than a private benefit, it is a public good. An educated workforce is not only more likely to be able to sustain individuals in the style to which they are capable of achieving, but a society, as well. We meet and counter the trends toward social disintegration, crime, disease, poverty, disenchantment, and hopelessness by providing our people with opportunity and gainful employment. We preserve our culture and buttress our democracy when we make quality education universally available. We provide a context for the masses of instantaneous information and the anxiety it provokes when all of our people are educated, and when training is an expectation of citizenship. Education is therefore more of a fundamental of economic growth and social stability now than ever before. We ignore the opportunity it provides at our peril.

Embracing momentous change requires a reevaluation of our national resources. Our most important resource is our people. Domestic investment in human capital is one critical first step in our preparation for engagement in the global village. It is, however, a step that is central to defining the terms of that engagement.

My view is that what is evolving—or needs to be articulated—is a new paradigm. People will support engagement in international organizations and efforts only when they see them as related to their own interests. This paradigm, one of shared prosperity through partnership, proceeds from an understanding that we are all in this together, that as Americans our well-being is directly linked to the well-being of people throughout the world.

Shared prosperity through partnership recognizes that if developing nations do not have cash, or the means to access capital, then they cannot purchase goods and services from America and the rest of the developed world. As such, support for the efforts of the World Bank in providing development assistance in Africa, for example, must be understood and seen as investment in new and potential markets and, therefore, as seeds for job creation here at home.

Technology transfers and debt forgiveness are therefore less charity than self-interest. By assisting development abroad, we can create business at home and provide jobs for our people in the process. Such a paradigm is not paternalistic. It rejects the notion of handouts, it promotes self-sufficiency, encourages responsibility, and demands accountability.

Our leadership in worldwide development is nothing less than an aspect of our domestic responsibility. By providing for growth in the rest of the world, we can provide opportunity here at home. By preparing our people to take advantage of that opportunity, we can counter the trend toward social disintegration.

This partnership requires reciprocity. It requires that everyone bring something to the table. In the case of the developing world, structural barriers to real market performance and free trade must be reduced, and political stability based on democratic participation must be achieved. Impediments to the free flow of capital and private enterprise must be diminished as a part of the development of a healthy market economy. Governments that do not support economic policies that give confidence to their partners will be challenged increasingly from within as well as without. Human rights and democratic reforms are a necessary focus and outgrowth of a partnership for prosperity.

Some time ago, I read a book titled, *The Growth of Economic Thought*. I was as much struck by the concept that economic thought was evolutionary as by the fact that economic laws are constant. What changes is our ability to learn those laws—from experience or otherwise—and to adjust our responses based on such learning.

We are now called on to shape our responses to global developments based on our greater knowledge of world affairs. What that greater knowledge inescapably tells us is that the consequences of our actions on the world stage are multifaceted, and so are the consequences of our inaction. We are challenged in our time to "connect the dots," recognize the relationships, and consider the impact—as we create a postmodern policy architecture.

Since the end of World War II, international organizations, principally the United Nations and the Bretton Woods institutions—the International Monetary Fund, the World Bank, and its affiliates— have played a central role in the economic development of the world's economies. Along with the United States, these international donor institutions provided Europe and Japan with the support required to rebuild their war-torn economies. Regional security organizations supplemented that support by providing a stable environment in which those economies could grow.

In the heady and optimistic days following the end of the war and colonialism in Africa and much of the Third World, these and similar international institutions were the conduit for international development, literacy and education, and improvement in the status of women and indigenous people. Somehow, we have lost the language of celebration of those achievements, and have allowed a negative spirit to so infect our response that America no longer feels embarrassed by its failure to honor its financial commitments to the United Nations and the International Development Agency, our links to the poorest nations of the world.

Yet, these institutions are another one of the keys, I believe, to a reformed policy architecture. The waste and inefficiencies for which they have been criticized should be eliminated, but by no means at the expense of the objectives they are uniquely situated to serve. The World Bank, with the direction embraced by its new leadership, recognizes the value of investment in human capital and people's needs as an approach to development. Nongovernmental organizations, NGOs, should be supported in their efforts to nurture local communities and held accountable for their activities in so doing. Education and training at home, development abroad, investment in human capital as a touchstone for domestic policy as well as foreign policy, all of these various iterations of a people-centered approach to public policy ought to characterize our response to the momentous change we face.

It is most important, however, to recognize that as we speak unequivocally about the connections between people and between nations, we are essentially talking about who we are and about our generation's stewardship of this planet. It is no more nor less than the colloquy between Alice and the Cheshire Cat. When she asked which way to go, the Cat replied, "that depends on where you want to get to." Our direction may not be carved in stone, and indeed, it may "work contrariously," but so long as we keep in mind the values that drive our endeavors, we will be "all well borne without defeat."

# Acknowledgments

This book has been a collective enterprise in more ways than one. The Ford Foundation, thanks to the support and encouragement of Christine Wing, provided the support that made possible the seminars and symposia from November 1995 to June 1996 at which these chapters were first presented. The Woodrow Wilson Center extended its usual warm hospitality for these meetings, in a setting particularly conducive to thoughtful inquiry transcending narrow academic specializations.

My debts to my colleagues in the Center's Division of International Studies are great. My friend Rob Litwak, the division's director, provided essential support and encouragement at every step along the way. The indispensable Michael Vaden oversaw every typescript and computer disk, putting each essay into finished form and editing many himself. Christa Sheehan Matthew likewise applied her deft editorial touch to several of the essays. Michele Carus-Christian organized the June 1996 "End of the American Century?" conference with her customary efficiency and good humor. P. J. Simmons, Andrew Grauer, Kate Sawyer, and Lucy Kennedy also provided invaluable assistance. I am grateful as well to the Woodrow Wilson Center Press and particularly to Senior Editor Carol Walker, for her skillful editorial oversight as well as her enthusiasm for the project.

The greatest credit and my deepest thanks go to the many contributors to this book, whose collegiality was as extraordinary as the quality of their thinking and writing. When we gave the enterprise the deliberately provocative title "End of the American Century?" we touched a nerve. Lots of people, it turned out, were similarly eager to see these topics treated in a way that got to the nub of matters rather than nibbled around the fringes. The series attracted an extraordinarily talented and diverse group of participants. Their partnership has made the editor's task a pleasure and a privilege.

R.L.H.
Princeton, New Jersey

# Index